Found Treasures

Stories by Yiddish Women Writers

FOUND TREASURES

STORIES BY YIDDISH WOMEN WRITERS

EDITED BY FRIEDA FORMAN,
ETHEL RAICUS, SARAH SILBERSTEIN SWARTZ
AND MARGIE WOLFE

INTRODUCTION BY IRENA KLEPFISZ

SECOND
STORY
Press

CANADIAN CATALOGUING IN PUBLICATION DATA

Main entry under title:
Found treasures: stories by Yiddish women writers

ISBN 0-929005-53-8

1. Yiddish prose literature – women authors. 2. Yiddish prose literature –
Translations into English. 3. Yiddish prose literature – 20th century.
4. Short stories, Yiddish – Women. 5. Short stories, Yiddish –
Translations into English. 6. Women, Jewish – Literary collections.
I. Forman, Frieda.

PJ5128.F68 1994   839'.09830808'09287   C94-930564-2

Permission credits appear on page 391

Cover photograph: *Members of the Jewish Workers' Bund in Poland 1908*
used with permission of YIVO Institute of Jewish Research

Printed and bound in Canada by University of Toronto Press

*Second Story Press gratefully acknowledges the assistance
of the Ontario Arts Council and The Canada Council*

Published by
SECOND STORY PRESS
720 Bathurst Street Suite 301
Toronto, Ontario
M5S 2R4

To the memory of our mothers and sisters,
and to continuity.

Yente Serdatzky

Kadia Molodowsky, Ida Maze, Rachel Korn

Rikudah Potash
1923

Esther Singer Kreitman

Malka Lee
1923

Blume Lempel
1959

Fradel Schtok
1910

Chava Rosenfarb
1950s

*Sarah Hamer-Jacklyn
1940s*

Celia Dropkin

Lili Berger

CONTENTS

PREFACE

Without remembrance there is no continuity.

FEMINISM TEACHES that to struggle forward we need to understand the women who brought us here. As longtime feminists we have spent the last quarter century exploring the lives, needs and concerns of women. Certainly, the breadth of literature available today detailing the experiences of women from all over the world is ever-growing, changing the way societies look at themselves and their histories.

Jewish feminists, however, have been slower to explore our own heritage. We have spent much of the last decades learning about women from other cultures and backgrounds but little time trying to better understand our own mothers and grandmothers, our own women writers, artists, teachers — all the women who helped shape our histories. For the most part, we have allowed them to remain lost, cloaked in a culture which, like many others, has hidden the experiences, struggles and accomplishments of its women.

In recent years Jewish feminists have been trying to rectify the situation. Various groups and gatherings have been organized, books written. In Toronto, a group of us from European backgrounds attempted to find our foremothers through their common language: Yiddish, the cultural core of *Ashkenazi* Jewry until it was almost obliterated by the Holocaust.

More than just a spoken language, Yiddish was a way of life, a rich culture and a literature which linked several million Jews in Eastern Europe with those who immigrated to North America before the Holocaust. There were Yiddish books, newspapers, literary journals, theatre, research centres, publishers and a whole world of artists, musicians and writers — all destroyed by the nazis, along with the people who spoke and read Yiddish. Today there remains only an echo of this golden era of Yiddish. Yiddish writers whose works have been translated into English provide us with impressions of Eastern European and North American Jewish life through their works — but only from a male perspective. Where are the voices of the women?

Guided by Frieda Forman, we discovered that the biographical dictionaries of Yiddish literature published from 1927 to 1986 document over three hundred Yiddish women writers. It became the aim of our study group, our *leyenkrayz*, to find and read the original works by these women. As we continued to read, we discovered a wealth of writings by Jewish women whose works are accessible only to Yiddish readers.

Formed in October 1990, our group was unique in Canada, perhaps in all of North America. We were diverse in age, background, politics, feminist commitment and Yiddish fluency. Our ages ranged from early twenties to late seventies. Some of us were Canadian born, others came to Canada in the first half of this century as young children; still others were Holocaust survivors and children of Holocaust survivors. Some were native speakers of Yiddish; others came to Yiddish later in life. Some had spoken it in their parents' home but had never formally studied the language. Others went to Yiddish secular schools, still others to traditional Yiddish schools where they studied Yiddish language and literature as youngsters; others learned Yiddish in university courses.

But we all had several important things in common: we all loved the Yiddish language and were committed to finding our foremothers' writings — our lost treasures. To study Yiddish literature after the Holocaust is a political statement; to study the works of Yiddish women writers seemed to us a doubly potent statement.

We wanted to read about women's experiences in the *shtetls* and cities of Jewish Eastern Europe, about their lives as immigrants to North America and Palestine/Israel, and to learn how their perceptions differed from those of their male counterparts. We also wanted to find out more about ourselves, to discover who we are, based on our Jewish women's heritage. Just as I. L. Peretz, Sholom Aleichem and Isaac Bashevis Singer had captured the spirit of patriarchal life in Eastern Europe, so we sought the writings of the women who could illuminate the world of our mothers, our grandmothers, our great grandmothers.

Not surprisingly then, the idea for *Found Treasures* came out of our group. Our next task was to make these women's writings accessible to a much larger audience, both Jews and non-Jews, so that we could share the treasures we had found. Translations from all languages are important, but they are especially important from Yiddish, the vanishing language and culture of an almost forgotten female heritage. And so, we began to translate ....

For all of us — the editors, translators and readers — the project has been a labour of love. At the same time, we recognize that *Found Treasures* is as much a document of history as it is a literary work. It is a window which permits us to retrieve the worlds of our mothers. Without translation there is no window, not one from their perspective, a perspective of ordinary women confronting everyday situations and extraordinary and sometimes horrifying events. Without translation their lives remain invisible, at best vague visions, sometimes footnotes, unmemorable and unremembered. Without remembrance there is no continuity.

Because it is the first volume of Yiddish women's writings, we have attempted to enrich and inform the prose with complimentary material. The introduction by Irena Klepfisz contextualizes the collection of stories, memoirs and sketches. Headnotes are included to situate the individual pieces and the biographies to give a fuller portrait of the writers and translators themselves. A glossary has been included to clarify vocabulary, spelling and pronunciation for the reader. All these components create a work which we hope will be accessible and lead the reader to further exploration.

As the editors of this collection it is our wish that this book not be viewed as the definitive text on Yiddish women writers. It is, rather, a first book. As the collection was being compiled, more and more writers were coming to our attention. And there are certainly many more whom we simply have not yet come across. It is our hope their work will appear in other anthologies in the not-too-distant future. We hope this book will be relevant to Jewish women and inspirational to all who are committed to reclaiming the voices of women from all cultures.

We would like to take this opportunity to thank Shmuel Blatt, Taffy Cass, Chana Erlich, Ellie Kellman, Judy Levitan, Shmuel Pupko, Nokhem Reinhartz, Sylvia Lustgarten, Rusty Shteir, Miriam and Julius Teitel, Ellen Tulchinsky, John Pitman Weber, Laura Weintraub, our editor Rhea Tregebov, whose dedication helped us through some difficult times, and the wonderfully patient women at Second Story Press — Louise Azzarello, Karen Farquhar, Elizabeth Martin and Lois Pike — whose unfailing commitment, trust and support gave us the time and space to allow this project to develop to its best potential.

— Frieda Forman, Ethel Raicus, Sarah
Silberstein Swartz and Margie Wolfe
OCTOBER, 1994

QUEENS OF CONTRADICTION

A FEMINIST INTRODUCTION TO YIDDISH WOMEN WRITERS

Irena Klepfisz

> *Ikh heng tsvishn do un dortn —*
> *Di malke fun stires.*
>
> I hang between here and there —
> The queen of contradictions.
> BLUME LEMPEL

ENGLISH TRANSLATIONS AND THE YIDDISH WOMAN WRITER

From a feminist perspective, English translations of Yiddish literature can be briefly summarized. Until the last fifteen years, though translations appeared occasionally, there was little interest in making Yiddish literature available to English readers. Recently, however, English language literary anthologies, novels, histories of Yiddish culture and bilingual texts have become more popular. Among these, Yiddish women poets are minimally visible, while women prose writers are hardly acknowledged to exist.[1]

In 1954 Irving Howe and Eliezer Greenberg defined and popularized *yidishe veltlekhe kultur/*"worldly" or secular Yiddish culture for English readers through their extensive introduction and selections in *A Treasury of Yiddish Stories.* This culture — intellectual dialogues, arts, and history — appeared to be devoid of women and women's concerns, except as depicted and interpreted by men. In 1967 an almost exclusively male canon and tradition was given further credibility by Lucy Dawidowicz's popular anthology *The Golden Tradition: Jewish Life and Thought in Eastern Europe.* By 1976, this tradition was an accepted historical fact which informed and titled Howe's massive history *World of Our Fathers.* Both Dawidowicz and Howe understood the complexity and richness of *yidishe veltlekhe kultur* with its probing intellectual controversies, bitter political debates and artistic expression. Yet their histories, distorted by their omissions, have been perpetuated by other scholars and translators. Until now, English readers — non-Jews and Jews — have had little access to women's individual and collective roles and achievements in Yiddish-speaking communities on both sides of the Atlantic.

There is abundant "Yiddish proof" of women's active participation in secular Jewish life. For example, during the early post-Holocaust period, two comprehensive Yiddish *yisker bikher/*memorial books were published in the States: one for the *umgekumene/*perished teachers of CYSHO — Yiddish acronym for the Central Yiddish Shul Organization (1952-54; 568 pp.); and the other, the two-volume *Doyres bundistn* [Generations of Bundists] (1956; 1,000+ pp.) for the socialist and pro-Yiddish movement of the Jewish Labour Bund. Together they provide over 200 biographies of women political leaders, pedagogues and intellectuals.

We find a similar situation in Yiddish literature. *Yidishe dikhterins* [Yiddish "Poetesses"], a 390-page anthology by E. Korman (1928) contains an introduction and the poetry, biographies and photographs of approximately seventy women poets, sixty-five of whom published between 1900 and 1927. The multi-volume *leksikonen*/lexicons of Yiddish literature include the biographies and bibliographies of almost 300 women journalists, poets, essayists, and fiction writers. Since modern secular Yiddish literature is barely 150 years old, the existence of hundreds of women documented in Yiddish histories, anthologies and bibliographies is astonishing, their absence in the English/Yiddish canon even more so.

Some Jewish feminists have been aware of the discrepancy between the original and translated versions of Yiddish culture. In 1980 Norma Fain Pratt identified fifty women writers in her article "Culture and Radical Politics: Yiddish Women Writers, 1890-1940." Since then two histories of Eastern European Jewish women have been published: Sydney Weinberg's *The World of Our Mothers* (1988) and Susan A. Glenn's *Daughters of the Shtetl* (1990). The research of Chave Weissler, Debra Weissman, Shulamis Berger and others has also broadened our knowledge of women in observant Yiddish-speaking communities and the Yiddish texts they used. Most recently, Naomi Shepherd's *A Price Below Rubies: Jewish Women as Rebels & Radicals* and my own article "*Di mames, dos loshn*/The mothers, the language: Feminism, *Yidishkayt* and the Politics of Memory" have brought to the forefront important Eastern European women activists whose Yiddish writing has been inaccessible.

But even when citing liberally from the original, all criticism, including feminist criticism, remains interpretive and second hand. Despite advances in feminist Yiddish scholarship, the woman writer's Yiddish voice has barely been audible in English. Some women poets (usually Molodowsky, Heifetz-Tussman, Korn, Dropkin) have been included in anthologies and Rachel Korn and Malka Heifetz-Tussman each have had individual collections published in English; however, no English collection of Yiddish women poets has yet appeared which indicates the history and breadth of Yiddish women's poetry.

Even fewer women prose writers have been translated: four complete works — the 17th-century memoirs of *Glückel of Hameln* (New York) and 20th-century Bella Chagall's *First Encounter* (New York), Esther Kreitman's *Deborah* (London) and Chava Rosenfarb's *The Tree of Life* (Melbourne); a handful of stories by Korn, Rosenfarb and Kreitman have appeared in Canada and England, and about ten all together by Serdatzky, Schtok, Kreitman, Molodowsky, Berger and Lempel in the States. The North American feminist magazine *Bridges* is the sole institution currently committed to publishing Yiddish writing by women in the original and in translation; but it alone cannot make up for such gross neglect.

Given this history, I can hardly overemphasize the significance of the present collection. *Found Treasures* presents for the first time a body of Yiddish writing by women who speak to us directly. It increases exponentially the number of English translations of women's prose by offering us the Yiddish fiction and memoirs of eighteen women artists, intellectuals and activists who, from the beginning of this century, have been productive writers in Europe, the United States, Canada and Israel. Ten are making their English debut, eleven as prose writers; four — Berger, Gorshman, Lempel, Rosenfarb — are writing today. For feminists accustomed to searching for Shakespeare's and Singers' sisters, the recovery of this secular women's Yiddish literature, while not surprising, is certainly long overdue.

However, neither *Found Treasures* nor original Yiddish sources such as the lexicons prove that women experienced equality in Yiddish-speaking communities. On the contrary, the women writers and intellectuals who participated in the blossoming Yiddish secular/cultural worlds at the end of the 19th century found themselves in a peculiar position: on the one hand, male Yiddishists and intellectuals championed "the women's cause" as part of their progressive agendas; on the other, the same men were trying to legitimize their own work by breaking with an older Yiddish literature strongly associated with women and a women's audience. Despite their desire to encourage women to engage in the evolving literary, political and artistic milieus, male Yiddishists must also have felt a need to distance themselves from them. As a result, Yiddish women writers were trapped by the conflicting motives of the men who exercised power and control over Yiddish journals, newspapers and presses. The following, necessarily brief, history of Yiddish literature from a feminist perspective provides a more detailed picture of these women writers' predicament.

FEMINIZATION AND YIDDISH LITERATURE

Yiddish — a unique fusion of German, Hebrew-Aramaic and Slavic components — emerged over one thousand years ago among Jews living in Ashkenaz, Loter, a region now recognized as part of Germany. Responding to anti-Semitism and economic necessity, many began as early as the 11th century to migrate east — to Poland and eventually to Russia. They took Yiddish with them, incorporating along the way elements of the Slavic languages of their new surroundings. Though in the past intellectuals and linguists argued about what Yiddish should be called — *loshn-ashkenaz*/language of Ashkenaz, *yidishtaytsh*/Judeo-German, *taytsh*/German, *zhargon*/jargon —

"ordinary" Jews have for centuries called it *yidish* and *mame-loshn* or *muter-shprakh* — mother tongue.

Throughout Europe Yiddish was a spoken language — a language of ordinary life, home, business and social relations — and became linked with the "secular," with feeling and women. Hebrew, on the other hand, was the written language — *loshn-koydesh*, the language of holiness, of *tanakh*, religious observance and *halokhe*/Jewish law — and was equated with moral and intellectual discourse and with men, the only ones allowed to study Hebrew texts. Yiddish became stigmatized by its "lowly" associations with women and the uneducated, while Hebrew was revered for its association with "higher pursuits," scholars and rabbis.

However popular or convenient, this contrasting depiction of the two languages is oversimplified, for the centrality of the synagogue and Judaism in pre-19th-century Jewish life precluded drawing strict boundaries between the secular and the religious. Neither *mame-loshn* nor *loshn-koydesh* were rigidly confined to women's and men's spheres.

First, Yiddish contains a large *loshn-koydesh* component and is not only spoken, but written in the Hebrew alphabet. Second, though Jews have always valued study (it is a *man's* highest duty *tsu lernen toyre*/to study Torah), for centuries they lived in abject poverty; most men could not afford to devote their lives to study. Many were illiterate; others never acquired more than a rudimentary knowledge of Hebrew. Being compared to a woman may have been humiliating, yet many men were no different than most women whose only language — oral or written — was Yiddish. Also, some learned men valued Yiddish. A known leader like the Vilna Gaon (18th century) insisted his daughters *and* sons learn Yiddish prayers. Rabbis spoke Yiddish among themselves, corresponded, mediated conflicts, interpreted *halokhe*, pronounced judgments and issued laws, divorce papers and legal settlements in Yiddish.

Third, there were women who studied religious texts, and in some cases became Biblical scholars. Opinions of them were polarized: admiration for mastering a "man's domain"; revulsion for trespassing. There was the *zogerin*/woman speaker/sayer who explicated passages and rituals, helped women with their prayers behind the *mekhitse*/women's section of the synagogue and, like rabbis, interceded on their behalf; the *rebetsn*/rabbi's wife advised women, influenced her husband and tutored girl children. Fulfilling traditional communal roles, these women, though not scholars, were often literate in Yiddish and Hebrew and served as sources of wisdom. They wielded power, demanded respect.

There was other blurring in the male and female, religious and secular domains of Hebrew and Yiddish. *Mame-loshn* was the medium for moral guidance of the (Hebrew) illiterate — women and men. In Eastern Europe, there developed a popular religious Yiddish literature strongly associated with women and set in a special *vaybertaytsh*/women's German typeface to distinguish it from Hebrew texts. Though Yankev ben Yitsik Ashkenazi, the author of the *Tsene urene* (16th century), stated on its title page that his work was meant "to enable both men and women ... to understand the word of God in simple language," it quickly became identified with women. Consisting of Biblical stories, *medroshim*/interpretations and commentaries, it is still popular among orthodox women who read it at home on *shabes* while the men pray in *shul*. The *Tsene urene* is an example of a Yiddish text, which, intended for the Jewish masses, became "feminized" and relegated to the women's sphere.

Most *tkhines*, on the other hand, were Yiddish prayers written specifically for women addressing their domestic duties, relations with husbands, sexuality and reproduction (menstruation, pregnancy, and birth). Though some were meant for the synagogue, most were recited by women in their homes at times of prayer or in conjunction with their household duties and contrast starkly with men's communal Hebrew recitations in the synagogue. Some appeared in print as early as the 16th century in small books and pamphlets bearing Hebrew titles and introductions (inaccessible to most women); their authorship is unclear since men commonly used women's pseudonyms for credibility with their readers. Two known 18th-century women authors of *tkhines* were Sarah Rachel Leah Horowitz and Sarah bas Tovim. The latter's *Tkhine shloyshe she'orim* [*Tkhine* of three gates], one of the most widely read, was repeatedly imitated/plagiarized by men wanting to cash in on her popularity.

Also popular between the 16th and 19th centuries among Eastern European Jews were Yiddish pamphlets on ethical conduct and the very popular *Ma'ase bukh* [Story Book] which, despite liberal use of folk tales and myths, never lost sight of its Biblical sources, nor of the primary reason for its existence: the moral elevation of the reader. The more secular *Bove bukh* [Book of Bova] drew on non-Jewish sources (Italian, French and English); it too, was immensely popular, its audience often characterized as *"vayber un proste mentshn/*women and common people."

It was common among 19th century critics and intellectuals to refer to women readers and the masses as if they were two discrete groups. This attitude isolated women at the same time that it merged/equated them, their tastes and interests with those of ordinary men. It feminized secular and religious pre-19th-century Yiddish texts by characterizing them as "women's literature," though they were written by men and their intended audience included men and women.

In the eyes of 19th-century Jewish male intellectuals, this feminization and automatic denigration of Yiddish literature passed on to the language itself. Even religious texts like translations of the Bible did not redeem Yiddish because of their (falsely) exclusive association with women and their (assumed necessary) simplification of the originals. After all, what could women — and by extension, illiterate men or the common masses — understand? Only Yiddish.

For a brief moment at the end of the 18th century, Yiddish gained stature among some Eastern European Jews through the early Hasidim who rebelled against rabbinical authority and insisted that a Jew's (that is, a man's) communication with God need not be mediated by Hebrew texts or rabbis. This populist approach valued emotion over reason, spontaneity over memory and scholarship, and the *mame-loshn* of the illiterate over the *loshn-koydesh* of the learned elite. Early Hasidism legitimized for men what had been standard practice for women: using Yiddish for religious expression. A Hebrew-illiterate or minimally educated man no longer needed to feel inferior for his ignorance of Biblical texts and rabbinical commentaries. These Hasidim "defeminized" Yiddish by endowing it with the dignity reserved for *loshn-koydesh*. But defeminization was not pervasive nor long-lived; the next Hasidic generation fragmented into competing sects each promoting rabbis and *tsadikim*/holy men who headed rival courts and *yeshives*. Yiddish was again feminized and Hebrew texts remained central to Hasidic men's observance.

ZHARGON AND THE POLITICAL CONTEXT: JEWISH LANGUAGES AND THE JEWISH FUTURE ... AND THE "WOMEN'S CAUSE"

Early (male) Hasidic attitudes to Yiddish demonstrate what feminists have found in other western cultures: women's perspectives and contributions are deemed inferior or insignificant until men decide otherwise, legitimize them through defeminization and claim them as their own.

The Hasidic revolution, however, was not about language, but about religion. For mid- and late 19th-century Yiddish male writers, legitimizing Yiddish was the core of their struggle, one which became entangled in the political debate on "the Jewish question": how were Jews to define themselves and how were they to relate to the non-Jewish environments in which they had lived for more than a thousand years? As a result of the debate, Eastern European Yiddishist intellectuals (those committed to legitimizing Yiddish) who advocated modernizing Jewish life found themselves trying to meet what they must have felt as conflicting demands which ultimately affected their attitudes towards women's writing.

Early Eastern European Yiddishists were *maskilim*/followers of the *haskole*, the enlightenment which originated in 18th-century Western Europe, in Germany. Ironically western *maskilim* shunned Yiddish, since their attitude to all Jewish matters was shaped by their desires (1) to absorb scientific/secular knowledge excluded from Jewish life by religious orthodoxy; and (2) to gain full citizenship. To obtain the latter, they abandoned Jewish customs, dress and languages — anything associated with peoplehood — and adopted those of their gentile neighbors. This included giving up Yiddish, which German Jews pejoratively called *zhargon*, a mangled version of German, and Hebrew. Western *maskilim* viewed "Jewishness" as neither culture, ethnicity, nor nationality, but religion, whose sphere was confined to prayers recited and holidays observed in non-Jewish languages. Looking to gentile cultures to shape their lives, many, especially German Jews, assimilated, then converted.

The *haskole* reached Eastern European Jews in the 19th

century but with different results. Because nation states were more ethnically diverse, claiming citizenship was a complex matter in territories encompassing many minorities who differed in language, culture and religion, some of whom were demanding independence. It was in this context that Eastern European *maskilim* urged incorporating modern ideas and science into Jewish life, but without giving up their Jewish identity. In doing so, some retained observance; others rejected it but, despite feeling at home with non-Jewish intellectuals and admiring their cultures, sustained strong roots in the Jewish community. Like members of other minorities, they believed they belonged to a distinct people; unlike other minorities, they had no territory to claim in Eastern Europe. Secularists — those Jews who abandoned observance, certain Jewish customs and dress — held on to Jewish languages as defining their national territory. Depending on their politics, this territory was either a convenient metaphor (Yiddish) or an anticipated reality (Hebrew).

Even before political ideology determined their choice, many Eastern European *maskilim* preferred Hebrew. Paralleling the orthodox, they regarded Hebrew as quintessentially Jewish and dignified, with its ancient roots and its association with men and learning. They too deemed Yiddish "*zhargon,*" vulgar and common, associated with women and illiterates, lacking the purity and beauty of Hebrew and of gentile languages like Russian. Its use in secular entertainment did not help the Yiddish cause. Mid-19th-century Yiddish romances, even those with didactic endings, were still "low brow," as evidenced by their popularity among the ignorant masses, especially women. As the century progressed, Yiddish secular writing (much of it aimed at women) seemed to pander to the lowest tastes; intellectuals called it "*shund*/trash."

Yet some remained committed to Yiddish and they were helped by circumstances and political ideologies. By the end of the 19th century, when pogrom followed pogrom and the Eastern European *shtetl* seemed beyond economic rescue, the linguistic debate became politicized. Secularists committed to Jewish survival offered different solutions to "the Jewish question" and split primarily into two linguistic camps. Arguing that anti-Semitism would never be eradicated, the Zionists (originating in the west, now proselytizing in the east) advocated a return to Palestine and the adoption of Hebrew, untainted by the *goles*/exile experience. Since most Jews understood only Yiddish, some Zionists established Yiddish papers and journals. A small minority, like those from *Poaley tsion*, supported Hebrew *and* Yiddish. But all Zionists agreed on ending Jewish exile and using Hebrew in the future Jewish state.

The Zionists' chief opponents promoted radical socialist ideology as an answer to the "Jewish question," maintaining that revolution and international class struggle would eliminate ethnic conflicts, including anti-Semitism, and that Jews could and should remain where they were. These intellectuals/radicals also originally accepted the practical necessity of using *zhargon* in their propaganda and literature when teaching and organizing Yiddish-speaking workers; unlike most Zionists, they eventually came to value Yiddish both as the language of the working class and as a cornerstone of Jewish identity. Thus, for the early theoreticians of the Jewish Labour Bund — some of whom at first could not even speak Yiddish — expediency was transformed into Yiddishist ideology which created a linguistic bridge over the cultural and class chasm separating them from the masses. In the political battle between Yiddish and Hebrew, these Yiddishists clearly had an edge since a vast population already spoke the language which they were promoting.

If the secularists disagreed about strategies for Jewish survival, they agreed on the need to modernize Jewish life and, within that context, on the importance of the "the women's question." All *maskilim* or progressive men urged Jewish women to become educated and many critiqued the compulsory roles of housewife and mother. Radicals, whether Zionist or communist, though differing in how they integrated women in their movements and in their vision of women's roles in future societies, called on them to become politically and socially active, and, in some cases, sexually liberated.

Jewish women responded. Middle-class women, mostly non-Yiddish speakers from assimilated backgrounds, were sent by their parents to Polish, Russian and foreign *gymnasiums*/high schools and universities, where they absorbed radical ideologies and joined revolutionary conspiracies. Committed to liberating peasants and workers, they were actively recruited for social and political causes which needed their physical, intellectual and artistic talents. Poor working women in urban centers were also valued and recruited; educating themselves and studying marxist theory, these Yiddish-speaking women became worker organizers and political leaders. A new type of woman emerged: a *"kursistke"* — a woman who studied (took courses) and prepared herself for revolution.

Among these — both middle and working class — were aspiring women artists who also found the atmosphere encouraging. In *gymnasiums*, universities, political *krayzn*/study circles, women were told their intellectual and artistic talents were equal to those of men and were urged to develop them. On the surface at least, it appeared that future Yiddish women writers were entering an open and supportive literary arena eager to publish their writing.

On the surface ... for male Yiddishists were probably more conflicted over women's presence in their circles than they were willing to admit. Not satisfied to see Yiddish used solely as a language of political debate and propaganda, eager to gain for it the respect and prestige that Hebrew enjoyed, they wanted to "legitimize" Yiddish as a medium of secular artistic, moral and intellectual expression. To do so they needed to defeminize it, to dissociate it from its recent "degenerate" history and its older demeaning connection with women and illiterates. But such a course contradicted their own pro-women principles. It was "*di klasiker*," the classical writers, who resolved the dilemma.

THE "CLASSICAL" PERIOD:
THE DEFEMINIZATION OF *MAME-LOSHN*

At first, 19th-century Eastern European Jewish intellectuals adopted the western *maskilic* attitude to Yiddish and referred to it as "*zhargon.*" But as they came to identify more and more as Yiddishists, they required a name for their language that was not only dignified, but also reflective of Jewish cultural autonomy. By the end of the century they replaced "*zhargon*" with the name used by ordinary Jews, "*yidish*" (the language of the Jews) and, almost simultaneously, began to use in their published articles the more informal and affectionate, "*mame-loshn.*" Within a decade, for intellectuals, "*mame-loshn*" became synonymous with Yiddish itself.

The timing was not accidental. Throughout the 19th century, Eastern Europe was swept by national movements which glorified the "common man" and admired his untutored intellect. Influenced by these movements, Jewish intellectuals and radicals turned to the Jewish masses to strengthen and to prove Jewish nationhood. Affirming a common man's language, a historical "mother tongue," was part of the process. A growing sense of cultural autonomy also led Jewish scholars in the late 1800s to begin collecting the "innate" wisdom of *dos folk*/the people," their customs, myths, tales and proverbs, and to develop Yiddish scholarship and linguistics, ethnography, musicology and history. Their research into the rich, "raw" material which they had "discovered" conferred respectability on them as scholars and on their subject. The organizing first of *zhargon komitetn*/jargon committees (late 19th century), then of networks of *yidishe folkshules*/Yiddish secular schools (early 20th century), the standardizing of orthography and grammar also raised the status of Yiddish. In 1927 this legitimization culminated in Vilna with the founding of YIVO, Yiddish acronym for *Yidisher visnshaftlekher institut* [Jewish Scientific Institute] (now located in New York City and called Institute for Jewish Research) which was to become the repository, codifier and promoter of Yiddish language and culture.

For all its advances, however, it is ironic that the era in which male intellectuals defined, created and placed under their control Yiddish studies and literature was the same era in which they institutionalized the term *"mame-loshn"* and permanently endowed Yiddish with an essential feminine nature. Most likely these intellectuals accepted Yiddish as *"mame-loshn"* precisely because it was "folksy," associated with the "common man" while conveying a sentimental attachment to women and motherhood. Also, as *"mame-loshn,"* it embraced the past and gave scholars and nationalists continuity and authenticity.

Gaining popularity at this time was another term, derived from the title *Bove bukh* [Book of Bove], which in early 20th-century reprints had become *Bove mayse* [The story of Bove]. In speech, *"Bove"* became *"bobe,"* and *"bobe-mayse"* — literally

translated as "grandmother's story" — came to mean nonsense, fabrication, or an old wives' tale. Thus, *"mame-loshn"*
— referring to Yiddish — and *"bobe-mayse"* — referring to
women's story-telling and Yiddish literature — articulated
polarized attitudes towards women: deferential, if not reverential, and dismissive and patronizing.

In this climate and amidst the growing interest in Yiddish
scholarship, "classical Yiddish literature" was born through
the works of Shalom Jacob Abramovich, better known as
Mendele Mokher Sforim (1835-1917), I.L. Peretz (1852-
1915), and Sholem Rabinovich, better known as Sholom
Aleichem (1859-1916). All three published in Hebrew before
Yiddish (Peretz began writing in Polish) and all continued
writing in Hebrew throughout their lifetimes. For all three,
writing in Yiddish was a (self)conscious and an inherently
progressive act: an identification with the masses through
their spoken language. Yet all three expressed ambivalence to
both Yiddish and the masses: Mendele likened writing in
Yiddish to having an affair with a stranger and the new
Yiddish literature to an "illegitimate issue"; Sholom Aleichem
wondered how he could bring himself to write in a language
which "everyone speaks"; Peretz was convinced that "the
common people" would not understand him.

Their ambivalence towards Yiddish differentiated the
writers from scholars, who were inventing Yiddish studies
and legitimizing *mame-loshn* through its roots and long history among the masses. By contrast, secular writers were burdened by Yiddish literary history: after all, was it not all *bobe-
mayses?* To gain respect, they had to reinvent Yiddish literature by providing it with a clean slate.

The aim of Sholom Aleichem's famous declaration that he
was Mendele's literary heir was more than just self-aggran-
dizement and erasure of other serious writers. The young

writer knew that despite Mendele and despite theory and politics, Yiddish was on shaky ground as a medium for serious writing. What better way to show that contemporary Yiddish literature was not a continuation, but a break from its illiterate and women's roots than to fictionalize Mendele, at fifty-two, as its "*zeyde*/grandfather" (and creator) and Sholom Aleichem himself, at twenty-nine, his "*eynikl*/grandson"? By making literature in *mame-loshn* patrilineal rather than matrilineal, Sholom Aleichem instantly created a male Yiddish literary dynasty which mirrored the rabbinical scholarly dynasties whose legitimacy and fame were rooted in Hebrew. Just when Yiddish was being championed as an authentic national *mame-loshn*, Sholom Aleichem declared — and everyone agreed — its literature now belonged to the fathers.

Undoubtedly this defeminizing and separating the new from the old, the male from the female, were meant to "universalize" a literature which, until then, had been seen as rooted in the women's sphere. But, as feminist criticism has shown, western concepts of the "universal" assume the primacy of *men's* feelings, experiences and perceptions; they treat women's experiences as trivial or fail to differentiate them from men's. In either case, women's experiences are erased.

Such a false "universality" is present in classical Yiddish literature, which is dominated by male perspectives and concerns. To state the obvious: the classical writers wrote *as men*, often using first-person male narrators who presented the world and the women in it through men's eyes. In the early fiction, the frequent negative depiction of women, especially those from the *shtetl* — wives, market women, unmarried women as shrewish, conniving and gossipy — helped male writers to bond with male readers and to establish a male audience.

The "grandfather" set the tone and content. Typical is his

popular *The Travels of Benjamin the Third* (1878), where, from the start, Mendele, as narrator, unabashedly reveals his assumptions: " ... gentlemen, I want to tell you about one of our brethren... ." This man-to-man address is intensified by Mendele's "citations" from Benjamin's own first-person narrative; thus, both narrators collaborate in their depiction of women as shrews whose sole purpose in life is to torture their husbands. Though Benjamin and his friend Sender (demeaned by the nickname "Housewife") are fools, their wives are cruel stereotypes whose plight in the decaying social and economic world of the *shtetl* is never articulated, unlike the plight of the two anti-heroes.

Sholom Aleichem's earlier fiction, novels written in part to elevate the popular genre of women's romances, depicted the "modern" Jewish woman, in one case even the woman artist. But it was precisely his inability to come to terms with this modern woman, with her relationship to her Jewishness and to men, that led him to abandon the genre. Whatever his progressive feelings, those conveyed in the "message" of the early *Stempenyu: A Jewish Romance* (1889) seemed to have won out: a woman's most valued role is that of wife and mother supporting her husband's business and raising his sons.

Because his narrators are gentler, Sholom Aleichem's portraits of traditional women are gentler than those of Mendele. Tevye, for example, is soft and highly emotional, often crying like a woman. Though he denigrates his wife Golde and complains about being burdened by daughters, Tevye also expresses large-heartedness and love for them. The daughters gain in significance as each comes to represent an aspect of late 19th-century Eastern European Jewish life. Here too, as in earlier work, Sholom Aleichem records the emergence of the modern woman, whose images were a major breakthrough and exhilarated some women readers. But their depiction is limited, for we know them only through Tevye; we never hear *their* views or witness the process of their modernization. They are literary vehicles enabling Sholom Aleichem to explore men's feelings about contemporary Jewish issues.

Of the three classical writers, Peretz openly championed "the women's cause," understanding the price women paid for men's unreflective piety and the need for social reform. But like many who argue for a political position theoretically, Peretz never internalized it as a moral imperative and it is conspicuously absent from much of his writing. Critics have described *Monish* (1888), his first Yiddish literary endeavor, as expressing the feelings of a whole Jewish generation. Yet *Monish* is a man's poem about men's conflicts, sexual needs, attachments to Judaism and artistic aspirations. Peretz's interest in Hasidic tales, as well as his conceptualizing of "*di goldene keyt*/the golden chain" of Jewish tradition in terms of a male dynasty, contributed to the defeminization of Yiddish literature. In the early stories of *Impressions of a Journey through the Tomaszow Region in the Year 1890* and in the later, more overtly political ones, when not focussed on the plight of women, Peretz reverts to stereotypes. This is true even in his famous "Bontshe the Silent" (1894), whose title character embodies passive Jewish masses incapable of protesting his/their oppression or conceptualizing a future. Among Bontshe's burdens is a cruel wife who abandons him and the son he is unaware is not his. This story calls for workers' liberation from their own passivity *and* for men's liberation from women's basic deceitfulness. Bontshe, Everyworker, is a "universal" man.

So not only how these writers viewed themselves, but also what they wrote, point to a desire to create a literature by men and for men. The use of male narrators who had the freedom to travel and observe the world, the focus on boy-hood, young men's coming of age and adolescence, the male artist, the establishment of fictional and literary male dynas-ties, even tales of the Hasidim — all testified that literature in *mame-loshn* was now rooted in the male domain.

This was already evident in 1908 at the First Yiddish Language Conference in Czernowitz, which, permeated by Hebraist and Yiddishist tensions, legitimized Yiddish as *a national language* of the Jewish people. The published invita-tion — signed by, among others, Mendele — was addressed to "Honoured Sir!" and announced a conference on "our precious mother tongue." The conference itself was an almost exclusively male gathering which included such lead-ing scholars, linguists and writers as Nathan Birnbaum, Chaim Zhitlovsky, Peretz, Sholem Ash, and Avrom Reisen. The sole audible and very passionate woman's voice was that of the still Bundist-identified political theoretician and leader Esther Frumkin, who supported the adoption of Yiddish as *the national language*. Perceived as divisive, some blamed her for single-handedly ruining the conference. Unwilling to compromise, Frumkin eventually stormed out.

Frumkin's critique appeared in a post-conference report. Grounded in Bundist socialism, she was angry at the partici-pants' ambivalence to Yiddish. A democrat committed to class struggle, she also argued that the conference was not legally constituted because its "delegates" had not been elect-ed; it represented no-one and had no mandate or authority to do anything. She accused the delegates of having nothing in common except the ability to pay the fare to Czernowitz and of distancing themselves from local Jews, who were not allowed to attend. To Frumkin, the conference was an elite body cut off from "the folk."

The charge of elitism is interesting because it was aimed

at intellectuals whose politics identified them with the (male) masses. It is common today to approach classical Yiddish literature, particularly that of the *shtetl*, with a tearful and nostalgic eye and to depoliticize Mendele, Sholom Aleichem and Peretz, whose writings expressed complex feelings about Yiddish and Jewish life: deep affection, disgust, anger and frustration. Their work addressed the social and political issues facing Jews, their unalleviated poverty and vulnerability (to anti-Semitism) in the *shtetlekh* and exploitation by factory owners (often Jews) in urban centres. Each writer's political vision fueled his interest in *dos folk* and gave texture to his art's tone and content: depiction of *dos folk* in its own language, scathing critiques of *shtetl* life (especially by Mendele and Peretz), and anger at religious orthodoxy for not addressing material problems. Frumkin, aware these were concerns shared by most intellectuals, simply highlighted the contradiction between professed theory and practice.

This contradiction — with a different twist — was also noted by Bundist leader Ane Heller Rosenthal. In her memoir, Rosenthal recalled that in the early 1890s members of Vilna's *Zhargon komitet* were desperate to find appropriate reading materials. Rosenthal said most Yiddish-speaking workers whom the *Zhargon komitet* was trying to organize were illiterate; those who did read found Peretz incomprehensible. It seems that before Yiddish education had become firmly established, the "classics" were not as accessible as we sometimes believe.

To Frumkin and Rosenthal political concerns were a "given" and contradictions were easier to detect. Today, looking back, both are often rendered invisible because *shtetl* life and Yiddish literature have been wrapped in a veil of nostalgia which obscures their true complexity. For feminists to indulge in such nostalgia is particularly dangerous because it discourages criticism, fosters ignorance of the true condition of Eastern European Jewish women and, in this case, erases the magnitude of the classical writers' failures both in promoting the "women's cause" in their writing and in their relations with women writers.

In the two instances just cited, neither Frumkin nor Rosenthal spoke as women; yet they both showed a sensitivity to segments of the Jewish masses who — because of class, illiteracy, or lack of literary sophistication — initially found the emerging Yiddish culture and its creators inaccessible and distant. Frumkin's critique of Czernowitz was rooted in her class consciousness. But as its sole woman speaker, she must have also been aware of her own "otherness" vis-a-vis the male delegates and of the discrepancy between what these writers stated publicly about women's roles in politics and art and what she knew they whispered behind her back. Considered by some the Bund's most brilliant mind, Frumkin undoubtedly experienced much sexism in her political work.

By the time of the 1908 Czernowitz Conference, Yiddish literature had been transformed. Its perspective, its voice and its content were male, aiming to please the men in its audience. This new "classical" literature was now the reference point, the norm against which all subsequent Yiddish writing would be measured. To the men at Czernowitz, the sight of an independent, fearless and passionate woman like Esther Frumkin arguing for *mame-loshn* may well have been unsettling. It is also not hard to imagine what these men of letters must have felt when simultaneously with their efforts to sever *mame-loshn* from its women's roots, countless women writers interpreting the world through women's eyes and perspectives began creating a Yiddish literature focussed on women's experiences. As intellectuals and progressive men they were, theoretically, devoted to the "women's cause." But as men writers insecure about the stature and history of Yiddish, the possible emergence of a strong literary women's voice — diverging drastically from newly defined male norms — must have been an alarming prospect, one which could sabotage their own efforts.

WOMEN'S COUNTRY: A COUNTRY OF SECRETS

The translator and editor Joseph Leftwich has inadvertently provided a metaphor which captures the Yiddish literary world's attitude towards women at the end of the 19th century and later. Among the 140 poets in *The Golden Peacock: A Worldwide Treasury of Yiddish Poetry* (1961), Leftwich includes twelve women, the largest English representation of Yiddish women's poetry before or since. The book is organized according to the countries where writers were born or published. Following the last two, "Romania" and "England," Leftwich added two more sections, ostensibly to fulfill the "worldwide" promise of his title: "Women Poets" and "Hassidic Poets." The Hasidim's distinct traditions and strict separation from non-Jewish cultures give the segregation of their poetry some logic. However, wrenching women writers from their roots and from the geography and collective history of Ashkenazi Jews is bizarre. As Leftwich presents it, "Women Poets" is a country unlike any other: without borders and without connections to Jewish history and communal life. The contradiction: the existence of women writers is acknowledged, while their place *within* Jewish literary history is denied. The women writers are anomalies, the male writers the norm.

Far from being physically isolated, the lives and careers of Yiddish women writers were informed and shaped by modern Ashkenazi history. Of those in *Found Treasures*, only Rokhl

Brokhes never wandered from her native soil and perished in the Minsk ghetto during the Second World War. The others, like millions of Jews — adults and children — were swept up in waves of Jewish (im)migration, spending years, sometimes most of their lives in foreign countries. In 1907, for example, Yente Serdatzky at age thirty, Fradel Schtok at seventeen and Ida Maze at fourteen left Lithuania, Galicia and White Russia, respectively; Serdatzky and Schtok settled in New York City, Maze in Montreal. Celia Dropkin at thirty emigrated from Russia in 1912 for Chicago, Sarah Hamer-Jacklyn at nine from Poland in 1914 for Toronto.

But for some, political ideologies (especially Bundism, communism, and Zionism) and European upheavals inevitably complicated resettlement. In 1924, Shira Gorshman, eighteen, left Lithuania for Palestine; in 1930 her communist ideology led her to the Soviet Union where she worked in the Crimea towards building Jewish communal life. Having survived Stalinist purges and the Second World War, she returned in the late 1980s to Israel, where she now lives. In 1929 Blume Lempel at nineteen left Galicia for Paris; in 1939, on the eve of the Second World War, she relocated again, this time to New York City and today she lives and writes on Long Island. Lili Berger studied in Brussels and in 1936, at twenty, also immigrated to Paris. Active in the French Resistance during the Second World War, she survived the war and out of a socialist commitment returned to Warsaw. But the Polish anti-Semitic purges of the 1960s forced Berger to leave again for Paris, her current home. In 1936, the year Berger first left Poland for France, Kadia Molodowsky at forty-one left Warsaw for New York City. She seemed permanently settled there, but in the early 1950s moved to Israel. Two years later she was back in New York. As a teenager Rachel Korn spent the First World War in Vienna and then returned to her native Poland. Almost twenty-five years later, she fled the nazis to the Soviet Union where, like Gorshman, she survived the Holocaust. She next returned to Lodz, and then permanently immigrated (via Stockholm) to Montreal. At twenty-three, Chava Rosenfarb, a survivor of the Lodz ghetto and Auschwitz, settled in Belgium; five years later she too immigrated to Montreal, her present home.

But these women reflected the patterns of European Jewry in other ways. Some did not automatically accept Yiddish. Dropkin first began writing in Russian, Lee in German, Korn and Rikudah Potash in Polish. Both Korn and Potash took up Yiddish in reaction to Polish pogroms, in part a gesture of relinquishing hope of Jewish-Polish integration. Dropkin and Lee began writing in Yiddish after they had immigrated to the States, reflecting both their desire to assert their Jewishness culturally and linguistically and the dynamism of North American Yiddish-speaking communities in the early part of this century. While living in Poland and the Soviet Union, Berger and Gorshman wrote, in addition to Yiddish, in Polish and Russian respectively. Only Schtok turned away from Yiddish all together and, a few years before her death, published a novel in English.

Their education was predetermined by geography, economics, the Jewish orientation of the family and attitudes towards women. In different decades and places, girls' options varied, ranging from traditional Jewish *kheders*, later to secular Yiddish and Hebrew *folkshules*, Polish-Jewish schools, Polish and Russian *gymansiums*, and Jewish teachers' seminaries and European universities. Serdatzky, Brokhes, Schtok and Raskin — all of whom began writing during the "classical" period — represent a cross-section of Eastern European Jewish life at the turn of the century. Serdatzky's

father, a used furniture dealer, was a *lamdn*/scholar committed to educating his daughter. She attended a girls' *kheder*,
but cut off her formal education at age thirteen to become a
seamstress' apprentice. Still Serdatzky mastered Hebrew and
German and some Russian. Brokhes' father, a *maskil* and an
unpublished Hebrew author, insisted she be fluent in Hebrew
and study *tanakh*. Dropkin studied with a *rebetsn* until she was
eight, and later completed a Russian *gymnasium*. Schtok was
said to have been an excellent student who recited Goethe
and Schiller; Raskin undoubtedly received a socialist and
Yiddish education through Bundist *krayzn*.

Among later writers, Molodowsky, the daughter of a
melamed/teacher, studied *khumesh* and *gemore* along with her
father's other students and later graduated from Warsaw's
Hebrew teachers' seminary. Dora Schulner's father was also a
melamed who owned a fine library. Though orphaned at an
early age, she was influenced by her early surroundings.
Malka Lee, from a Hasidic background, attended a Yiddish
folkshule and a Polish *gymnasium* and became fluent in
German (she went to Hunter College in New York City).
Hamer-Jacklyn attended Toronto public schools; Rachel Korn
went to Polish-Jewish schools and took private Polish lessons.

These biographical details — from the lexicons (which
tend to focus on the father) and from book prefaces — indi-
cate that these particular women began life, for the most
part, in surroundings which encouraged them to study and
learn; for some, poverty more than sexism was initially the
barrier. Their formal education may have been too brief and
not pedagogically sound, but the *idea* of learning, of pursuing
intellectual activities, was not taboo for them as young girls.

The literary and political circles (Yiddish, Polish and
Russian) which they joined must have also encouraged and
motivated women to write and to publish. One indication is

the age at which they made their literary "debuts" (provided by the lexicons). Between 1899 and 1927, Brokhes, Potash and Lee debuted at age nineteen; Schtok and Korn at twenty; Dropkin at twenty-four; Serdatzky and Molodowsky at twenty-six. Serdatzky, Potash and Molodowsky belonged to writers' groups based in Kovno, Lodz and Kiev. Some also had contact, support and appreciation from well-known male writers. Serdatzky was encouraged by Peretz, who published her first story in *Der veg* [The way]. Schtok was declared by Melekh Ravitch to be one of the finest story writers of her generation. Dropkin's talent was recognized by Avrom Leyesin; Schulner was encouraged by Professor Max Weinreich of YIVO; Sholem Ash admired Potash, naming her "the Jerusalem poetess." Molodowsky, Rosenfarb and Korn were recipients of various Yiddish prizes awarded during the post-Holocaust era.

Above all, women writers published individual books and fiction and essays in national and international Yiddish journals and newspapers. At least half the writers in *Found Treasures* appeared in New York's *Tsukunft* [Future], where some also made their literary debuts: Schtok in 1918, Raskin in the 1920s, and Rosenfarb in 1946. Many were contributors to New York's *Dos naye land* [The New Land] and *Der forverts* [The Jewish Daily Forward] edited by Avrom Reisen and Abraham Cahan respectively; in the post-Holocaust Israeli literary journal *Di goldene keyt* [The Golden Chain], edited by Avrom Sutzkever and the post-Stalinist *Sovyetish heymland* [Soviet Homeland]. Wherever they lived, they sent their work to local and other Yiddish journals in Montreal and Toronto, Chicago and Los Angeles, Mexico City and Buenos Aires, and Paris and Tel-Aviv.

A number were also prolific. A volume of Serdatzky's collected writings appeared in 1913. Brokhes was the author of two hundred short stories. When the nazis invaded Poland, a volume of her collected prose was already typeset; but the book was never printed and the manuscript did not survive. Gorshman wrote over thirty novellas and novels. Molodowsky, Korn, Berger and Rosenfarb each have published significant numbers of novels, collections of stories, essays and memoirs.

However, their rootedness in and identification with Jewish life, commitment to Yiddish and publications never secured them an honoured place in Yiddish cultural history. Despite the record of their writings, not a single woman prose writer has ever received attention and respect comparable to those accorded male writers during and since the classical period. The origins of this erasure can be traced to Yiddish cultural leaders and writers whose ambivalence towards them and their work left women in a limbo, a women's country from which most could not escape.

Despite the professed "pro-woman" politics of progressive Yiddish secularists and culturalists, the anarchist *Fraye arbeter shtime*[Free Voice of Labour] was the rare paper which had a genuine interest in women's writing. On the whole, women's prose was published only sporadically. For example, in the late 1910s, *Tsukunft* ran a series of Ester Luria's articles on famous women (Jews and non-Jews); all were either dead or had no connection to contemporary Yiddish culture. During the same period of more than three years, *Tsukunft*, a monthly, published nothing about Yiddish women writers, nor anything by a woman about Jewish social issues; creative contributions by women consisted of two short stories and about six poems. Thus, any woman's writing which was published in *Tsukunft* in this period was more a personal triumph than a feminist breakthrough.

There are probably many reasons why the response to women's prose was more negative than to the poetry. Prose tends to be associated with intellectual matters, poetry with feeling. Women prose writers tend to be less accepted for interpreting and commenting on Jewish life than women poets for expressing emotions. For example, it is significant that the term "*maskil*" — a follower of the enlightenment, the modern European Jewish intellectual and progressive who embraced secular ideas and science — is never used in Yiddish in relation to a woman. A woman could be the mother, wife, and/or daughter of a *maskil*, but she herself was never described as one. The whole *haskole* movement of the *maskilim* has always been conceived of in male terms.

Also, unlike poetry, prose requires a commitment of space from an editor to a writer. Especially at the end of the 19th and the beginning of the 20th centuries — during the establishment of a male norm and audience — editors were probably reluctant to give much space to women writers. Editors might accept individual pieces which may or may not have dealt with women's issues, but — consciously or not — they would have limited women's contributions to prevent the feminizing of their audience.

Their use of Yiddish should have placed women writers within the Jewish literary sphere; yet early Yiddish women writers were outsiders. The literary sphere had been shaped by centuries-old quarrels from which women had traditionally been excluded. For example, women writers' inner conflicts over Yiddish, unlike the men's, involved non-Jewish languages, not Hebrew. Before the Hebrew *folkshules*, the great majority of women never received the education which would have enabled them both to draw on and rebel against Hebrew traditions. By writing out of their own experiences as girls and women, daughters and mothers, intellectual women single and married, women writers were creating a literature unlike that of contemporary male writers. Their literature was alien and conveyed a different reality and different contradictions within Jewish life.

Superficially, many women's themes do not differ from those of men and include: childhood; education; the impact of the *haskole* on the Eastern European *shtetl*; political movements; immigration and its effects on Jewish life; the Holocaust and post-Holocaust life; the artist, etc. But these themes were inevitably *transformed* when presented from a woman's perspective. They lost their "universality" (male focus): childhood (boyhood) became girlhood; political struggle (of men workers) became, in part, the struggle against "progressive" sexism; the artist (male) became the woman artist. Such transformations are inherently radical and challenge both the norms and assumptions of literary traditions and of the society from which those traditions spring.

The covert resistance which women faced both among the progressives and in society in general took its toll. At the end of the 19th century, most Jewish women — especially those from poor and working-class backgrounds — had few options. The main "profession" open to them was that of seamstress, a step up from various types of factory work. (Later on, teaching became a primary option.) In secular, just as in observant communities, marriage remained a necessary strategy for survival, though often it brought poorer women even greater burdens and responsibilities. Early writers like Serdatzky and Dropkin were overwhelmed by earning a living and/or taking care of their families — Serdatzky was a cook and took in boarders, Dropkin raised five children. The combined difficulties of finding time to write, of being taken seriously enough to be published, resulted sometimes in the deadening of creativity as described by Tillie Olsen in *Silences*. Serdatzky, Schtok and Dropkin stopped writing for long periods and dropped out of literary circles all together.

The date of Schtok's death in a mental sanitarium is uncertain because no contemporary literary figure was concerned with her fate.

The double messages are familiar. Whether at the end of the 20th or the 19th centuries, the process of giving up and sharing power (progressive rhetoric not withstanding) has never occurred willingly nor easily. Thus, early Yiddish women writers were acutely aware of the unfulfilled promises of secular liberation, but also of the impossibility, for them, of returning to observant life. In looking back, some writers presented graphic depictions of confining orthodox roles which forced women into arranged marriages and denied them full autonomy. Brokhes' *"Fartshadet"* [Dazed],[2] Schulner's "Reyzele's Wedding" and Schtok's *"Opgeshnitene hor"* [The Shorn Head], provide intimate views of a woman's revulsion at the prospect of marrying and having sexual relations with a man she does not know, a girl's helplessness against traditional and parental authority, and the long-term consequences of early widowhood on a young woman.

The awareness of women's unequal status in the progressive secular world led to different types of stories. Miriam Raskin in her autobiographical novel *Zlatke* describes with subtle irony the lack of understanding by Zavl, her heroine's suitor/comrade, of women's new role in the workers' (Bundist) struggle and in future society. Dreaming of economic independence, *Zlatke* has trained as a seamstress in order to be "self-sufficient; [so that] no-one at home could tell her what to do." Zavl too has his dreams, through which Raskin reveals her awareness of the differences between men's and women's concepts of women's equality. Zavl, we are told,

> would see himself and Zlatke sitting at the table eating a supper which she had prepared. Zlatke, happy and cheerful,

wearing a white apron, presiding over their domesticity. Their family would grow, children would come. All the while they'd remain dedicated fighters in the movement; one thing had nothing to do with the other.

Committed to Bundism and to women's equality, Raskin was obviously aware, as many other women must have been, of the absurdity of the idea of "let's do things differently, but keep things the same."

Serdatzky's critique was far angrier. In *"Vide"* [Confession], the main character Mary Rubin complains of parasitic male intellectuals and radicals who use up women in political work and in their own sexual gratification and then discard them. Miriam Karpilov, of the same generation as Serdatzky, published in 1918 *Tog-bukh fun an elende meydl* [Diary of a Lonely Girl]; the novel's subtitle tells all: *Der kamf kegn fraye libe* [The Struggle against Free Love]. According to both writers, the liberation of women from traditional roles did not include liberation from men's continued exploitation.

Women's fiction about forced marriages or seduction of immigrant girls by unscrupulous men paralleled male fiction critical of these and other aspects of traditional and modern life and was probably unthreatening to male editors. However, it is unlikely that critiques which implicated progressive political allies and fellow writers would have been welcomed or popular; it is understandable that some women writers avoided these issues altogether.

But anger can never be totally repressed and a number of writers offered coded critiques. Through creative and artistic female characters, they expressed their own preoccupations and frustrations with the "modern" woman's condition. Dropkin's "A Dancer" is perhaps the most telling and explosive. Its main character, Gysia, is an artist manqué, a woman unable to express the artist in her. Yearning to become a dancer, but acutely in touch with reality, she understands the discrepancy between what she thinks, feels and wants, and what she will be allowed to express and do. Her final withdrawal into silence stems from her well-grounded fear that any disclosure to her husband of her true feelings and thoughts will lead to her being institutionalized.

Other writers also created women characters whose aspirations moved beyond home and family. Sheyndl, in Schtok's "*Opgeshnitene hor*," is a young widow who expresses her rebellious and artistic nature by allowing her hair to grow back beneath her *sheytl*/wig and by sewing exotic clothes which she can never wear in her *shtetl*. Brokhes' *zogerin*, Gnesye, is another unfulfilled artist who has spent a lifetime putting all her creative energy into other women's prayers, but never into her own. When we meet her, she has finally snapped and is raging in frustration at being left poor and empty. And there is the ten-year-old heroine of Hamer-Jacklyn's "My Mother's Dream" whose only solace after her mother's death is the nightly dreams in which she imaginatively brings her mother back to life. But the girl, like Dropkin's Gysia, instinctively knows that others (especially her father and grandfather) will misunderstand and destroy these visions; so she too retreats into silence, telling no-one but the reader of her pain and comfort. Repeatedly these stories present the creative/artistic Jewish woman/girl as an outsider, someone depleted by society and by those closest to her, someone unable to risk speaking the truth for fear she will not be heard or will be considered mad or immoral.

Like much of classical Yiddish fiction, many of these stories are first-person narratives or use narrators closely identified with the women protagonists; it is useful to compare them to Sholom Aleichem's classical narrator/talker, Tevye.

Wanting to show off his "scholarly" knowledge and to create a bond with the reader (or Sholom Aleichem), Tevye depends on an engaged listener and respondent. As one critic points out, this kind of encounter between "two Jewish males" is "a natural form of... [Yiddish] literature." In this case, Tevye's engaged monologues confirm what his readers suspected all along: things are bad, they may get worse, and God's reasoning remains a mystery. Throughout, Tevye rightly assumes his readers are like him, that he and they inhabit the same world, share the same human condition.

But in many of the women's stories, there is no engagement or common ground between the narrator and the reader. Serdatzky, Brokhes, Rosenfarb and Lempel — writers who represent the earliest secular women's literature and the most recent — all have speakers who, unlike Tevye, address either unsympathetic listeners or no-one. In Serdatzky's "Unchanged," the nameless narrator, on the verge of suicide, tells her life story of sexual liberation and betrayal to a writer who is listening only because she is in search of new "material." Gnesye the *zogerin* rages over the injustice in her life, but her eleven-year-old grandson does not understand her; the women in the courtyard do and consider her insane. Lempel's "Correspondents" begins and ends with the destruction of letters. The first written (and immediately torn up) by the nameless narrator expresses her feelings for a young woman. The second, from the young woman herself, is also destroyed by the narrator who cannot face its lesbian overtones. Rosenfarb's narrator Rella in "Edgia's Revenge" addresses no-one, is terrified that her *kapo* history will be revealed.

It is an inherent paradox that these stories' structure and content simultaneously focus on speech and on silence. Rather than monologues, many are soliloquies which do not demand a response. Readers learn of hidden feelings and secrets only because they are reluctant eavesdroppers. The narrator/protagonist of "Correspondents," Rella of "Edgia's Revenge" and Gysia of "A Dancer" speak to the reader through a wall of silence; only the reader has any inkling of what they think or feel. Their speech never creates a bond because they speak about what no-one wants to hear. If as readers we do identify, it is often about something we would not want to admit to.

An astonishing number of these stories revolve around unexpressed feelings, thoughts and secrets. Manya, in Schtok's "The Veil," has no-one to talk to and is muffled by her mother as she is led away from the wedding festivities. Dropkin's Gysia keeps her artistic nature a secret. The Bundist Sadie, in Raskin's "At a Picnic," though bonded with her former comrades, is unable to express her secret disappointment in her sons' lack of political commitment and stoically keeps it from her friends. Lee vividly describes her father's attempt to destroy her manuscripts and Gorshman the inability of a mother and daughter to speak to each other about the past. Slucka-Kestin tells of the silence between Paula, married to an Arab, and her family, Berger of the silence surrounding a hidden Jewish child adopted by Poles.

In Berger's story, Katerine's stepmother decides to help her find her true identity; Lee's mother also helps her daughter establish an independent life. But these instances of women supporting each other are rare and, for the most part, women receive neither comfort nor support from other women. Serdatzky's narrator ("Unchanged") complains that women's compassion over her misfortunes too quickly transforms into envy and malice when her luck changes. Gnesye the *zogerin* hates and, in turn, is unsupported by the women in her *shtetl.* For Rella, it is a woman, Edgia, who is the great enemy. In other stories, we read of lifelong, unresolved tensions between mothers and daughters (all recounted from the daughters' points of view): mothers demanding daughters sacrifice their girlhood (Raskin's "Zlatke," Schtok's "The Veil"); mothers allowing daughters to be married against their will (Schulner's "Reyzele's Wedding"); mothers withholding comfort (Gorshman's "Unspoken Hearts"). The picture is of women extremely isolated from each other.

It seems likely that the sense of isolation evoked in these stories reflected, in part, these writers' isolation from each other — especially those of the early period. Though it would be unrealistic to expect them to have the consciousness to create the kinds of networks some women writers have today or even to have formalized their concerns, it is disappointing that they seemed unsupportive of each other. Awareness of the need of such support did exist as is evidenced by the Bundist Ane Heller Rosenthal who not only founded YAF (*Yidishe arbeter froyen*) — the Bund's Jewish Working Women's Organization — but also paid tribute, in an article on the Bund's fortieth anniversary, to its women organizers. Yet not once in *Svive*[Environment], a literary journal which she controlled as editor and publisher, did Molodowsky write or ask someone else to write an essay on the individual and collective contributions of women writers to Yiddish culture. In fact, nothing like Rosenthal's article seems to have been written about women writers by one of their own. Had it been otherwise, it is doubtful so many of women's *published* writings would have been forgotten so quickly. The causes for this need to be further investigated.

But it is important not to jump to conclusions. Feminist Yiddish critics are just beginning to consider these questions and to look at original Yiddish sources. Forms of support may have existed which are not evident to us at this time. What is evident is that women's prose contributions to modern

Yiddish literature are now being recovered only because of feminist efforts. This work is motivated by scholarly interests, but also by Jewish women's needs to reconstruct and claim an authentic past in which women are included. Without it, most of us feel unrooted and incomplete. *Found Treasures* is a major step towards such reconstruction.

It is still too early to formulate broad theories about Yiddish women's writing. Yet it is clear that many of these women individually remade Yiddish literature every time they sat down to write. Their stories contain faint echoes from an older women's literature, especially that of the *tkhines*, Yiddish women's prayers — their secrets, their pain, their wish for release. But if indeed these are *tkhines* transformed, then we need to recognize that they are spoken in stories without a religious framework, without a sympathetic overhearer.

The classical writers left us images of Jewish life which lend themselves to nostalgia and to the fabrication of a coherent and orderly past. These women's stories do not allow for such fabrication. More resistant to nostalgia, they provide a past which cannot be romanticized and which, for women, does not differ in many ways from the "liberated" present in its contradictions and challenges. The Yiddish women's writing anthologized in *Found Treasures* is truly unique in its insistence on its own perspectives, its own truths, and its own tradition.

NOTES

1. Statistics on the representation of women in popular and scholarly English collections are: Howe and Greenberg, *A Treasury of Yiddish Stories* (1953) — 23 writers, 620 pp., no women; Dawidowicz, *The Golden Tradition: Jewish Life and Thought in Eastern Europe* (1967) — 57 writers, 502 pp., 3 women, 25 pp.;

Rosenfeld, *Pushcarts and Dreamers: Stories of Jewish Life in America* (1967) — 10 writers, 254 pp., no women; Leftwich, *Great Yiddish Writers of the Twentieth Century* (1969) — 82 writers, 840 pp., 1 woman, 5 pp.; Howe and Greenberg, *Voices from the Yiddish: Essays, Memoirs, Diaries* (1972) — 22 writers, 328 pp., no women; Neugroschel, *The Shtetl: A Creative Anthology of Jewish Life in Eastern Europe* (1979) — 20 writers, 569 pp., no women; Fishman, *Never say Die! A Thousand Years of Yiddish in Jewish Life and Letters* (1981) — 48 writers, 763 pp. (oversize book), 4 women, 30 pp.

The field of poetry is as follows: Betsky, *Onions and Cucumbers and Plums: 46 Yiddish Poems* (1958) — 14 poets, 250 pp., 1 woman, 12 pages; Leftwich, *The Golden Peacock: Worldwide Treasure of Yiddish Poetry* (1961) — 141 poets, 722 pp., 12 women, 32 pp.; Howe and Greenberg, *A Treasury of Yiddish Poetry* (1969) — 58 poets, 369 pp., 6 women, 20 pages; Whitman, *An Anthology of Modern Yiddish Poetry* (1979) — 14 poets, 135 pp., 3 women, 22 pp.; Harshav and Harshav, *American Yiddish Poetry: A Bilingual Anthology* (1986) — 7 poets, 700 pp., 1 "poetess." 35 pp.; Howe, Wisse and Shmeruk, *The Penguin Book of Modern Yiddish Verse* (1987) — 39 poets, 703 pp., 5 women, 50 pp.

2. All my comments refer to the stories in this collection, except for: Brokhes' *"Fartshadet"* [Dazed], Schtok's *"Opgeshnitene hor"* [The Shorn Head] and Serdatzky's *"Vide"* [Confession], as well as Miriam Karpilov's novel *Tog-bukh fun an elende meydl* [Diary of a Lonely Girl].

SELECTED BIBLIOGRAPHY

Baum, Charlotte, Paula Hyman and Sonya Michel. *The Jewish Woman in America*. New York: Dial, 1975.

Berger, Shulamis. *"Tehines*: A Brief Study of Women's Prayers." In *Daughters of the King: Women & the Synagogue*, 73–83. Edited by Susan Grossman and Rivka Haut. New York: Jewish Publication Society, 1992.

Dawidowicz, Lucy. "Introduction: The World of East European Jewry." In *The Golden Tradition: Jewish Life and Thought in Eastern Europe*, 5-90. New York: Schocken, 1967.

Falkovich, E. *"Ester — der lebensveg fun der groyser revolutsyonern"* [Esther (Frumkin) — The Life of a Great Revolutionary]. *Folkshtime* [Folk Voice] (1965), 20: 1-6.

Glenn, Susan A. *Daughters of the Shtetl: Life & Labor in the Immigrant Generation*. Ithaca: Cornell University, 1990.

Goldsmith, Emanuel S. *Modern Yiddish Culture: The Story of the Yiddish Language Movement*. New York: Shapolsky and Workmen's Circle, 1987.

Howe, Irving and Eliezer Greenberg. "Introduction." In *A Treasury of Yiddish Stories*, 1-71. New York: Schocken, 1953.

Howe, Irving. *World of Our Fathers*. New York: Harcourt Brace Jovanovich, 1976.

Kagan (Kohn), Berl. *Leksikon fun yidish-shraybers* [Lexicon of Yiddish Writers]. New York: Rayah Ilman-Kagan (Kohn), 1986.

Klepfisz, Irena. *"Di mames, dos loshn*/The mothers, the language: Feminism, *Yidishkayt*, and the Politics of Memory." *Bridges*, IV: 1 (1994), 12-47.

——. *Dreams of an Insomniac: Jewish Feminist Essays, Speeches and Diatribes*. Portland: Eighth Mountain, 1990.

——. "Jewish Feminism 1913: Yente Serdatzky's 'Confession'." *Bridges*, I: 2 (1990), 77-78.

Korman, E. *"Forvort"* [Forward]. In *Yidishe dikhterins antologye* [Yiddish Poetesses Anthology] vii–lxv. Chicago: Farlag L. M. Shtayn, 1928.

Korn, Rachel (Rochl). "Bronia" and "Bluma Zelinger." Translated by Abraham Boyarsky. In *Canadian Yiddish Writings*, 51–63, 65–88. Edited by Abraham Boyarsky and Lazar Sarna. Montreal: Harvest House, 1976.

———. "Earth." Translated by Miriam Waddington. In *Canadian Jewish Short Stories*, 1–22. Edited by Miriam Waddington. Toronto: Oxford University Press, 1990.

Leksikon fun der nayer yidisher literatur [Lexicon of New Yiddish Literature]. New York: Congress of Jewish Culture, Inc., 1956, 1958, 1961, 1965, 1968, 1981.

Lempel, Blume. *"Bilder fun a nakete kanve"* [Pictures on a Bare Canvas]. In Yiddish and English. Translated by Sheva Zucker. *Bridges* (1993), II: 2, 12–25.

Levin, Nora. *While Messiah Tarried: Jewish Socialist Movements 1871-1917.* New York: Schocken, 1977.

Luria, Ester. *"Sholem Aleykhem un di yidishe froy"* [Sholom Aleichem and the Jewish Woman]. *Tsukunft* (August 1916), 710-713.

Miron, Dan. *A Traveler Disguised: A Study in the Rise of Modern Yiddish Fiction in the Nineteenth Century.* New York: Schocken, 1973.

Molodowsky, Kadia (Kadya). "The Lost Shabes." Translated by Irena Klepfisz. In *The Tribe of Dina: A Jewish Women's Anthology*, 145–147. Editors Melanie Kaye/Kantrowitz and Irena Klepfisz. Boston: Beacon, 1989.

———. "Gone." Translated by Irena Klepfisz. *Jewish Currents* (July-August, 1990), 42: 7, 31–33.

Niger, Samuel. *Bilingualism in the History of Jewish Literature.* Translated by Joshua A. Fogel. Landham MD: University Press of America, 1990.

———. *Di yidishe literatur un di lezerin* [Yiddish Literature and the Woman Reader]. Vilna: Vilner farlag, 1919.

Norich, Anita. "Portraits of Artists: Three Novels by Sholom Aleichem." *Prooftexts* (September 1984), 4: 3, 237-52.

———. "The Autobiographical Imagination." In *Homeless Imagination in the Fiction of I.J. Singer*, 87–96. Bloomington: Indiana University Press, 1991.

———. "The Family Singer and the Autobiographical Imagination." *Prooftexts* (January, 1990), 10: 1, 91–107.

Ozick, Cynthia. "Sholem Aleichem's Revolution." In *Metaphor & Memory*. New York: Random House, 1991, 173-198.

Pratt, Norma Fain. "Culture and Radical Politics: Yiddish Women Writers 1890-1940." *American Jewish History* (1981), LXX , 60-91.

———. Editor. "Eastern European Jewish Women Immigrants: To America and to Pre-State Israel." Special issue of *Shofar* (Summer 1991), 9: 4.

Reizen, Zalman. *Leksikon fun der yidisher literatur, prese, un filologye* [Lexicon of Yiddish Literature, Press and Philology]. Third edition. Vilna: Vilner Farlag fun B. Kletskun, 1927, 1928, 1929.

Rosenfarb, Chava. "The Greenhorn." Translated by Miriam Waddington. In *Canadian Jewish Short Stories*, 111–121. Edited by Miriam Waddington. Toronto: Oxford University Press, 1990.

Rosenthal, Ane Heller. "*Bletlekh fun a lebns geshikhte*" [Pages from a Life History]. *Di yidishe sotsyalistishe bavegung biz der grindung fun "bund"* [The Jewish Socialist Movement until the Founding of the "*Bund*"], *Historishe shriftn* [Historical Writings]. Vilna: YIVO, 1939, III, 416-437.

Roskies, David G. "Yiddish Popular Literature and the Female Reader." *Journal of Popular Culture*, X: 4, 352-358.

Schtok, Fradel (Fradl). "The Shorn Head." Translated by Irena Klepfisz. In *The Tribe of Dina: A Jewish Women's Anthology*, 190–193. Editors Melanie Kaye/ Kantrowitz and Irena Klepfisz. Boston: Beacon, 1989.

Seller, Maxine S. "World of Our Mothers: The Women's Page of The Jewish Daily Forward." *The Journal of Ethnic Studies* (1988), 16:2, 95-118.

Serdatzky, Yente (Yentl). "*Vide*" [Confession]. In Yiddish and English. Translated by Irena Klepfisz. *Bridges* (1990), I: 2, 79–92.

Shepherd, Naomi. *A Price Below Rubies: Jewish Women as Rebels & Radicals*. Boston: Harvard University Press, 1993.

Sinclair, Clive. "Esther Singer Kreitman: The trammeled talent of Isaac Beshevis Singer's neglected sister." *Lilith* (Spring, 1991), 8–9.

Sokoloff, Naomi, et al. editors. *Gender & Text in Modern Hebrew and Yiddish Literature*. New York: Jewish Theological Seminary, 1992.

Waddington, Miriam. "Mrs. Maza's Salon" and "Rokhl Korn: Remembering a Poet." In *Apartment Seven: Essays Selected and New*, 3–8, 190–199. Toronto: Oxford University Press, 1989.

Weinberg, Sydney. *The World of Our Mothers*. Chapel Hill: University of North Carolina, 1988.

Weinreich, Max. "Internal Jewish Bilingualism." In *History of the Yiddish Language*, 247-314. New York: University of Chicago Press, 1980.

Weissler, Chava. "Prayers in Yiddish and the Religious World of Ashkenazic Women." In *Jewish Women in Historical Perspective*, 159–181. Edited by Judith R. Baskin. Detroit: Wayne State University, 1991.

Weissman, Debra. "*Bais Yaakov*: A Historical Model for Jewish Feminists." In *The Jewish Woman: New Perspectives*, 139-48. Edited by Elizabeth Koltun. New York: Schocken, 1976.

Wisse, Ruth, editor. "Introduction." *The I. L. Peretz Reader*, xiii-xxx. New York: Schocken, 1990.

——. "Two Jews Talking: A View of Modern Yiddish Literature." *Prooftexts* (January 1984), 4:1, 35-48.

MY MOTHER'S DREAM

Sarah Hamer-Jacklyn

❦

Like many stories in this collection, "My Mother's Dream"
functions as a yisker bikhl *commemorating the destroyed*
Jewish communities of Eastern Europe. Hamer-Jacklyn
recreates the shtetl *which she had left behind forty years*
earlier with vivid details of both language and image.

Judaism, like all patriarchies, favours males over
females and in its orthodox expression it adds a religious
dimension: the son, the kadesh, *is designated to perpetuate*
the memory of his parents by reciting the memorial prayer
for them. It is an indication of the author's subtlety and
perception that Sorele, the young protagonist, is complicit
in her culture's devaluation of the female, while it is her
grandfather who rejects a rigid interpretation of Jewish
law and custom.

SHABES AFTERNOON. Father was napping. Mother was reading the *Taytsh-khumesh* and I was listening to the beautiful
tale, drinking in every word.

Suddenly the door opened and my grandmother entered,
looking angry and upset. She snapped a "Good *Shabes*," sat
herself down at the window and, sullen, looked down at the
street. Nervously she tugged at the slider of her gold chain,
pulling it up and down. She said not a word. Mother closed
the *Taytsh-khumesh* and got up from her chair. A blue silk
jacket trimmed with lace helped conceal her heavy body, but
I knew that she'd soon give birth. Slender, of medium height,

her figure bent stiffly with the weight of her belly. Large, gentle brown eyes shone from her pale, expressive face. With a white silk handkerchief she wiped the sweat from her high forehead and straight, thin nose. Patting her *sheytl*, which looked almost like her own hair, she asked her mother-in-law, "Would *Shviger* like perhaps a glass of tea?"

"I don't need any tea!" replied grandmother angrily, and she added, "Nice things I hear about you!"

Mother was confused. Then it dawned on her, "No doubt *Shviger* is thinking of my visit to Dr. Mitlman for an examination."

"Exactly! Now I ask you, why would a good Jewish-daughter go to a male doctor? You've already had five children, may these three live long years, and always with a midwife. Why suddenly a doctor? It's a sacrilege."

Mother soothed her, "In any event, I didn't find him at home."

"So, it's all for the best," replied grandmother, relieved.

"I think so too. It's probably destined that this time too I'll manage without a doctor. Still, there's something I, myself, don't understand, *Shviger*," complained my mother, "with the other children I never felt so unwell ..." and she bent towards grandmother, whispering something quietly into her ear.

"So!" With a wave of her hand, grandmother dismissed my mother's secret. "It's nothing, foolishness; it'll pass. We're all in the hands of the Almighty. But tell me, whose idea was it that you go to a doctor?"

"Mrs. Shashevsky's."

"Oy!" and Grandmother clapped her hands. "That heretic! She's actually kept her own hair, refuses to wear a *sheytl*; doesn't go to synagogue on *Shabes* and — they say — she doesn't even keep a *kosher* home. How did you get to her in the first place?"

"She comes into the store; happens to be a nice woman,

and a good customer; always asks me how I am. So we got to talking and I told her how everything about this pregnancy was different. So she insisted — and wouldn't let up — that I go to the doctor immediately."

My grandmother practically jumped out of her chair. "*That* woman shouldn't be allowed into a Jewish home and *my* daughter-in-law should certainly not follow her advice." Mama agreed, and my grandmother, mollified now, requested a glass of tea.

To me she said, "If your mother has another girl, your value will diminish." Her words scalded me. Ever since my mother had become pregnant everyone had teased me. If it wasn't a boy this time either, they said, I'd be worth even less. That had frightened me terribly: If God forbid, it was a girl, I'd soon be worth nothing at all. The question of what Papa would say bored endlessly into my child's mind.

I felt such pity for him. I still hadn't forgotten what had gone on when my third little sister was born. I remembered exactly how my father stood at the door of the birthing room, agitated and with great anticipation, waiting for the announcement that his *kadesh*, a son, had come into the world. During my mother's pregnancy he had made a pilgrimage to the *Rebe* to offer a large contribution, certain that this time the child would be a male. I was standing beside him, ready to carry forth the news. A terrible scream was heard and, soon after, the muffled cry of the infant. Minutes later, Malke, the midwife, appeared and announced, "A girl!"

My father hadn't responded. Close to fainting, he collapsed into a chair and stayed there, confused, bitter, silent. With all of my eight years, I had understood my father's grief and shouldered my mother's guilt. Quietly I asked, "What should I say Mama had, a boy or a girl?" My father came to. "Hmmm. Oh, yes, tell *Bobe* and *Zeyde* and the rest of the family that it's a girl; but to others, to strangers, say that it's a boy. They'll learn the truth soon enough."

This time, if, God forbid, Mama had a girl, I wouldn't tell a lie. I'd say that it was a girl; I didn't want to be called a liar later.

Night and morning, after prayers I pleaded, "Dear God, let the new child that you send us be a brother for me." Then it occurred to me that a little girl's prayers might not reach the heavens for the Almighty to hear. After much thought, I decided that the most suitable messenger to God would be my devout grandfather. He was, after all, the eldest trustee to the great and holy Reb Yekhezkele of Radom and was himself immersed in the holy books day and night.

Early Sunday I ran straight to *Zeyde's* but came to a stop near the house. His *Gemore* chant was drifting through the open window. I tiptoed in to the little alcove and remained at the door. *Zeyde*, completely absorbed, swayed over the pages of the open *Gemore*. He turned and saw me, straightened his skull cap and smoothed his grey beard. His parchment-yellow face broke into a smile. With contained pleasure he asked, "Why so early, Sorele?"

"I want to ask you for something."

"Aha, I understand ...," reaching into his pocket.

"No, no, I don't want any money."

"No money? What else would one want from a *Zeyde*?"

"That you ... that you ... should pray ...," I stammered, not knowing how to tell him.

"Pray? Pray for what?"

"To the Almighty ...."

He smiled broadly. "But what shall I pray for?"

"That my mother have a boy," I uttered in one breath.

His smile vanished. His face suddenly darkened and he spoke sternly, "It is not for a boy that you should be praying, my child. We should pray that your mother come through this safely."

And once again he plunged into the tome, swaying more fiercely and reciting even louder, with greater passion and devotion. I lingered a while longer, but it seemed my grandfather had somehow forgotten me. Frightened, I shuffled out of the house and sadly went home.

Friday night as my mother swayed devoutly over the *Shabes* candles, I heard her add to the usual blessing, "Lord of the Universe, Master of All Worlds, small and insignificant am I, a sinful woman, unworthy of pronouncing Your holy name, a mother of three cherished children, I ask of You: show Your kindness and graciousness and keep Your right hand over my delivery, that I may be privileged to nurture my children."

"Amen," I whispered piously. Mama looked at me through tear-filled eyes.

Father came into the house with a cheerful "Good *Shabes!*"

"Without a guest?" Mama asked, disappointed.

"Before I could look around properly," he said, "the visitors had all been snatched up."

He made *kidesh*, washed, said the blessing over the *khale*, and cut a "*hamoytsi*" for each of us. Mama served *gefilte* fish, soup with noodles and chicken with sweet carrot stew. Papa asked her, "How do you feel?"

She nodded and answered quietly, "Praised be His name."

Having eaten, she remained at table, exhausted. Her eyelids drooping like a chick's, she fell asleep. The last golden flames of the flickering candles guttered and shadows veiled my mother's pale face. Papa gestured to us silently, a finger over his lips, not to be noisy, not to waken Mama.

Minutes later, she awoke with a start, her eyes wide open,

staring in alarm. Then, as if grasping something horrible, she broke into stifled sobs. Shaken, we tried to understand the meaning of her outburst. Mama said that she'd had a bad dream. When Papa asked her to tell us her dream, she answered, weeping, that you mustn't relate a bad dream.

Father was a Gerer *khosed*, so he advised her to journey to the Gerer *Rebe*. Let her tell her dream to the *Rebe* and he would interpret it. She didn't want that either, but in the end she did promise to step in to the Radomsker *Rebe*, Reb Yekhezkele. All week she went about as in a dream. She looked at her children through teary eyes. She scrubbed their hair, inspected their ears, washed their little necks; she sewed on buttons and took their shoes to be repaired.

One day, unexpectedly, she said to me, "Come, Sorele, I'll show you how to change the bed linen." I didn't want to. After a day at school, I was ready to run out into the street and play with the children. Mama kept me back, however, explaining, "You are the oldest girl, *kayn eyn hore*, almost a *kale moyd*, more than ten years old. Should something happen to your mother, heaven forbid, *you* must take her place.

Terror and an unknown dread took hold of me. "*Mameshie* dear, why do you say things that frighten me?"

"My child." She put her hands on my shoulder. "I want to teach you to be a *baleboste*. It sometimes happens that a mother falls ill. The oldest daughter must then know how to do her mother's work. A well brought-up child ought to know everything and it's a mother's responsibility to teach her."

I imitated everything that Mama taught me. I kept pulling the pillow cases on and off and she kept saying, "No, not like that, again, this way, once more." Till finally she smiled with satisfaction and said happily, "That's fine, quite fine, Sorele ... enough for one day ... you may go out and play now."

That whole week she walked about in a black depression.

She visited the *Rebe*, went to the cemetery; there she left a note of supplication in the prayer house where the most saintly are buried. She visited the graves of her two dead children and of my great-grandmother; then she came home, eyes red from weeping, and began a fast. Her spirits were not restored at all. She moved through the house like a shadow, continuing to work quietly, sighing and throwing coins into the alms box of Rav Meyer, the Master of Miracles.

Friday night following my mother's dream, Papa brought with him two *Shabes* guests. Mother was overjoyed with the visitors, serving them with great respect. As they were leaving she handed each a parcel of food.

In the middle of the night dreadful moaning woke me from a deep sleep. I opened my eyes, terrified, and to my great astonishment saw my father striking a match and lighting the gas lamp. "Papa!" I cried out in a voice not my own, "It's *Shabes*; you mustn't!"

"Mama is going under, wake the neighbour. I'm going for the doctor!" and he ran out of the house.

Wild-eyed, I ran to my mother's bedside. She was lying in a pool of blood, her face white as chalk.

"Mama, dearest, I'm scared." I fell down at her bedside. "Don't go away ... don't leave us," I pleaded, half faint. I felt her ice cold fingers stroking my face; her glazed eyes stared unseeing.

Her pale lips whispered, "I'm not going; I'll be with you ... always be together ... with my little swallows."

I sobbed softly. She was breathing heavily, the air forcing through her nostrils. "I won't abandon you, Sorele ... don't cry ...," her voice fluttered. "Go, call the neighbour!"

I tore myself from her side and rushed to our neighbour,

Bashe. I woke all the neighbours in the courtyard. Soon our home was full of women but still no doctor had arrived. They didn't want to crawl out of a warm bed late on a rainy night.

At last Papa returned with Malke the midwife, a stout woman of sixty carrying a small satchel. She grumbled that she should not have been called out in such weather since my mother was not yet due and that no-one had any pity for a poor lonely widow. She had barely reached my mother's bed when she began wringing her hands, screaming, "A calamity, a hemorrhage! Quick, cotton batting, get me towels, cold water, a pan ... hot water!"

The women set to work, saying that only merciful intercession would save Mama. They chased me from her room and told me to pray for her health.

I ran trembling to the synagogue, my light child's steps echoing in the empty night alleys. Demons seemed to pursue me. The pouring rain soaked my hair; drops ran down my face mixing with tears which flowed endlessly. In the synagogue I found my father and other men from the congregation already reciting Psalms. I ran from there to wake the rest of the family. *Bobe* wouldn't let me go home. Before leaving, she instructed *Zeyde* not to let me out until my clothes had dried.

Zeyde looked at me beseechingly as he recited the Psalms in a loud tearful voice. I shuddered, feeling insignificant and guilty for having asked him to pray for a boy. Bewildered, I drifted from room to room.

At the first hint of dawn I ran home, coming to a stop at the window, afraid to enter. I could hear muffled voices. Dragging myself into the house I saw a crowd around my mother's bed. Someone called, cried out, "Freyde Rive, open your eyes! In whose hands do you leave your children?"

Somebody pushed me to the bed.

"*Mameshie, Mameshie!*" I screamed.

With all her strength my mother forced her glazed eyes open and looked at me for a long time. She moved her lips to say something, but no sound came. Her eyes closed slowly and locked forever.

That was *Shabes* morning.

Late Saturday night and early Sunday carts and buggies brought uncles, aunts, relatives and friends from surrounding villages. With pious trembling they prepared themselves for the confinement of the dead woman which had to take place before the funeral.

My mother, covered by a white sheet, lay on the ground, a heavy copper pan on her large belly, a burning candle at her head. The mirrors were shrouded, the clock on the wall was mute. Burning candles were on the table and men in prayer shawls swayed devoutly over open prayer books. The rabbi and Moyshe Khayim the scribe stood white-robed before them. Moyshe Khayim held a *shoyfer*.

The women were assembled in another room, straining to hear. Anxious and fearful, they listened to every rustle as the pious men conducted a trial over my dead mother. They were demanding that she give up the unborn child.

Moyshe Khayim the scribe struck the table, "Silence!" The rabbi, Reb Mendele Gushnitser, wrapped himself deeper into his white robe and, swaying to the rhythm of his own words, summoned my mother.

"Freyde Rive, daughter of Shloyme the renowned sage and grandchild of the great Reb Hersh Volf, may his memory be blessed, we charge you to give up the child willingly. It is a terrible transgression, a disgrace, to carry away an unborn soul within you ...! Cleave the child from your flesh: that you may enter purified into paradise ...!"

All eyes were on the dead woman. A quiet sobbing was heard from the women.

"It seems to me she's moving!" Kayle startled, poked my grandmother. "Quiet in there!" Moyshe Khayim yelled at the women.

Reb Mendele Gushnitser continued to address my mother, "We promise that if you give up the child, you may take it with you to your grave. You'll not have to part from one another, only to separate!" It was horribly quiet. From time to time, one heard the buzzing of a fly, the weeping of women. Everyone's strained and fearful gaze was directed towards my dead mother.

My grandfather, an illustrious *Toyre* scholar, had consistently opposed the trial. The religious court and the community, however, intruded and carried out the sentence without his consent. Even my father had agreed. Dejected as he was, he did not want to pit himself against rabbinical law and the community. *Zeyde* stood isolated in a corner of the room. Sunk in great sorrow and pain, he kept pulling at his grey beard and smoothing his sidelocks.

Since his arguments and pleading with my mother had been of no avail, the rabbi ordered Moyshe Khayim to blow the *shoyfer*. A trembling murmur passed through the stifling room: "*Teki-o.*"

And instantly, a *shoyfer* call like the one on *Rosheshone* echoed through the rooms and out into the courtyard, which was black with people.

"*She-vo-rim ... tru-o ...* ," the rabbi continued prompting Moyshe Khayim.

A terror fell over the gathering; a fearful weeping broke out among the women.

"*Te-ki-o-o ...* ," the rabbi's lips continued to tremble.

Suddenly, from his corner, my *Zeyde* emerged. His frail

figure stretched and seemed somehow taller. He banged on the table; the candles swayed. With a harsh and stern voice he commanded, "Stop! Stop tormenting her! Don't shame her! She wasn't due yet. She can't release the child to you! She was a righteous woman; let her pure soul, together with her unborn child, rest in paradise!" He walked over to Moyshe Khayim, took the *shoyfer* from his hand and called out, "Women, perform her rites now and let us proceed with the funeral."

After the funeral I saw my mother in every corner of the house, heard her voice in every rustle of the trees, in the whistle of the wind, in the sound of the steaming kettle on the stove. In every whisper around me, I heard her speak.

Days, then weeks, passed and still my mother was not dead for me. She followed me always and everywhere, watched over me and comforted me. At night, when frightening winds howled, I went down from my bed, quietly opened the window and instantly heard my mother's voice.

"Sorele, put on your warm undershirt — you'll catch cold, heaven forbid. Watch over Khavele and Tsipele: make sure they eat their food and drink their milk."

I confided to my father, "You know, Papa, I talk to Mama every night."

He said, "My child, your mother is far from us now. She is in paradise and you must stop talking such foolishness ...."

But I assured him, "Yes ... it's true! I talk to her!" My father grew despondent. "I'll take you with me to the *Rebe* ...."

Worried that the *Rebe* would separate me from my mother, I stopped telling about my visions and conversations with her.

I fell ill and for a time hovered between life and death. Throughout this period, my mother nursed me, gave me medicines, cooked nourishing soups for me, applied compresses to my forehead, and rubbed me with salves and herbs.

When I opened my eyes, my grandmother, my father and Dr. Mitlman were at my bedside. The doctor said that the crisis was over and I'd soon be well again.

Only after my recovery did I finally comprehend that I was truly an orphan and that my mother was dead.

TRANSLATED BY FRIEDA FORMAN AND ETHEL RAICUS

THE NEW WORLD

Esther Singer Kreitman

❦

This is the story, real or imagined, of the circumstances of Esther Kreitman's birth. Kreitman points out the discrepancies between the attitudes towards men and women, especially within the Hasidic milieu in which she was raised, where the male is valued far above the female. We see that in Kreitman's world a woman's feelings of powerlessness began very early, perhaps even at birth. In a sense, the story is symbolic of Kreitman's entire life: she wanted to be "born" — to be creative, to experience a full life — and from the day of her birth, she was pushed back into darkness and passivity.

How much of this story is based on fact is unknown. However, her son later noted that Kreitman's deep depression later in life was the direct result of early ostracism — beginning with her first three years of life spent under a foster family's table.

FROM THE START, I didn't like lying in my mother's belly. Enough! When it got warm, I twisted around, curled up and lay still ....

But, five months later, when I felt alive, I was really very unhappy, fed up with the whole thing! It was especially tiresome lying in the dark all the time and I protested. But who heard me? I didn't know how to shout. One day, I wondered if perhaps that wasn't how to do it and I started looking for a way out.

I just wanted to get out.

After pondering a long time, it occurred to me that the best idea would be to start fighting with my Mama. I began throwing myself around, turning cartwheels, often jabbing her in the side; I didn't let up but it didn't do any good. I simply gave myself a bad name so that when, for instance, I'd grow tired of lying on one side and try turning over, just to make myself a little more comfortable, she'd start complaining. In short, why should I lie here cooking up something, it didn't do any good — I had to lie there the whole nine months — understand? — the whole period.

Well (not having any other choice), I consoled myself: I'll simply start later! Just as soon as they let me out into God's world, I'll know what I have to do .... Of course, I'll be an honoured guest, I have a lot of reasons to think so. First of all, because of what I often heard my Mama tell some woman who (as I later found out) was my Grandma:

"It does hurt a little but I almost don't feel it," Mama would say. "I'm glad! I was so scared I was barren. A trifle? It's already two years since the wedding and you don't see or hear anything .... Minke the barren woman also said she would yet have children. And why should I be surer of it?"

"Well, praised be the one who survives. With God's help, it will come out all right; and God forbid, with no evil eye," Grandma would always answer.

From such conversations, I assumed I would be a welcome guest.

I knew that, here in the other world, where I lived ever since I became a soul, when an important person came, he was supposed to be greeted with great fanfare. First of all, a bright light was to be spread over the whole sky. Angels (waiting for him) were to fly around; merry, beautiful cherubs who spread such holy joy that the person only regretted he hadn't ... died sooner. It was quite a novelty that

I, an honoured, long awaited guest, expected to be born into a big, light home with open windows, where the sun would illuminate everything with a bright light ....

Every morning I waited for the birds who were supposed to come greet me, sing me a song. And I was to be born on the first of *Oder* — a month of joy. "When *Oder* begins, people are merry."

But right here "it" comes — the first disappointment.

Mama lay in a tiny room, an "alcove." The bed was hung with dark draperies, which completely screened out the light. The windows were shut tight so no tiny bit of air could get in, God forbid; you shouldn't catch cold. The birds obviously don't like screened out light and closed windows; they looked for a better, freer place to sing. Meanwhile, no happiness appears either; because I was a girl, everybody in the house, even Mama, was disappointed.

In short, it isn't very happy! I am barely a half hour old but, except for a slap from some woman as I came into the world, nobody looks at me. It is so dreary!

Grandma comes in and smiles at Mama. She looks happy — probably because her daughter has come through it all right. She doesn't even look at me.

"*Mazl tov*, dear daughter!"

"*Mazl tov*, may we enjoy good fortune!"

Mama smiles too but not at me.

"Of course, I would have been happier if it were a boy," says Mama. Grandmother winks roguishly with a half-closed eye and consoles her.

"No problem, boys will also come ...."

I listen to all that and it is very sad for me to be alive. How come I was born if all the joy wasn't because of me! I'm already bored to death. Oh, how I want to go back to the other world.

All of a sudden, I feel a strange cold over my body: I am jolted out of my thoughts; I feel myself clamped in two big, plump hands, which pick me up. I shake all over. Could it be — a dreadful idea occurs to me — is she going to stuff me back in for another nine months? Brrr! I shudder at the very thought.

But my head spins, everything is whirling before my eyes, I feel completely wet, tiny as I am! Am I in a stream? But a stream is cool, pleasant, even nice. But this doesn't interest me as much as the idea of what the two big, clumsy hands want to do with me. I am completely at their mercy.

Thank God, I am soon taken out of the wet. I am brought back to the alcove, already violated, sad. I am carried around the alcove: everybody looks at me, says something. At last, I am put back to bed. Mama does put a sweet liquid thing in my mouth: I am really hungry for what is in the world.

Mama looks at me with her nice, soft eyes, and my heart warms. A sweet fatigue puts me to sleep and I am blessed with good dreams ....

But my happiness didn't last long, a dreadful shout wakes me with a start. I look around. Where did it come from? It's Mama!

People gather round.

"What happened? Where did that shout come from?"

Mama gestures, tries to point, her lips tremble, want to say something and can't. She falls back onto the pillow, almost in a faint.

Seeing they won't get anything out of Mama, they start looking for the reason in the closet, under the bed, in the bed.

All of a sudden, a shout is heard from the nurse, who keeps repeating in a strange voice, "Cats, oh dear God, cats!"

The people look up, can't understand what she's saying.

But, except for the word "cats," they can't get anything out of her — so upset is she.

Grandma is also very upset. But she takes heart, makes a thorough search in the bed and, laughing to hide her fear, she calls out, "*Mazl tov*, the cat had kittens. A good sign!"

But apparently, this isn't a good sign. The people are upset.

"On the same day, in the same bed as a cat? Hmmmm, a person and a cat are born the same way," says one brave soul.

They calm Mama. But again, nobody looks at me. Mama falls asleep. And with that, my first day comes to an end. I am, thank God, a whole day old and I have survived quite a bit.

The third day after my birth was the Sabbath. This time, a big, red gentile woman puts me in the bath. I wasn't so scared any more, already familiar with the way it smells.

Once again, I lie in bed with Mama. Mama looks at me more affectionately than yesterday. I open my eyes, I would like to look around a bit at the new world. I am already used to the darkness. All of a sudden — it grows darker for me than before.

A gang of women burst into the alcove. I look at them. They're talking, gesturing, picking me up, passing me from one to another, like a precious object. They look at me, they look at Mama, they smile.

Meanwhile, Grandma comes with a tray of treats.

The women make her plead with them, pretend they don't want to try any of the cookies, whiskey, preserves, cherry brandy, berry juice or wine; but, Grandma doesn't give up, so they open their beaks, and finally consent to do her a favour.

Males also stuck their heads into the female alcove. They talked with strange grimaces, gestured, shook their beards, went into a fit of coughing.

With them, Papa succeeded, not Grandma. And I am named Sore Rivke, after some relative of his.

Now they need a wet-nurse. Mama is weak, pale, with such transparent, narrow hands without sinews, she can hardly pick me up. A middle-class woman, she cannot breast-feed me. I am the opposite: a healthy, hearty gal, greedy, I restrain myself from shouting all I want is to eat.

"Not to a *goyish* wet-nurse," says Grandma. Not for all the tea in China. And she can't find a Jewish one. The pharmacist says I should get used to formula, which is better than mother's milk. But I say I don't want to get used to it and I throw up all the time.

This is bitter! Grandma is upset. Mama even more. But Papa consoles them, saying the Holy-One-Blessed-Be-He will help. And He does.

Our neighbour remembers a wet-nurse named Reyzl. She has the voice of a sergeant-major and two red eyes that scare me. She can't come to our home. She has six children of her own but there is no choice.

All the details are worked out, she is given an advance and may everything work out all right.

Reyzl picks me up out of the cradle, takes out a big, white breast, which looks like a piece of puffed up dough and gives it to me to suck, as a test. Well, what should I say? I didn't drown. Even my eyes fill with the taste of a good wet-nurse.

Reyzl looks happily from one to the other,

"Well, what do you say?"

Mama and Grandma glance at each other furtively and are silent ....

I have the good fortune to be a tenant at Reyzl's! Not that she needs another tenant because she lives in a flat not much bigger than a large carton. When Reyzl brings me home, her husband comes to greet me carrying their smallest one in his arms and the other five heirs swarming around him. He seems to be pleased with my arrival.

"Well, what do you say about this, eh? Ten gulden a week, my word of honour! Along with old clothes and shoes. Along with the fact that, from now on, they'll give all the repairs only to you! You hear, Beyrish?"

Beyrish is silent. He turns around so his breadwinner won't see his joy.

"You're more of a man than me, I swear. You can earn a gulden faster ... ," he thinks to himself. But right away he becomes serious. "Where will we put the cradle?" They ponder a long time.

But Reyzl's husband, who is an artist at arranging things in his tiny flat, smacks his low, wrinkled forehead with his hard hand and calls out joyously, "Reyzl, I've got it! Under the table!"

So in a tiny cradle, I am shoved under the table.

With open, astonished eyes, I look at the filthy wood of the table, covered with a host of spider webs, and think sadly, "This is the new world I have come into? And this is its heaven?"

And I weep bitter tears.

TRANSLATED BY BARBARA HARSHAV

THE ZOGERIN

Rokhl Brokhes

❦

The zogerin *is virtually unheard of in Jewish communities today but in the communities of Eastern Europe she
played a central role in women's religious participation.*

*Traditional Jewish services were highly structured, led
by a male, with men and women separated. The women's
section was apart from the centre of the formal service;
women were not permitted to touch the holy objects, especially the* Toyre.

*To counteract their distance from what they considered
holy, women designated a* zogerin — *a speaker or teller
— a position which was highly respected and admired. The*
zogerin *read the prayers aloud for the women, leading
them in the service. The* zogerin *had a special significance
in representing the illiterate. Individual women would also
ask her to intercede on their behalf for something personal.
This could include anything from the serious, like the
health of a child, to the more material or frivolous.*

*In the following story Rokhl Brokhes confronts us with
Gnesye the* zogerin, *a woman angry and frustrated,
whose life of praying for others seems to have given her little but bitterness. Gnesye is the "madwoman behind the*
mekhitse."

"NO, I SAY; ENOUGH is enough! On their behalf I prayed, for
their benefit I cried my eyes out. Enough! I say, no! May I be
struck dumb if I will say one more word, not even my name,

Gnesye." She had a strong chin. She was a *zogerin*. A very good one and she argued:

"*Reboyne-sheloylem*, kind Father, You alone know how I have prayed both summer and winter, never missed a *Shabes*, never stinted on a *tkhine*. On their behalf what have I not prayed for? Wealth, length of days, pleasure from the children … . Comes *Reshkhoydesh*, my heart simply melts, my soul leaps. It's no small thing, *Reshkhoydesh*! I pray for everything, everything! Weep for everything! My heart, my heart … not to even mention the *Yomim noroim*. Every year I leave the synagogue absolutely sick, hoarse, distraught, worn out. Had I been chopping wood or digging ditches I couldn't have worked so hard. It's no small thing to be a *zogerin*!

"So many women around me, maybe more than twenty … the air, stifling … the din … the bickering and complaining among them — this one doesn't hear, she's sitting too far away, she wants to be closer. Another one is leaning too close to the one beside her. Yet another one thinks that I'm ignoring her, that I failed to remember her grandmother during the *yisker* service. This one, that I forgot about her Khatskele; that one, that I didn't pray for her Iserl."

She complained and fumed, standing in her little room, peering out strangely from under her brow as if searching for something. On the edge of a bench her grandson sat restless. He was some eleven years old. Perplexed and afraid. What was the matter with his grandmother? She was so angry today, bad-tempered and swearing … he wanted to say something to her, ask her not to scream or cry so much. He felt today her crying was not like other times. This time her tears were different. He lifted up his thin little hand silently and then let it drop again.

Her heart was pounding. "Better to fall ill, better to be struck dumb than to have wasted my life praying for fat Teme that she might have such a grand house and so many stores; for Faytl's daughter Shtishe, a rabbi for a son-in-law and such good grandchildren; for that scabrous Tsipore a legacy of ten thousand. For whom have I not prayed and for whose sake have I not pleaded? And what have I gotten from it all? They paid me only a fiver a week and that's *enough*! All they paid me was a pittance to keep my mouth shut. 'Here, choke on it and shut up, for you that's enough.' Can you believe it?"

Her wig askew, eyes blazing, lips foaming in anger, her thin hands fanned herself, here, there and everywhere. Her whole body shook.

"Did I not find a spot for them? They came to the *besmedresh*, that precious Dina, so high and mighty, all puffed up. Pshaw! Came in silk and velvet, a neck thick with pearls. No small thing! And me, Gnesye the *zogerin*, I don't know where to seat her ... and I sob and I pray on her behalf, for wealth, for all that's good and what does she give me? A sixer, a copper, from her munificence! One sixer, for all that I pleaded, for all that I sobbed .... She gave me only one sixer and nothing more. She, the rich one, while I, Gnesye the *zogerin*, Gnesye the pauper ...."

The little boy became even more frightened. His grandmother paced the tiny room, screaming. What was the matter with her? He wanted to come up to her saying, "*Bobinke sha, Bobinke* don't cry, be quiet *Bobinke*," but he was afraid. The entire night she had sat up on her cot; leaning over his bed, waking him, speaking to him and to herself, not budging even an inch to eat the evening meal, that's how angry she was.

"It happened one *Shabes*," she complained. "It was a winter day, my bones were aching. My throat was so swollen I couldn't swallow and all my limbs were aching. It seemed to me, maybe a person could have stayed in bed resting herself, but no, to that I didn't pay any attention. Off I hurried to the *besmedresh*. I moaned, I pleaded. When I came to the *tkhines*, I absolutely melted away, so intense was my prayer."

"*Bobinke sha, Bobinke* be quiet," the child spoke out. Women were standing in the doorway.

"Don't you know?" she screamed, grabbing his hand with her burning one, her eyes crazy clear.

"*Bobinke*, stop," the child begged.

"Be quiet; you don't know, you can't know. All this is not your concern. It's mine. I lamented, I pleaded before the *Reboyne-sheloylem*. All He gave me were my bloody tears. This is all me and my prayers, you hear, Shmertsik? Me and my prayers. Do you hear, Shmertsik, all mine and they repay me with a penny, a fig, like a beggar at the door. My whole life, twenty years, I pleaded for them, on their behalf I fasted. About myself I forgot altogether. I am poor. You see how I wear an old worn-out shirt .... You see how I eat only a dried out crust of bread .... *They* live in palaces and sleep on soft beds, silken dresses *they* wear. All that is *mine, my* hard-working prayers for more than twenty years."

Actually, the little boy wanted to plug his ears to keep from hearing his grandmother's tirade, wanted to hide himself to elude her gaze.

"Listen, Shmertsik, do you hear? My tears, my widow's tears pierced the very heavens, and all for them. Shmertsik, my child, my bitter little orphan, you are the only one left to me from my seven children. Did *they* want to hear what was in my heart? I knocked on all their doors. No, *that* doesn't belong to them! Everything they own is mine, mine! You hear, Shmertsik? Mine! That Faytl's daughter Shtishe, she wouldn't even give me a scrap of food to feed you with and Hertse's daughter Zlate, she wouldn't give me an interest-free loan from *gmiles khesed*. Teme's daughter Zundl didn't

even want to enroll you in the new *Talmud Toyre*. I went to
that scabrous Tsipore. In front of her I wept, told her all that
was in my bitter heart, 'have pity, help me with something for
my little one, my poor orphan' but she had no time for me.
She was too busy. In the middle of the week, she won't even
acknowledge that she knows me.

" 'Mama, some kind of poor old woman wants to see you,
probably needs a hand-out,' her daughter says to her. 'A
strange woman.'

" 'Mother is not at home, we tell you.' So angry, this
daughter.

"Naturally, on *Shabes*, she is entirely different, she has an
entirely different hide *then*, she becomes so gentle. Then she
needs me, Gnesye the *zogerin*.

" 'Cry, plead on my behalf,' she says. 'I am a wealthy
woman. My tears are so precious, they're worth silver. *My*
eye, *my* heart, I need to save them for the good things in life.'

"No! I say, do you hear, Shmertsik? Enough!"

Right away the little boy began to cry, sobbing; that's how
frightened he was. "*Bobinke sha*, *Bobinke* be quiet," he stammered. "Look, *Bobinke*, how all the women are staring at us
from the window, from the doorway, see?"

She became quiet, pensive. Her eyes bored deeply into
herself. She bowed her head low and her old wrinkled face
lost its angry red colour. All at once she became deathly yellow. The women at the door and the window went off slowly,
whispering and telling secrets quietly among themselves. The
little boy practically fell apart from pity. They were talking
about his grandmother, but he didn't know what to do, how
to calm her.

"Ha," she said, and her gaze fell on the child, an angry,
hard look and her voice became entirely different, strong
now and full of venom. "No," she said again and stomped her

foot. "No, I'll show them. Do you hear, Shmertsik? I'll go on praying, I'll go on weeping but now I'll pray for me, just for me. I'll pray for a disaster to fall on them, on all my enemies ... they are my worst enemies. They took away my prayers, my tears, my years .... Do you hear, Shmertsik? All that they have is mine. I'll pray for it back. I'll take it back, you hear, Shmertsik. I'll take it all back. I'll be avenged on them. My prayer will be a prayer of revenge, do you hear, Shmertsik ... ?"

"Be quiet, *Bobinke*," the child whimpered. "Look how they are watching, wondering, the women are shaking their heads."

"Shmertsik, are you listening? I'll ask for it all back. I'll pour out my heart in tears. I'll plead for my own sake and with an outstretched hand. I'll pray for myself. Do you hear, you women, you can plead for yourselves." With out-stretched hand, wild voice and flashing eyes, she lunged towards the door. The women moved away.

"Look out," whispered one of the women, "look out. Gnesye the *zogerin* is out of her mind." "God help us! The Lord's miracles!" "It's dangerous to let her out on the streets. She could hurt someone," said a third. "The poor little grandson." "Sh, sh, she's coming."

But she stayed in the tiny room. Only her voice, angry and vengeful, could be heard echoing far, far, all the way into the third courtyard.

TRANSLATED BY SHIRLEY KUMOVE

REYZELE'S WEDDING

Dora Schulner

❧

Life for women in the shtetls *of Eastern Europe was highly prescribed. Depending on the family's wealth and background, a girl of marriageable age was expected to behave in a predetermined manner. Her reputation was almost as important as her dowry in a world where arranged marriages were part of the norm. And with a community relatively small and tightly knit, there was little that escaped the eyes or ears of its members.*

"Reyzele's Wedding" is the section of Dora Schulner's memoirs of shtetl *life in which she tells about a young woman who "strays." Reyzele is the object of gossip simply because she dares to explore beyond the accepted boundaries set by her community. Reyzele's story illustrates the tensions between tradition and changing ideologies and social movements.*

BORUKH THE *KVAS*-MAKER was famous in all Radomysl for his skill in *kvas*-making. There were many in our town who put up *kvas*, but none came near him in *kvas*-making — it was real apple wine. In this his wife Brokhe helped him, and both would put on tremendous airs about the secret that made *their kvas* taste like real wine. The other *kvas*-makers were furious and never missed an opportunity to vent their spleen whenever they spoke about Borukh and his wife.

There were four in the family — father, mother and two daughters. Libe was a seamstress but the other daughter,

Reyzele, didn't work. The town indeed had good reason to gossip, for Reyzele could be seen evenings walking — not unaccompanied — in remote gentile neighbourhoods. In short, Borukh the *kvas*-maker didn't make his living selling to our Jews. While gentiles got to enjoy his *kvas* to the very last drop, Jews envied him and had good reason to gossip.

We lived next door to them and, even though Libe was older than I, she befriended me. Libe worked for herself as a dressmaker; I at that time belonged to the *Bund* and every Saturday hurried to the woods for meetings. In the evenings I would either take walks near the labour exchange, or read books by serious writers; Libe enjoyed my reading aloud to her.

I worked in Yosele Orenshteyn's cloth mill. Many girls my age worked there but they were nothing like Libe. So I would eat quickly after work and run into Libe's house. To hear them talk or sing was a special joy. Libe talked and sang softly. In a beautiful, moving voice she would weave her songs into a musical fabric. The machine would accelerate and Libe's sweet voice mingled with its hum. She sang: "How many notes and letters I have sent him and he has not delighted me with even one." Tears flowed from Libe's lovely eyes. She wept out of longing for her lover serving in the army.

Big tears rolled down her pretty pale cheeks; her brown hair, her brown eyes with long lashes, a shapely nose. A beauty. But everyone avoided her because her sister was that sort. Her mother too was a source of gossip, and it was precisely because everyone else talked that I would hang around there night and day. My mother worried herself sick that I would somehow learn "nice" things, but I learned nothing since nothing I saw in that house was any different from ours.

As I said before, Borukh the *kvas*-maker and his wife put

up *kvas*. Libe's mother was a stylishly dressed woman, wore a peruke and earrings that danced from her ears whenever she moved her head. Neither parent was friendly, and I would feel uneasy whenever Libe's father would look at me from the corner of his eye. He was a tall man with a blond beard and cloaked eyes who never met anyone's gaze.

There were three rooms in their house: a parlour with a window, an alcove, and a large kitchen. Libe worked in the kitchen, while the parlour was elegantly furnished. Borukh put up his *kvas* in the dark alcove where it was stored behind the oven. The cleanliness was a pleasure to behold. A pretty tablecloth was always spread on the table, on which stood a very bright lamp. Libe's machine stood at the window to provide her with daylight, and at night the lamp offered light. I was attracted by the cosiness of the place. Evenings, I would sit with Libe, help her with her work and wait for her to go with me to the labour exchange.

I saw little of Reyzele; she was never home evenings. From Libe's terse comments I gathered that Reyzele was straying from the straight and narrow path.

On those occasions when Reyzele didn't go out she, like her father, could never look anyone in the eye. She'd gather up her things, humming the well-known song, "In the wild forest alone, where no-one can see." My eyes followed her every movement and I envied her for her beautiful, shapely arms and legs. She would often smile but that smile was to herself.

In the evenings Borukh and his wife would sit at the kitchen table counting the day's take. Reyzele, if she were at home, would go into the parlour. By that time Libe would be ready for her walk with me. I wondered how members of the same family could be such strangers to each other. But Libe's smile convinced me that things would sort themselves out.

"Let's go to the labour exchange, Dvoyrele. *Your* friends are waiting for you."

She would always tell me that it was *my* friends who were waiting for me, because she was her own boss and I was just a worker.

One evening, when Libe and I had decided to go to Potshtov Street, she was in high spirits and very talkative. That evening Reyzele didn't go out. She stood at a wash basin washing her sparkling white things, a fine figure. Libe was whispering to me about her young man, who had stayed with them when he came to report for military service. At that time Libe had promised she would wait for him till he was discharged. Then he would come for her and marry her — no matter what. A burst of loud laughter startled us. Reyzele was laughing hysterically. Her beautiful eyes were full of tears. There she stood over the wash basin of soapy water holding up a pair of delicate lace-trimmed underwear, water streaming from them and tears streaming from her eyes. Suddenly she threw down the underwear and began to sob. At that very moment, the door opened and her mother and father walked in.

Still crying, Reyzele picked up her underwear and finished washing them. The parents exchanged a silent look. Libe asked me to wait; she'd soon go with me. Reyzele kept on crying.

Her mother started setting the table and began speaking to Reyzele about how good it would be for her if she were smart enough to understand what her parents wanted.

"First of all, my child, remember, Arn is a wealthy man, owns a stable with as many horses as a country squire. No small catch, Arn the coachman! His first wife lived like a queen. The most important people ride in his coaches. Wherever you want, my daughter, you'll be able to go. And his house! May all my dear ones have such homes."

The mother talked and talked; Borukh the *kvas*-maker was silent. Libe and I looked at each other. Reyzele threw herself upon her mother, crying bitterly that he was such an old man. At that, her father jumped up enraged, yelling at her mother for spoiling her.

All property matters had been settled. The marriage would take place after *Shabes*. I was flabbergasted and couldn't wait to escape from that house.

I keep remembering that *Shabes* afternoon after which the wedding was to take place. Reyzele was lying on the sofa, her pretty face drawn. Her eyes were filled with a deep sadness. Libe and I had been reading Nomberg's story, "Be Silent, Sister." I read and they listened. But when I looked up from the book, I saw both sisters crying. Reyzele jumped from the sofa; her eyes glistened with tears. She threw herself upon my neck crying bitterly.

"What have I done to deserve this?" she pleaded.

But how could I help her? The wedding was already set for after *Shabes* and Arn the coachman would make Reyzele happy — so her parents said.

After *Shabes* the city was abuzz. The marketplace came to life. The women at their stalls woke as from a sleep. The slightest event forced people from their humdrum lives. Storekeepers would sit at their open doors in the market for days on end. It was midsummer, around *Shabes Nakhamu*; the days were hot and there wasn't much business being done then. This was like a theatre for them, a theatre with no actors. They all took their own parts, spoke their own lines, laughed at their own jokes, and ridiculed the beautiful wedding that was to take place in the *kvas*-maker's house.

The day of the wedding at the *kvas*-maker's house was very sad. My mother used to say about me: she weeps over

every death and graces every wedding. My mother bemoaned
the fact that I would in no way be coaxed to leave the *kvas*-
maker's house. My sister Rokhl continued to maintain that
her prophecy would come true; Reyzele would come to no
good. I cleverly extricated myself from this talk and helped
Libe prepare for Reyzele's wedding.

The *kvas*-makers had bought ready-made cake, a bottle of
liquor, wine, several herring and fresh bread; they had
enlarged the table and spread a pretty white cloth on it.
Borukh and his wife from the *besmedresh* had invited a few
book pedlars who used to peddle small religious and other
books. Itskhok the *shames* and Khayim the *shames* were both
there, and Reb Bunim their landlord was also there. Then
the groom arrived with several other coachmen. Arn wore a
new long gabardine over a white shirt, his long, thick beard
freshly combed. He looked like a *goy* on his way to church on
Sunday. And this old man was about to marry Reyzele.

Almost everyone had arrived. They all acted as though
they'd been hired for a quiet wedding. No *klezmer* played;
no-one rejoiced. It felt more like someone had died. The
bride herself was pale and frightened. Libe had told me her
father had brutally beaten Reyzele, had threatened to tie her
up, to kill her rather than see her go astray! Her mother
looked dejected. Everyone now waited for the sanctification
of the vows.

Finally Moyshe the cantor arrived with Yosl the *shames*.
The mood seemed to lighten. They brought in four poles
and tied the *khupe* to them. Four men held the poles. Under
the *khupe* stood Arn the coachman with Reyzele. The cantor
said the blessing quietly. The *shames* handed the ring to Arn,
who recited: "Behold thou art consecrated unto me." I can
still see Reyzele's tears.

After the ceremony, the mood grew livelier. Men crowded

around the table taking sips of whiskey, eating cake, then eagerly attacking the herring and fresh bread which they washed down with more whiskey. They congratulated the bride and groom, danced a bit to their own singing, amusing themselves with their own little bit of fun. Strangers by now felt like family and joined in the merry-making.

The *kvas*-maker and his wife were very subdued. Nonetheless they saw to it that the men had food and drink, half-heartedly responding to their jolly good wishes. Finally, wishing bride and groom long life, the guests left, weaving their way unsteadily home.

Arn the coachman was now left alone with the family. Until now he had stuck close to the other men and had also tossed back quite a few. The parents had looked the other way, and pretended not to hear. Libe and I stood by Reyzele. There was no point talking to her. She moved stiffly about like a bound calf. When she looked at both of us, her beautiful eyes held the misery of a poor creature being led to the slaughter.

Reyzele's mother wept as she packed her daughter's trousseau into a leather case. The old father, Borukh the *kvas*-maker, sat at the table, his chin cupped in his hand, staring into space. His face no longer looked angry. It was heartbreaking to look at this miserable father who had forced his daughter into marriage.

We were all roused from our numbness by a loud snorting sound which might have come from a half-slaughtered ox. It was Arn, exhausted, who had collapsed on the sofa and, old and drunk as he was, had fallen into a deep sleep.

This image remains alive for me still. This is how Reyzele, the daughter of Borukh the *kvas*-maker, was forced into marriage.

TRANSLATED BY BRINA MENACHOVSKY ROSE

THE VEIL

Fradel Schtok

❧

*Fradel Schtok's evocative portrait of a young girl's longing
for the world beyond the* shtetl *is placed in the setting of
an Eastern European wedding. Like any adolescent,
Manya is stirred by music and romance but is constrained
by circumstance.*

*Her father's disappearance has left her mother an
agune, unable to marry again unless he grants her a
divorce. This has severe consequences for the entire family,
especially for Manya who, as the eldest child, must bear the
brunt of family obligations, poverty and social stigma.*

THE VEIL WAS BROUGHT into the house along with the myrtle. Manya put out a bowl of water and set the myrtle in it.

Tsirl's daughter Beyle was getting married today. When
she was betrothed four weeks earlier, the family had thought
it a miracle. Beyle was getting on in years, and no-one
expected her to marry.

"True, he is an older man, but on the other hand he has a
well-stocked store." That's what Zlate, Manya's mother, had
told them.

Manya had not been overjoyed, because she knew that she
would not be at the wedding even though they were relatives.
Ever since Manya's father Itskhok has disappeared and Zlate
was left an *agune*, she didn't allow the children to raise their
heads. Never did they go to a wedding, nor hear the *klezmer*
play, except from a distance. And Manya loved the *klezmer*.

More than once she got up at night, opened the window, and listened as they walked through the town playing and moving further away. They played some sad melody that drifted in through the window keeping people awake half the night. Some sadness would then grip the heart so you wouldn't know what it was you wanted.

Her heart would always tremble. And what made it tremble? — at times the ringing sound of the scythes on a summer evening, or a handsome gentile lad on a hay-wagon, or a song of the oppressed at night behind her window.

She had always wanted to go to a wedding, and her mother had never allowed it. For that matter, where did her mother ever allow her to go? Not even to the circus when it came to town! *She* had to stay home and help her mother sew bed-linen for others. So, of course, she didn't really know how to behave in company, and when on *Shabes* at the pre-wedding party she had reached for another piece of strudel, she was glad that her mother had stepped on her toes.

Sunday morning the bride's mother, Tsirl herself, had come in and burst into tears, pleading with Zlate to allow at least Manya to attend the wedding. No garland-maid had yet been chosen. Zlate's face took on a strange pensiveness. "Maybe." When the younger children had heard that "maybe," they began to beg her. Pesi, the neighbour, and Pesi's daughter Leytshe had also beseeched her. Tsirl kept wiping her eyes. Only Manya had been silent; being the eldest, she understood. Nevertheless, her heart trembled, her face turned pale. At last Zlate looked at Manya and said, "All right. Iron your muslin dress, garland-maid."

The veil and the myrtle had been brought in and the house was turned upside down. Leytshe hugged Manya, telling her that the new flutist would play at the wedding. Who was the new flutist? A student — from Vienna! — who played the flute. He had quarrelled with his father, left for another city and become a *klezmer* to spite his father. And oh did he play ….

Manya bent over the bowl to sniff the myrtle. The small green branches had swelled in the bowl, drinking their fill of water. And they released their scent through the house, redolent of bride, white veil, *confiture* and *khupe*.

Royze, the hairdresser, came to weave the garland. She used grey thread to tie the small branches as she braided, tried it on Manya's head for size and then added more at the forehead so it would look like a crown. Then she took the white veil out of a box and shook it out over the room. The room seemed filled with veil. Manya's heart fluttered — so much veil ….

Manya stood stock still, to the tips of her fingers respectful of the whiteness and transparency of the veil. Then she moved the neighbours who had come in into the corners of the room. As Royze shook the veil out across the whole room, she trembled, afraid it would be soiled.

"Royze, you'll dirty the veil. Spread something under it …."

"What shall I use?"

"My muslin dress."

"You're crazy!"

Later the veil lay spread out under the green garland, drops of water dripping onto it from the myrtle.

Manya's heart trembled. "A veil that can cover an entire room, and is so … I don't know … ahhhh."

When the time came to take the garland and veil to the bride's house, Manya carried it as one would a breath of air that could at any moment evaporate into nothingness. And when she put the garland on the bride, she bent her own head so as to catch the drops of water dripping onto it from the myrtle.

The *klezmer* were playing for the bride at her house. Manya, wearing her muslin dress, was standing near a lamp that gave her face a rosy glow. She didn't look at the new flutist, but held her head in such a way that she could observe him looking at her.

She heard no-one, only his flute. Suddenly she began to feel ashamed in the presence of the flute, ashamed that Tsirl — her own relative! — was forever going to the *gmiles khesed* for an interest-free loan for her stall, ashamed that Tsirl was toothless, that Tsirl's husband was associated with the Karlsbad waters affair, and that Tsirl's son had a bandaged neck.

She was ashamed that everyone was crying; to her it seemed like water dripping from a frozen roof when the sun suddenly shines on it.

To her eyes, Leyzer's long face looked as it did on *Rosheshone* at *tashlekh* when she saw him shaking out all his sins into the Zbrukh River to rid himself of the burden and to square things with God.

She looked at the *klezmer* — whose music had buried more than one Jewish bride — and it seemed to her they were smiling behind their moustaches. She sensed the truth of what was said when the wedding trumpet sounds, "This too will be your fate, this too will be your fate ... " and the fiddle laments, "Oh, how you will be blighted!" while the bass angrily booms, "Just like this, just like this."

A horse-drawn cab took them to the hall for the wedding meal.

Manya sat near the bride, continually straightening Beyle's garland, spreading the veil over her shoulders, her face, her legs, gathering it at her knees, and she kept wiping each droplet of water that fell from the myrtle on Beyle's forehead. She felt she was carrying the weight of the world. She had never before understood what it meant to be a garland-maid; to care for the bride's garland, attend to the bride's veil!

And inside, again all she heard was his flute. Manya didn't look at him but felt his eyes on her.

When she danced the Lancers, she bowed politely to the flute player.

She had many occasions to approach the *klezmer* — a garland-maid has to make sure that everyone dances. And when unintentionally she did look at him, what she saw was chestnut-brown hair, dark eyes, a thick lower lip — and felt him bow to her close, too close.

"*Fräulein* ... you dance divinely ...."

Later he whispered in her ear many words, words of passion. He said casually, "*Fräulein*, this is of course sweet madness."

And he began to laugh, straight from the heart, and for Manya this laughter burned in her ears, and they turned crimson.

"It is certainly sweet madness ... sweet."

Leytshe called her away. "I have to tell you a secret," she moved her head closer. "He, the flutist ... is asking about you, asking 'Who is this girl? Oh, what a fine girl.' "

Manya looked at Leytshe, her black teeth, and thought lovingly just how attractive black teeth could be after all ....

She went up to the bride and put her flushed face under the veil, straightening the myrtle on the bride's head.

Suddenly her mother came up to her in her everyday dress to say it was three o'clock, she was to go home. The younger children had been carried home sleeping.

She stopped as if she were in a fog, knew nothing of what was happening to her; even the music seemed strange and distant. Suddenly a man's grey sheepskin coat materialized and Manya slipped her arms into it, letting her mother wrap it tightly round her neck, and it seemed to her that was the worst part — it was her mother tightening it closely round her neck.

TRANSLATED BY BRINA MENACHOVSKY ROSE

ZLATKE

Miriam Raskin

❦

The Bund, *a Jewish socialist workers' movement, was the driving life force for its followers. All encompassing, it provided a structure and social milieu of values, ideals and goals through which members transformed themselves into practising revolutionaries. Raskin frequently uses religious language and metaphor to express Zlatke's revolutionary fervour, which is rooted in traditional Jewish concepts and yearnings.*

In these excerpts from the novel Zlatke, *Miriam Raskin, herself a* Bundist, *provides a glimpse of the* Bund's *impact on Zlatke, a young activist. Raskin shows how her heroine's commitment to the movement overrides traditional parental authority and provides a new sense of class consciousness. The piece is also a telling commentary on men's and women's contrasting views of gender equality.*

I

LIKE A PIOUS, devoted Jew who performs all deeds in God's name, Zlatke was dedicated to her ideals, to serving the movement with all her might. To begin with, she wanted to learn a trade, to become a seamstress. Then she'd be self-sufficient; then no-one at home could tell her what to do.

Zlatke had already discussed her plans with Zavl the quilter. He was now the one closest to her, with whom she could talk about personal matters. Their closeness no longer frightened her; she knew he was reliable, a wall of steel.

They never spoke of love; Zlatke wouldn't allow it to cross his lips. She also insisted that they not be seen together often, lest people talk. For all that, she loved the gentle voice in which he spoke to her and was flustered by his passionate gaze. To herself she would say: Revolutionaries must harden their hearts, not let feelings overcome reason.

Without meaning to, they often stayed behind after their work in the cell. One evening when Zavl accompanied her home, she told him of her decision to train as a seamstress.

"What do you say, Zavl?" She sought his opinion.

"What do I say?" Zavl stopped in the middle of the road. He gazed at her, his broad-boned, vibrant face radiated with pleasure. Now, she would be a true proletarian like him; the differences and distance between them would dissolve. Zlatke stared at him for a moment. His jacket was slung over his shoulder, the Russian blouse with its sash revealing his strong body. He was closer to her now than at any other time.

The autumn night was mild and in the pale moonlight the sleepy houses on the street took on a magic. They walked to Zlatke's house in virtual silence, understanding each other without words.

Zlatke could see difficulties in speaking to her parents about her decision. Her mother would certainly oppose it. There were no tradesmen in their family up to now. Poor as they were, Zlatke's mother protected their status, hiding their poverty. In the *shtetl* Zlatke's father had a reputation as a fine Jew and scholar. Her mother often boasted about her husband to neighbours: how learned he was, that he had received rabbinical ordination.

Zlatke fixed upon Saturday evening to broach the subject. It was already dark when she came home earlier than usual. Mother recited the prayer for the end of *Shabes*: "God of Abraham, Isaac and Jacob ... ." She remained seated at the window, still and pensive. *Shabes* was gone. Here was Father back from *shul*. Zlatke lit the kerosene lamp and he said *hav-dole* over a thick braided candle. "A good week, may it be a full week, a providential week," he called out. He was still wearing his *Shabes* caftan, his beard beautifully brushed. But on his gentle, pale face the week-day cares had already settled themselves. Zlatke plucked up her courage and approached her mother.

"I want to tell you something, Mama," she started breathlessly. "I want to learn sewing; I want to apprentice with a seamstress."

Aroused from her thoughts, Mama gave Zlatke a telling look: she knew what Zlatke had been up to and that she could now expect all kinds of wild behaviour from her. She turned, not to Zlatke, but to her husband. "Itskhok, d'you hear your daughter's talk?"

Father was pacing, hands behind his back as was his custom. In a voice both sorrowful and soothing he hummed "*Hamavdl ben koydesh lekhol* ... ." Puzzled, he stopped in the middle of the room and looked at Zlatke. Great affection existed between him and his eldest daughter, though they rarely spoke more than a few words to each other. He contemplated her silently for a while. How nicely she had grown, her face young and fresh; she was strong, self-possessed. All at once, his mood lightened. "How old is our Zlatke now?" He spoke half in earnest, half in jest. "Time to think about a suitable match."

Zlatke stood at the window, head lowered. She knew that what was being left unsaid between her and her father might now never be expressed and she was filled with remorse.

Her mother just shrugged and remained silent. She was angry at her husband, who never concerned himself with domestic matters, leaving all the worries to her.

After that night, her mother went about sullen and upset. She didn't want her daughter to become a seamstress, but even more disturbing was that Zlatke had not asked her.

"She no longer seeks her mother's advice; she's her own boss now," she kept repeating.

Zlatke's mother was known for her common sense. People came to her for advice, but she found it hard to understand her own child. How long since Zlatke had obeyed her in all matters? She already shared the burdens of the household equally with her mother, helping with the chicken and egg business and with raising the younger children. There were four other children at home: Sheyndl, next to Zlatke, the twins, Moyshke and Dovidl, and the youngest, Rivtshe, still a baby.

To tell the truth, Mother had her doubts about her eldest daughter's capability. She'd often blunder when sent on an errand, lost in the world of romantic books. "Zlatke, why are you day-dreaming?" she'd say, trying to bring her to her senses.

Gradually, her mother came to realize that she could no longer influence Zlatke. Too late. Her motto: If you can't climb over, you have to crawl under. Trying to persuade her husband, she said to him, "Come to think of it, Itskhok, it isn't such a bad idea. What would she do here, sitting at home? Let her start earning something; it'll come in handy."

Zlatke had been spending her evenings at home lately, so as not to provoke her mother. Perhaps her home had even become dearer to her, but that she would never let on. At home Zlatke saw her mother always working. Concern for her children never ended: this one's shoes need looking after; that one needs a warm garment mended now that winter's near. Her mother's step was firm and agile; dark eyes sharp and intelligent; a few silver streaks showed from beneath a white head-covering.

Sitting at the enamel stove, darning a sock, an eye on the steaming pot, she asked her daughter, "Which seamstress have you chosen? I want to speak to her myself." When Zlatke told her the name, Mama didn't approve.

"That seamstress does only alterations; I'll find you a tailor, the best in town. If you're going to do something, do it right."

Sheyndl, the younger sister, was tall for her age, slender and very mischievous. She played with boys, climbed over fences and hedges. When she flew into the house, wild from play, Mama would scold her.

"Such a big girl, time to grow up."

Her words were a warning that from now on, Sheyndl would have to take Zlatke's place in the house. Mama showed much love to the children only when they were small. As each grew, her love was transferred to the youngest child — and so it went. Zlatke remembered when she herself had been a child: her mother would comb her hair, braiding a ribbon into it, glorying in her daughter's long brown braids.

Now the two boys, Moyshke and Dovidl, had arrived home from *kheder* and immediately thrown themselves into their games. Silence fell on the room when Father came home.

"A good evening," he said in an unruffled voice and almost immediately began his afternoon prayers.

Then everyone sat down to the table and Mama apportioned the food, her face devoted and attentive lest she deprive anyone of a rightful portion. The smell of food filled the house. You'd think there was nothing to Mama's cooking, a workaday pottage of barley and potatoes in browned onions — but it was flavourful beyond description. A homey warmth and harmony enveloped the table, but Zlatke's heart ached: this wouldn't be hers for long. Late that night, in bed between her two little sisters, it seemed to her they cuddled more than usual, as if afraid she would leave.

Zlatke's first days in the workshop were hard ones. She was lost in unfamiliar noise and confusion. Fumes from the irons gave her headaches which lasted for days and she seemed to see everyone through a screen. Around the large work table, reflector lamps burning brightly, sat boys and girls, apprentices, joking and punning and laughing. Hands with threaded needles flew up and down to the rhythm of a song.

A substantial entrepreneurial stance, close beard, and eyes that saw and knew everything: that was the boss, the owner. He watched his people; his wife and sometimes one of their children helped him in this work. Their lowering looks seemed to Zlatke to follow her every turn as she sewed and she felt hemmed in. She came home bone weary, every limb aching, and ate her supper in silence. When questioned about anything she avoided answering, could hardly wait for bed time.

But Zlatke was not one to give up easily. What she had conceived, planned and plotted, she had to carry out. Before long, she was totally caught up in her sewing. She had a goal: to learn the craft as quickly as possible and become independent, a true proletarian. Her mother had prevailed upon the tailor that her daughter not become an errand girl like the other apprentices. Zlatke made progress: she could now be trusted to sew a pair of sleeves, to hem a dress with fine little stitches. These were skilled workers in the workshop, great artists who could make a coat or a dress of the most complicated fashion. Sewing was music in their hands and Zlatke watched them in wonder. Her trusting smile won their affection and they gladly taught her. "Just don't hurry, just don't rush," they advised.

Eight in the evening exactly, the workers began winking to one another: time to put down the work and go home. It was a tense moment; someone from the owner's family was always there just then, checking which of the workers would be the first to rise from the table.

Stories from the past were recounted in great secrecy. "There were times when we worked till twelve, till one o'clock at night, and on Thursday, or before a holiday, we would stay all night. What goings on, then! The more daring young apprentices were not passive. More than once a stone flew through the workshop window during the night. They would snatch the owner and pour oil on his face. The rebels were apprehended, sent to Siberia. No-one knows what became of them."

Zlatke listened to their stories breathlessly. These unknown heroes became her very own. To be sure, their methods of terrorism were not hers; in her organization, terrorism was forbidden. But those first ones forged the path and now others had to carry on.

II

Zlatke had planned to arrive in Bialystok shortly before *Peysekh*, at the start of the needlework season, when work would be readily available. Having received a letter of recommendation to the organization in that city, she was filled with excitement. Lying in bed at night, she tried to imagine her life in Bialystok, a noisy, crowded city dense with people and buildings; while here all around her was stillness. The windows of her house opened onto the meadows and trees. But she no longer needed these; she was no longer a child ....

How would Zavl receive the news of her leaving? He would come there later. In her mind she pictured how they would both live there: they'd have only one room and see little of each other. Evenings, they'd both be busy with work in the organization or in the Workers' Exchange. It would be a life full of struggle and danger. Should one of them be arrested, they'd send letters through the guards. She'd heard that there were some sympathetic prison guards.

One evening, after a meeting of their cell, she stayed behind in Zavl's little room, having chosen this as the time to tell him of her impending departure. Zavl was in a very good mood. An acquaintance had left him his mandolin for a few days. He had tried playing first working with his finger, then with the pick, and it was going well.

"Want to hear?" he asked jovially. Taking up the mandolin, pick held stiffly in his hand, he played her a tune. Zlatke was enchanted. She hummed along and they spent a long time like that. Zavl was beginning to wonder: usually at this time, Zlatke would be rushing to get home. But now ....

"How would it be if I were to leave here?" was how she put the question to him.

"Leave? Where to?" Zavl was shocked.

"I'm serious. I want to go to Bialystok, to work there. I've been thinking about it for a long time."

Zavl fell silent. She saw his face drain of colour, a forlorn look appearing.

"You don't want me to go, Zavl? Tell me the truth."

"How can I tell you what to do?" the words burst out, tense. He had always believed she knew more than he: she was, after all, well educated. He sat slouched on the chair, silent. Zlatke put her hand on his shoulder.

"You'll come there too, later on. You're a skilled worker, you'll easily find work."

She began to paint a picture for him of how they would live there. Everything was set and clear in her mind. She spoke for a long time, coaxing him with the warmth of her voice.

But Zavl was filled with dark thoughts: what would become of him when she was gone? She'd meet an intellectual in the big city, one who spoke easily, fall in love with him and no longer care for Zavl. He had often thought of their future together. During such contemplative moments, he would see himself and Zlatke sitting at the table eating a supper which she had prepared. Zlatke, happy and cheerful, wearing a white apron, presiding over their domesticity. Their family would grow, children would come. All the while they'd remain dedicated fighters in the movement; one thing had nothing to do with the other.

Zavl rose and suddenly asked, "Have you spoken to your mother about us yet?"

"No, not yet. What does it matter what my mother'll say? Am I asking her permission? If we love each other ... ." She was happy to see his face gradually brighten. He had accepted the necessity of her going.

Love had left him vulnerable and he began softly, "You probably think I'm very ignorant."

"Don't talk such foolishness." She nestled up against him.

Later that night, they went down into the thick darkness of the street. The town was sunk deep in sleep. Here and there, a night lamp flickered through a windows: probably a scholar who had risen early and was sitting over a page of *Gemore*, or a youth whom the movement had already touched sitting at a forbidden book, immersed in the new bible of socialism.

Quite by chance, Zlatke had a long talk with her mother. The town was already buzzing about her love affair with Zavl the quilter and the rumour had reached her mother. Mama refused to believe it, knowing her daughter was friends with the wealthy youth of the town. In her eyes, Zlatke had, as a result, greatly matured — and now such a rumour.

"Is it true, daughter, what they say about you and Zavl the quilter?" So started the conversation when they were in the house alone.

"It's true, Mother." Zlatke was glad to have it out with her at last; she ought to know.

Her mother barely knew Zavl. She'd only heard stories about him: how on a market day, a drunken gentile and his cronies had attacked some Jews and Zavl appeared out of nowhere. He'd let them have it, right and left, until the hooligans were driven from the market.

"I always thought you would choose a fine, learned young man, a noble-minded husband," her mother said in a soft voice.

"What are you saying, Mama?" Zlatke's face turned red. "Zavl is nobility itself. You don't know him and you shouldn't talk like that." In that instant she decided she would also tell her mother about her going, to prepare her. "Mama, I want you to know, I may be leaving very soon."

Mama was cutting bread for supper. She put down the knife slowly, giving Zlatke a sharp look. Minutes passed in strained silence. What could she say to her? The time was long gone when she could scold Zlatke. Now nothing would help: neither kindness nor severity.

"Think carefully about what you're doing," the words escaped. Her voice betrayed a mother's anxiety for her child. "Now she wants to embark on a journey, all alone, to an unknown place, and God knows what will come of it all."

The next evening, when Zlatke came home from work, she found her father pacing the floor restlessly. He knows everything, she thought. She felt a tug at her heart. Her father was ashen, and when she met his glance, she saw only deep sorrow. She could read in his expression a heavy reproach: What path are you setting out on, daughter?

That evening, he tried looking into the account books of his lottery sales but his mind was elsewhere. Then he walked over to his holy books, turning the yellowed pages. Soon he was again pacing back and forth as though the house were too cramped to hold him.

There was much talk in those days about a certain train which passed through the town. They said that one wagon, with barred windows, held the prisoners arrested for opposing the czar. Hersh-Leyb, the tavern keeper, who happened to be in the station waiting-room, saw the wagon himself and later told Zlatke's father about it. "Lost souls," Hersh-Leyb called them, his voice conspiratorial and frightened.

The town was full of the secret. *Shabes* in the synagogue, it was *the* topic of conversation; Zlatke's father did not join the circle. But at home, he devoted himself more than ever to his two boys. They were both good students in *kheder* and father tested first one, then the other, as if to insure their future as good, God-fearing Jews.

Zlatke bought a braided straw case in which to pack her things. It was very quiet at home, one of the last evenings before she was to leave. The children looked now at Zlatke, now at Mama, with apprehensive eyes. Mama had shouted at them to go sleep and they were afraid to make a peep. Silently, Mama prepared food for the trip and helped Zlatke pack. Her silence was her protest against her daughter's leaving. Then they all went to bed and Zlatke knew that neither her mother nor her father closed an eye that night.

Zlatke met with her cell comrades for the last time, but they spoke little about activities in the organization. All were distressed by Zlatke's departure. It was such a loss; they'd miss her, the best, the most energetic member. They wanted to organize a farewell party for her but on no account would she accept it.

"Not now; maybe when I come back," she begged.

After that, she stayed with Zavl in his attic room. They spoke little to each other that evening. In festive stillness, they both sat at the table drinking the tea she had prepared for the last time. Zlatke was even more distraught than Zavl; her eyes tear-filled, her face pallid, her lips puffed and red. During their goodbyes, she drew close and embraced him,

"I love you so, Zavl!"

The words leaped out in a trembling voice. Zavl touched her satin hair; he felt her body shiver and in that moment forgot that tomorrow she'd be gone. There was no-one in the world besides the two of them.

That night they pledged eternal love.

III

Bialystok, proletarian city, city of labour and struggle. Throngs of youth were drawn here, fresh from the provinces, from the tiny surrounding towns where life moved slowly, enveloped by the stillness of pine forests, wide fields and orchards. It was here that they came, the healthy, red-cheeked girls with thick black braids, burning eyes. Pallid boys came, with bony scholars' hands, fresh from the *yeshives* where for years they'd grounded themselves in the wisdom of the *Talmud*. The factories and workshops opened their doors wide to them. Together, they now constituted a great mass of true proletarians, future fighters for the revolution. As their vision cleared of small town dreaminess, their pace quickened and their step became more animated ....

Zlatke quickly sensed the fast pulse of the big city. She too wanted to move more quickly, more energetically. An accomplished artisan with a well-honed sense of her craft, she was already employed in a workshop. The more complicated the pattern, the greater her enthusiasm.

"These country bumpkins do a good piece of work, they don't bungle it," they said about her sewing.

Here too in the workplace the vibrant revolutionary mood could be felt. Not long ago, a strike had taken place in the needle trade and now they worked only nine hours a day, going home when it was still daylight. The owner of the workshop, an elegant and nervous lady, became even more nervous when she saw her girls get up from their work on the hour — exactly. If she needed a piece of work finished urgently, there was no way she could persuade any of them to do it.

"Just the hem, and the dress'll be finished," she pleaded in a tragic voice.

"Tomorrow is another day," was the girl's response. The time was long past when they'd give in to any boss. Lustily and proudly they rushed out into the street, Zlatke among them. She did not, heaven forbid, reveal her identity, her membership in the *Bund*. The girls looked down on her as one does with country people but Zlatke thought to herself: Wait, wait, you'll soon see who Zlatke is ....

After work, she walked home through the narrow, winding little streets of Piaskes, the working-class district. The old wooden houses with their grey, peeling walls and the poverty of the neighbourhood offended her proletarian pride. She consoled herself with the thought that their suffering would not last: the revolution would transform everything.

That same week, Zlatke went to Surazer Street, where the *Bundist* Workers' Exchange was located. Sheyne Rokhl, the daughter of the Mateses, with whom she was boarding, took her there. The street was flooded with workers, noisy with life and activity.

Here came the great weavers' trade, recognizable by their thin, drawn faces. Their children were also weavers, their daughters spoolers and threaders. Tribes of them came here. And then there were the gallant youth, the tanners and the delicate, pale-skinned girls from the tobacco factories. And the clerks with their dandy neckties and well brushed gaiters. And tailors and shoemakers and joiners and tinsmiths — all were there.

Workers brought their complaints against the owners and sought justice from the *Bund*: finagling a week's wages, violating hard-won agreements, dismissal without cause, the boss speaking coarsely to his girls. The *Bund* representatives were severe with the owners and those found guilty were punished. A strike was called when necessary and decisions made at the Workers' Exchange had to remain in force.

They were everywhere, the *Bundist* representatives, flying through the crowd on wings. They clarified obscure issues, answered questions. Their pockets were bursting with illegal literature which they distributed in stealth and trust to their people. Now a speaker sprang up from the thick crowd, forthright and free. His flaming words spoke of a better world to come, a future which will belong to those who produce everything with their own hands. With pride and faith the workers looked at the young speaker, his thin face framed by a dark beard, his eyes shining.

Here and there, a political leaflet fluttered through the air, secretly passed from hand to hand and the message it proclaimed was: The time is near, be prepared! In the midst of this tumult, Zlatke held firmly onto Sheyne Rokhl's arm and surveyed the sight with misty eyes, with a piety that recalled her childhood when she accompanied her mother to synagogue and saw the congregation at prayer.

Soon, Sheyne Rokhl got busy. She was an agitator, a

representative for her trade, and she sought out her people, distributed literature to them and answered their queries. She herself had been educated here, at the Workers' Exchange, had completed a course on revolutionary strategy she was now passing on to others.

No police were in sight; should a suspicious character appear, they knew he was a spy. One of the workers, a hefty youth, would meet him straight on with a light foot and a tight fist. The stranger took off and disappeared, the Workers' Exchange resumed undisturbed.

The other residents of Surazer Street — coach drivers, porters, rag dealers, and even shopkeepers — were not genuine proletarians and cared little about what went on in the street. Once in a while though, someone, perhaps a porter or a shopkeeper would, in passing, stop, fear and hope in his heart. Perhaps his salvation too would come from them.

Further on, way down at the corner of the long, narrow street, stood the City Hall, its clock on the pointed tower. Around it spread the market with its countless shops. There, life went on at its usual pace. Merchants, shopkeepers weighed and measured their goods, bustled, quarrelled among themselves and lured customers away from one another. During a quiet hour, the shopkeepers would look at that other street, dense with people. In hushed tones, they would talk, shaking their heads; something was in the works in that street, nothing good. And old Jewish eyes grew sadder still.

The activists from the Workers' Exchange looked down on the shopkeepers. They were the petit-bourgeois elements, unfit for battle and, according to socialist theory, condemned to extinction ....

When night fell and stars appeared in the sky, the crowd thinned out. A few groups of workers stood about here and there on the corners to finish an important discussion or a dispute which had been started earlier. Their voices echoed far in the now quiet surroundings.

Zlatke left for home with Sheyne Rokhl. She was elated and refreshed like someone who had splashed into an ocean wave on a hot summer day. Full of strong emotions, she didn't want to speak.

In their room, before going to sleep, Sheyne Rokhl said to her, "You know, I've already put your name forward; very soon you'll be admitted into the organization."

"Oh!" Zlatke exclaimed. She'd been waiting for this moment but now, suddenly, she was filled with self-doubt: was she sufficiently prepared for such responsible work? But she said nothing to Sheyne Rokhl.

The next evening, as soon as she had returned from work and eaten her supper, she went into her room and sat down to write a letter to her lover. "To my beloved and loyal comrade, Zavl," she began. "There's not enough ink and paper to tell you everything on my heart." She described everything she had seen at the Workers' Exchange: the great masses of workers, true proletarians of whom they had only dreamed at home during their strolls in the moonlit nights. She told him how happy she was to have come here and about her new friends. Zlatke had intended to write a long letter, but because of the conspiracy laws she didn't know what to include, what to omit. She wrote, crossed out, and the outcome didn't please her. Her longing for Zavl at that moment was intense. In the end, she wrote that she awaited his arrival; as they'd agreed, both would be fighters for their ideals. "Come quickly and I'll tell you everything in person." Signing her letter, "From me, your passionate Zlatke," she sealed it and sat in reverie.

Sheyne Rokhl came into the room on tiptoe, looking for something. The same age as Zlatke, she was more serious and staid. She spoke in an assured, decisive voice, without inner doubts. Although not well-read, she could intuitively grasp an issue and address it with confidence. She had a longish face, large, dark eyes and straight black hair parted in the middle. She always wore a white blouse with a long white tie. It was said about Sheyne Rokhl that she had an intelligent look. The blouse showed off her flat chest and Zlatke envied her flatness.

Zlatke didn't like her own appearance. Her pale face was still too round, her lips too red, her light brown hair too curly and unmanageable. When she was alone in their room, she would stand in front of the mirror critically examining herself. She was angry at her full, round body — "round like a pumpkin" — she scowled to herself grimacing at the mirror. She tried hard to walk hunched over, hoping to hide her full, high breasts. Immaturity on the verge of becoming was stamped on Zlatke. Deep within herself, she dreamt of rising in the movement, of girding herself with knowledge, perhaps becoming one of the leaders. Inside her coexisted all kinds of moods: anxiety, hope, joy and longing.

Late one evening, when Sheyne Rokhl had completed her rounds, Zlatke wanted an intimate, heart-to-heart with her friend, to confide in her about her lover and perhaps ask if she too had someone. But Sheyne Rokhl was stingy with words when it came to personal matters, so Zlatke directed the conversation towards serious matters, speaking about the movement and the books she had read. Sheyne Rokhl was amazed.

"You certainly know your way around a point," she told her.

And so everything went well with Zlatke. But sometimes

at night as she lay awake, her head burrowed into the pillow, she thought about home with a trembling heart. How were they all? How was Zavl? Did he miss her as much as she missed him? If only she had a glass to see far away, to glimpse through the window at all her near and dear.

TRANSLATED BY FRIEDA FORMAN

ESTER

Dora Schulner

❦

This is the first chapter of a novel by the same name which follows the life of a Jewish woman caught up in the various political, social and cultural movements around her — first in Russia, then in the United States — during a time of great upheaval.

The action in this chapter takes place in the Soviet Union not long after the October Revolution of 1917, when many old standards of behaviour were uprooted with the old regime, and sexuality was allowed greater expression. It was also a time of idealism which gave rise to social reform. Ester, the heroine, is involved with both a maternity home for unwed mothers and a children's home which takes care of her four children.

Stride lightly over these nearby hills,
And come to me joyously,
Do not plan to come in company,
Come alone, and think alone of me
So I may be your friend from now to journey's end.

IVAN TURGENEV

Soviet Union, 1922

A WINTER NIGHT descended on the town of R. Outside the frost was bitter. Inside the Maternity Home, all was warm and cosy. For Ester, the manager of the institution, today was a happy day. She had persuaded the medical office of the Children's Home to let her take her four children for a month's vacation. The children were well taken care of at the Children's Home, but Ester missed them. Permission had been granted. And now the children were with her.

The children were quiet as kittens the whole day. She had told them to be good because there were sick people there. Ester's children — two boys and two girls — were real angels, particularly the oldest girl. Rokhele looked upon her mother as an older sister and was always complaining that the children needed to be taught, that they were wild. At that Rokhele's dark eyes would fill with tears. Ester had soothed Rokhele, promising that she would obtain permission to take them for a vacation. Now they were asleep — Yankele and Hershele in one bed and Rokhele and Feygele in the other. Looking at the sleeping children, Ester felt joy in every limb. Ester herself still looked like a mere girl. She was all of twenty-eight, slender, supple, with short hair, a lively, expressive face, dark eyes, a mouth that smiled warmly. Friends said she had a fiery temperament, that the earth shook beneath her feet.

Her mother had married her off very early, afraid of her impulsiveness. And now, at twenty-eight, she had a mother's responsibilities. The children were asleep in their beds, but Ester couldn't sleep. She sat at the table in the reception room, the lamp shining brightly, its light making the room cosy. Her head leaned on her hands. She still felt the taste and warmth of her children, how they embraced her with their little hands and kissed her affectionately. Yes, it was warm and good to be a mother, but nature demanded she honour a debt she couldn't meet. She went to meetings, helped rebuild her ruined country and was content that she could conquer her longing.

It was now midnight. When Ester did not sleep well it was better to sit up late and read. However, she wasn't reading — pictures hovered before her eyes now as if projected on a screen: She saw the war, her husband going to the front lines, then the revolution, pogroms, herself running with her children to save them from evil, fear and illness. She hadn't heard from her husband since the war and the end of the revolution. That time belonged to the distant past. Now she was in a warm home, happy to be helping to build a new life as well as raising her own children. Ester herself had helped establish the Maternity Home. The town was small, yet there were women who needed help when their time to give birth came.

Christie, the miserable streetwalker, had rested her tired body here where she waited for her child to come into a beautiful, liberated world. The pockmarks on her face had faded. Ester was proud to hear Christie say, "Comrade manager, I feel so good here!" Other women, who used to think that this was a home only for those like Christie, also felt good here. The fire that had destroyed the town brought many women to this place. They were now grateful to the government for the home that gave them rest and peace.

Ester smiled to herself, remembering how difficult the work had been and how good it felt now.

The clock struck one. She got up, looked at herself in the mirror which showed her a fresh, young face. She still wasn't sleepy but sleep she must.

Suddenly she heard horses' hooves and men's voices. They wouldn't be coming to her because men weren't allowed here. Someone was probably lost. Then she heard knocking and a plea for permission to come in to warm up. She opened the door to two Red Army men stiff with cold who apologized for disturbing her; their military unit had just reached town at this late hour. The frost was burning; having found lodgings for almost everyone else, they themselves had nowhere to sleep.

Ester scrutinized her night visitors. They stood before her in greatcoats that told of their high rank; one in his forties, the other in his thirties. Smiling, they said, "Comrade, allow us to stay overnight here. We see that you have a stable; give us the key, we'll put the horses in and will remember you forever."

Ester stood lost. It was strictly forbidden for men to cross the threshold here. But how could one let people freeze outside? Without a word she opened the door wider. The younger one pressed her hand very elegantly and soon they were in the room.

Ester gave them the key to the stable; they led the horses in and came cheerfully back, taking off their greatcoats and making themselves comfortable. Ester examined both and her eyes lingered on the younger one: his athletic physique, curly dark-blond hair, fiery eyes — her heart leapt.

She asked them to be very quiet so that no-one should know they were in the house. They assured Ester they would. "The main thing, Comrade," they pleaded, "is to give us some tea, if you possibly can." Ester went to the kitchen and the younger one offered to help her put the samovar on. Ester filled it with water, he put in the coals, she poured on kerosene, he carried the samovar out, lit it and fanned the coals. Before long the samovar was boiling. The comrade took the samovar into the room. Ester put glasses, bread and honey on the table. All this in as matter-of-fact a fashion as if they had known each other for a long time.

Suddenly — she couldn't remember how it happened — the comrade was holding her tightly in his arms. A current ran through her. He pressed her tightly to himself and two souls became fused. Ester freed herself from his arms. Her face was aflame.

They called the other comrade in for tea. Now, as all three

of them sat at the table, both kept thanking her. The older one was tired; he apologized and went to sleep on the bed prepared. And now Ester remained alone with her young man. He told her he came from Odessa, that he graduated in architecture, that he was in command of the unit which would remain here in town for a while.

His bright handsome face beamed at her imploringly but she spoke to him as if he were a child. "Morning," she said, "is wiser than night." He didn't listen to her, however, and locked her once again in his arms, pressing her to his heart and kissing her passionately. She was weak with desire but tore herself away and ran into her children's room.

When the morning sun shone into the house, her guests were no longer there. No-one had even an inkling that anything had happened during the night.

Ester woke that morning with mixed feelings. Like every other day, she followed her routine, but her thoughts were far away. And when Ester looked at the morning paper, she read that a new military unit would remain stationed in their town for a while. Its commander, Vlassoff, was particularly praised. Ester read those lines under a spell. Commander Vlassoff was the younger of her two guests.

During the day her new friend came and brought his rations as a gift for her children, and for the two of them tickets to the municipal theatre. And when Ester wanted to refuse, without any embarrassment he called her "child" and took her and her children in his strong arms. The children rejoiced as if they had seen their own father.

Ester was exhilarated by the feelings he awakened in her. Until that moment, she had not experienced such turmoil. She had had children with her husband, she loved her children like her life, but this kind of love she had not yet understood.

In the evening they went to the theatre. Ester was happy. Everyone wondered how she knew him, when she had met him. They all already knew who Commander Vlassoff was and therefore the curiosity was great. Ester thought that it was not for them to know that the night had brought him to her; that her longing had showed him hers of all the doors he could have knocked on.

Vlassoff's time was limited but he did not let go of Ester. Ester's girlfriends surrounded him but he had eyes only for Ester and kept paying her compliments. Both men and women were wearing greatcoats and caps on their clipped hair. Ester also dressed that way, and was always told that it became her. Now it came in handy; Ester wanted to look pretty.

From that night her life had purpose. That winter she felt like a butterfly. Her children were back at the Children's Home. She did her work as usual, but in the evenings she was happy.

The winter went quickly and spring came, and with the spring her love blossomed again. Vlassoff had a beautiful voice and would sing operatic arias. After his daily duties he would come straight to Ester. Riding his beautiful horse to her window, he'd sing to her and give her his first kiss through the window. It seemed to Ester even his horse was happy with his master's love for her. Her days shone brightly. She was drunk with love; it seemed to her that only now had she discovered life. Until Vlassoff there had been no life. Her love for him was all-consuming; she saw no-one but him.

Rumours spread around the city. Ester's name was on everyone's lips. Her sister-in-law Sheyndl brought her all the gossip from town but Ester wasn't troubled by it. She was a slave to her feelings — Vlassoff knew how to love and Ester loved.

But happiness doesn't last forever: one autumn night, he held Ester in his arms and tenderly said, "Child, our unit is leaving town and I want to explain the situation to you." Silently she clasped her hands around his head and with a confused smile pressed herself against his heart. She did not cry; she had had too much happiness to cry now. She wanted to be happy in these moments; to give him her happiness to take away.

Vlassoff told Ester that if she wanted she could go with him. He was certain that they would both suffer when they were separated. "Child," he said, "come with me where I am going. Leave the children at the Children's Home."

Ester was startled. For many nights she hadn't slept, had only thought about the separation over and over again. During those sleepless nights she had seen her happiness and watched it disappear. She had known he wouldn't stay forever. She had compared those nights with the sleepless, lonely nights of the year before and concluded that she would never abandon her children; that pain is sometimes good, if only one can conquer it. She knew she was strong and was certain she would win. Ester was prepared to suffer, but she had wanted to be happy if only for the moment.

She heard her lover's words and wanted to tell him — "don't talk, it can never happen" — but she was silent. She drank the cup to the end. She pressed herself more strongly to her lover and closed his mouth with her lips.

And now the last night had arrived. Now they stood outside at the door, the same door through which she let him in that cold wintry night. Ester thought with pain that she would not abandon her children. She stood by his side and felt him in every limb. She knew that she was standing beside him for the last time. She heard his words. He was pleading with her, "Child, I am a soldier; I have to go where they send me. I love you and I want you to come with me. Leave the children in the Children's Home." Ester was silent. Her love for her children was stronger and it prevailed. Without the children there would be no happiness, and if she must long for someone, better to long for the lover ....

Vlassoff held her hands in his, looked silently into her eyes and waited. But Ester's trembling answer was — no. She freed herself from her lover's arms and pressed against his handsome horse, the one on which he came that night. The horse had stood there all the while turning its head from one to the other as if it understood their conversation. When the horse felt Ester's hands, its nostrils quivered. She embraced its neck, buried her head in its mane to hide her tears.

She found herself again in her lover's arms — the last kiss. He leapt on his horse, bent down to her. He said the most tender words to her. She heard his voice — "Be well, child." The horse's gallop woke her as if from sleep. Ester stood in the dark night alone. The horse's hooves could still be heard in the quiet of the night. The rider and his horse had disappeared.

TRANSLATION BY HENIA REINHARTZ

DINA

Ida Maze

❧

Ida Maze's autobiographical novel Denah, *left in draft form when she died in 1962, was prepared for publication by the Montreal poet Moshe Shafir in 1970.*

Set in White Russia at the time of the 1905 Revolution and the government-inspired pogroms during and after, it is a story of relationships: Jews and gentiles, Russians and Poles, mistress and servants; most passionately, Dina's attachments to animals, houses, the living, the dead, nature, and to the earth itself.

These selections take place after Dina's father, forced off his farm by his Polish landlord, had left for America. The reluctant thirteen year old Dina and her mother set out in 1907 to join him, thus becoming part of the great European Jewish immigration to the New World.

I

DINA'S MOTHER, PESHE, received a letter from her husband in America. Shloyme wrote that Malke, their firstborn, had, in a blessed hour, married and that he was lonely without a woman in the house. Peshe was to settle their affairs and join him as quickly as possible. Heavy-hearted, Dina began looking for ways to avoid the inevitable: this "America" on the other side of the world. She'd have to tear herself away from the soil where she'd been born and taken her first steps, from her very being, her whole world. She couldn't imagine what was ahead. She felt herself at the brink of a dark abyss and wanted to pull back.

On her way to Slutsk to buy a wedding gift for Malke, Peshe stopped off in Kapulye at her friend Rode's and left Dina there. In Rode's home Dina was, as always, a cherished guest. Everyone there felt saddened by her leaving.

Dina felt worse than all of them. She sat mute, neither speaking nor listening to those around her.

Motl, Rode's son, tried to console her, "After all, the world isn't that big. Soon, the time will come when countries will be closer together, when it will even be possible to ride or fly like birds from one country to another."

Dina lost patience with him. He believed in every kind of foolishness! "We'll fly like birds! And if we fall and are killed, God forbid, what then?" Better he shouldn't speak such nonsense. There's a limit to everything. Motl smiled at Dina's obstinacy.

She stayed upset, "It would be better if there were no ships crossing oceans .... No-one would leave home and no-one would drown. With a ship you can drown."

"But not with an airship!"

"But with an airship, you can, God forbid, fall down and be smashed to bits!"

These talks took place at night from their beds at opposite ends of the room. They whispered late into the night till Motl would tell Dina to go to sleep. Dina would begin her night prayers silently, interspersing all kinds of questions to God and answering them herself with heavy sighs.

Dina waited for her mother to come back from Slutsk to take leave of her children buried in the cemetery. Dina remembered how her mother had ailed after little Freydele's death. Itshe, the young revolutionary, dead after a beating by czarist agents, was, of course, older. She'd surely go to the cemetery to weep at the graves of her two children, begging their forgiveness. She would never leave them had Father not written that she must come.

Instead of Mama, a letter arrived saying that she was going straight back to their old home in Ulye and that Uncle Yankl would bring Dina to her on Friday. From there they'd start out to America. The letter came on Tuesday, leaving only three days for Dina to say goodbye to the town and to Rode's household. Mama wasn't coming and wouldn't be saying goodbye to her children. She was leaving them behind, abandoned for all eternity.

Dina went to the cemetery by herself that evening. She circled the fence, chose a low spot and clambered over. She found Itshe's grave and squatted at his tombstone till the cool wind chilled her and the evening grew dark. Then, sadly, she got up to look for the other grave, the little grave. She couldn't find it. So, climbing back over the fence, she crossed the field back to town, where lamps were already flickering in the windows.

II

With forced cheerfulness, Vasil said, "So you're going to America, Dinke?"

Dina answered sadly, "I don't know .... If Mama says we're going, we'll probably go."

"When you get there, tell your father to bring me out too. I'll serve him as I always have. Will you tell him?"

"I'll tell him. But why would you go so far away from here? And what will become of Olyana and the children?"

"I'll send for them as your father is sending for you and your mother."

"Don't leave, Vasil. Better to stay here. I don't want to go either. This is our home."

"Our home! Some home!" said Vasil angrily. "That vile

dog, may the earth refuse to hold him, drove your father from his own house and property, drove your father out and himself into the ground! May he rot! I took to drink ... out of despair. I drink, then come home and beat Olyana and the children."

Dina shuddered. "You beat Olyana and the children? You mustn't, Vasil. My father would never forgive you!"

"As God is my witness," answered Vasil, full of shame. "Dinkele, you know me. I've never hit anyone before. But this comes out of desperation. I can't find a place for myself. Promise me that you'll ask your father to send for me."

"Promise me you won't hit Olyana and the children any more and I'll ask my father to send for you — if I get there myself."

"What do you mean, 'if you get there'? You're going, aren't you?"

Dina replied in a self-satisfied tone, "They may still turn me back at the border because of trachoma, or blemishes on my body. I have a large birthmark on my foot. I may be turned back."

"God forbid."

"And I pray to God I won't be allowed through."

"You're a foolish girl, Dinke. What are you thinking? Everyone else will be in America and you'll be here?"

"That doesn't matter. Itshe stays here alone too — and Freydele."

Vasil crossed himself, "Holy Mother of God, what are you saying? They're dead, aren't they? How can they go with you?"

"That's even worse, Vasil. If they're dead and can't come with us, we mustn't leave their graves alone for all time, forever."

III

Dina closed the door behind her and stood looking at the large room that had once been their home. She touched the sun-drenched wall, then shuffled towards the empty kitchen. It was like a hollow cave. Long rays of sunshine cast lean shadows on the bare floor and everything looked fixed and ghostly, like a still-life behind glass. She stole into the large synagogue room; silence, like after a pogrom; mildew and spider webs over the holy ark, books, lamps and curtains.

Dina stood as still as the dead things around her, then turned back to the kitchen. The shelves that had once held gleaming copper and brass utensils were empty. Between window and door, where the large tub and water barrel with its copper dipper had once stood, there were only rings of mould. She looked till tears began to blind her.

Suddenly, a weak, thin mew from the wall where the oven was. Then, deep in the oven, like in an open grave, she saw a dusty, emaciated cat: Grulye!

The cat got to her feet and started towards the opening, her rheumy eyes fixed on Dina, who was now stroking the ash-covered fur. With a weightless leap she let herself down and began rubbing back and forth against Dina's feet, purring softly as if to tell of her suffering since the family had left. Dina picked her up and went for some milk. She filled a saucer and held the unfortunate cat over it. Grulye lapped it up; every few licks, she lifted her head to check with Dina.

The door opened and Olyana herself entered, arms spread wide. "Dinke! Look at that! Her patience has been rewarded. Just a cat, but she knows her mistress' touch. However often I called her, took her home and fed her like a child, however much the children nursed her, comforted her, tried to play with her — it made no difference! Before we even turned our backs, she was gone! Where was Grulye? Like yesterday — gone, back into the oven. It was such a pity to watch the mute creature.

"We've all lost. See how Vasil in his despair has taken to drinking, weeping, beating me and the children. *He's* permitted everything, everything. Isn't *my* heart broken too? It was my home too. I raised you children." She bent down and kissed Dina on the head.

"Oy, Dinke, Dinotchka, may the earth refuse to hold that landlord, that Polish dog. He's made us all miserable. Now my Vasil speaks only of going to America, to your father, and of leaving me and the children here in our misery.

Olyana wiped her eyes and Dina comforted her, "If he goes, Olyana, he'll send for you. He told me that."

"Good Dinkele. Not for nothing did I carry you in my arms and teach you the blessings. Remember when you wouldn't eat *matse* on *Peysekh*?"

Dina smiled, embarrassed. "I was little."

"Of course you were. You wouldn't do that now. *Peysekh* is *Peysekh*! You're a fine girl, Dinke; I know that. A fine girl."

Olyana made a place for herself beside Dina and sat stroking Grulye. "Dinke, did he really tell you himself that he'd send for us from America?"

"Yes, on our way back, this morning."

"Good Dinke. You talk to your father and I'll ask your mother. I served them faithfully, like my own parents. Vasil wants to leave. Even a dog needs its own place. We're worse off than dogs. We don't own a crumb of land. Even this miserable shack isn't ours. We can be thrown out just like your father."

Looking at the cat, Olyana grew thoughtful. "Like Grulye, like her, we'll be left without a home. She'll lie in that oven till she expires. I took her all the way to your Uncle Shimen's.

Your Aunt Khashe cried, looking at us. She took me in like one of her own, filled a sack with food and trifles for my children, put Grulye into her children's care and told me to go home and not to worry. They'd look after her. In less than two days, Grulye was back in the oven again; found her own way back. A dumb animal is more faithful than a person. It knows nothing of trickery. Put her down, Dinke. Let's see whether she tries to get back to the oven." Dina let the cat down. Grulye remained snuggling and purring at her feet, content.

IV

Peshe wanted to spend this last *Shabes* in Ulye, her former home. Knowing what to expect at her widowed brother-in-law's, she arrived laden with fish, soup, *khale* and puddings. It was, as the cheerful pauper Yankl had foretold, a *Shabes* fit for a king.

It was late, almost time to bless the candles, so Peshe immediately began planning with Olyana. "Tomorrow, they'll all be coming here to pray as a congregation. There hasn't been a *minyen* here in a long while and the prayer room is covered in dust and spider webs." What would become of everything after her departure was beyond Peshe's control, but for now Olyana was to warm some water and clean the prayer room as best she could. Olyana listened, her honest peasant eyes shining with joy. She'd do it immediately, the floor too and the windows. Her hands longed for real work.

At the Friday night table, Uncle Yankl glowed. His late wife's candlesticks stood on a little table covered with a sparkling white threadbare cloth. Under a cover embroidered with the *kidesh* lay two small *khales*. This cloth too was a reminder of Yankl's late wife. The gentle Rokhl had made it while still a girl.

The floor had been sprinkled with fresh sand. The three children were scrubbed and dressed in clean patches. Yankl wore a clean shirt, his long-neglected *Shabes* coat had been brushed and he had been instructed to dress in honour of the guests. All this had been wrought by the devoted Olyana so that her mistress might find peace and Sabbath joy.

The congregation had planned to have *kidesh* in Peshe's rooms after prayers. The torte and schnapps had been sent over the day before. Now, seated at the long table, each wanted to say something appropriate to Peshe, a "go in peace." But the atmosphere was heavy. Young Rokhl's shadow hovered. Everything they wanted to forget surfaced anew. Everything bore witness to the collapse of a home, a family and lives. They sat around the table like mourners.

Early Sunday peasants from the village saw Peshe off, kissing and weeping until Vasil screamed at Olyana, "That's enough! Let go of Dinke! Stop the kissing; you'll choke her! The horses won't stand still!" And he cracked the whip.

What did he have against these dumb creatures? Had he anyone else on whom to let out his bitter heart? The lashing was really meant for himself. How else to vent the terrible pain? A man doesn't cry except when he's had a glass of whiskey. Tears were choking him and he would have liked to turn the whole world upside down. But when you're no more than an ant, only the whip can bring relief.

The horses suddenly tore into a gallop, leaving the crowd behind. Through a fog of dust, they watched the wagon carry Peshe and Dina away from the village of Ulye. Vasil loosened the reins, and the horses, knowing the road well, slowed to a trot. Driver and passengers could at last think their own thoughts.

Just past the village young trees leaned out towards the road. Dina took leave in her heart of each little tree, and in her thoughts each one nodded and answered, "We'll miss you too." Lost in dreams, Dina seemed to hear a cat meowing. "Mama, I think it's Grulye!" Hearing her name, the cat answered with a strong, loud meow and kept running after them until they lifted her onto the wagon. Dina stroked her till she fell asleep.

In a last minute stop at Rode's, Peshe made her farewells quickly and told Dina to do the same. The day would not stand still and they had a long journey ahead, some of it after dark. Dina stood mute, with tear-filled eyes, not knowing where to begin. Her mother's urging merely increased her confusion.

Rode's niece came to her rescue. "*Nu*, Dinele, go in the best of health, but don't forget to write. You know how to write nice letters, don't you?" She kissed her lightly on both cheeks. Rode, weeping silently, kissed Dina again and again. "Go in good health, my child, and may God grant you all that you merit." Going out to the wagon, Dina passed Motl with averted eyes, but he stopped her. "Dina! Don't you want to say goodbye to me?"

"What good are farewells?"

"You're a strange one, Dina. Why then do people say goodbye?"

"I don't know. "

Motl offered his hand but Dina looked down and didn't take it.

"Well, Dina, go in good health. "

"Perhaps they'll turn me back. "

"Nonsense! They won't send you back. "

Dina was saddened and angry. "You don't want them to turn me back?"

Motl offered his hand again, "*Nu*, Dina, go in good health. Give me your hand!"

She blushed and bent her head so Motl wouldn't notice. She gave him her hand and withdrew it instantly, as if she had touched a fire. Dina then climbed onto the wagon. Vasil handed her Grulye and she turned her head so no-one would see her tears. Motl shouted after her, "I'll write to you Dina. Write back!"

The road stretched endlessly. Dina was remembering how Motl had spoken to her, her embarrassment when he had taken her hand and the tremor that had passed through her when, for a moment, their hands had touched. For all of that, it was mean of him to have said that they wouldn't turn her back at the border. He must want her to go. People are so uncaring. Grulye, with such devotion, had refused to part: a dumb creature, a cat, but more loyal than people. The sleepy cat seemed even dearer to her and she cradled her affectionately.

V

The wagon stopped at a long, open shed. Under its red roof, people were already waiting. Kerchiefed women guarded their belongings and every little while checked on their children name by name. The young perched on baggage like hens or dawdled underfoot. Dina crawled out of the wagon, and at her mother's bidding sat down to guard their large wicker trunk.

Soon heavy galloping was heard and everyone hurriedly dragged their bundles towards the road. The public coach appeared, pulled by four fine large horses. Two coachmen brought it to a clamorous stop. Dina once used to imagine herself flying in a chariot with light wheels and rose-blue wings pulled by four grey mares with silver manes; gracefully, with heads high, they had wafted her into space, through painted clouds.

Dina seated herself high up in the coach, leaned her head against Peshe and held on. With a jingle of harness bells the coach pried itself away and everyone swayed in response.

They travelled all night. Dina dreamt of the green fields and blossoming orchards of the village, of the barn full of hay, of her swing and how she and her girlfriend swung and laughed freely as the wind blew their light skirts every time they went up.

She woke with a start and couldn't remember where she was. The coach had stopped at the train station. Soon other wagons arrived and stood there in the cold grey dawn. Women and children crawled out as if they were crawling from midnight caves. Resigned, they huddled together seeking warmth. Half asleep, they watched the train station which stood like a fortress, doors and shutters locked.

Time dragged on. Morning, wrapped in a grey mist, refused to emerge and the damp settled into every heart. The younger children, overcome by fatigue, hunger and thirst, demanded what was rightfully theirs. Mothers could find neither hands nor words to quiet them: a hand over a mouth, a tug at a sleeve, arm included. "This isn't home, we're in the middle of a journey!" The young remained unappeased and sharpened their protests against life's injustice. All waited as if they were waiting for the Messiah.

A light carriage arrived and there descended one with yellow buttons on his hat and coat. He pompously passed packs and people without a glance, unlocked the door, entered, and shut it again. The crowd surged forward, their mood lighter. A second carriage arrived, grander than the first, and there emerged a being with even more and bigger brass buttons. He had a spiked moustache, flashing spectacles and a pointy cockade in his round, blue hat. For this personage the first opened the door wide. With a tinny purling the station clock struck six. The door opened and the crowd pushed in. Mothers feverishly unknotted the little sacks around their necks, groped for documents or coins, and approached the wicket. The official with the piercing spectacles and moustache stood hatless behind heavy bars like an exotic bird in a yellow cage. His forehead was red and ruddier still was his neck, pinched into the pale blue velvet collar of his uniform. Even at a distance, his glance was frightening. Periodically he stuck out a fat red hand three fingers of which, like hooped barrels, were encircled by three wide gold rings. That hand took the money already placed there for him. Without looking up, he barked just one question that echoed like an order, "Where to?" Then the wicket of the golden cage slammed shut. On command from the one with the smaller buttons, the crowd began to exit. They arranged themselves along the tracks, behind the mounds of baggage. Mothers commanded children to hang on and not to be frightened when the train pulled in. All stood at the ready, soldiers awaiting the enemy's attack.

A roar was heard and the earth shook under them. Trembling, Dina swayed forward ... Peshe caught her. "What ails you? Behave! Show some pluck! When you hear the train coming closer, close your eyes and cover your ears. Once we're in the train I'll give you a bit of brandy and you'll feel better."

The second roar of the approaching train was followed by an ear-splitting whistle. Dina hid her head between her raised shoulders as if expecting a blow, and covered her ears with both hands. The train stopped with a crash. The locomotive gasped and died. Peshe tugged at Dina, "Well, how long are you going to stand there like a Jew at prayer? The train has stopped."

Dina lowered her hands and saw a kind of iron stew-pot with a roof, doors and windows. As her fear lessened, her wonder grew. A long black house that flies on wheels over shiny, narrow rails, that whistles and moans and belches and steams. It's not really a living being. Where does it come from?

The shoving now turned into pandemonium and Peshe grabbed Dina's arm, pushing her onto the narrow step and into the train. Dina groped her way in the half-dark wagon, found a bench and sat down. Looking around, she saw spittle on the floor and lifted her feet with revulsion. Peshe sighed deeply. "Thank God we're in the train." Dina, choking on the stale, smoky air, felt the cold creep from the bench through her clothing to her skin like the touch of a stranger's icy hand and shivered.

The tumult subsided as they began to arrange themselves and even to feel at home in the cold and dirt. Mothers began to serve from little white sacks: an apple, a chunk of white roll. Then again silence and waiting.

The conductor paraded past and told them to be ready. Mothers put their arms around their children. Along with a thwacking thump, slow, then urgent, wheezing, panting, and moaning, came a sudden shrieking, wailing whistle. And over it all, the terrified howling of the children.

The train lunged forward. Faster and stronger it struck into the unending distance. Dina, feeling dizzy, gripped the seat. She had been pried from the earth and was now being carried away on thousands of monstrously wild wings to the accompaniment of grotesque noises; far, far away, endlessly, incomprehensibly far.

TRANSLATED BY ETHEL RAICUS

UNSPOKEN HEARTS

Shira Gorshman

❦

This strongly autobiographical story is set in Lithuania during the period between the 1917 Revolution and the Second World War when Lithuania was independent of the Soviet Union. At the time, the Jewish communities in Lithuania and the Soviet Union were separated by borders as well as by the secularization of Russian Jewish life.

"Unspoken Hearts" is about a visit of reconciliation between a daughter living in Moscow as a liberated proletarian and the family she left behind in Lithuania, where Jewish life remained uninterrupted. Her visit is cut short by the approach of the German armies.

IT WAS ALMOST TWENTY years ago that Khane had left the little town she was now approaching on the Kovno train. She was nervous and troubled, more than you'd expect even of someone returning after a long absence. Though she was a capable, mature person, she felt very apprehensive. She couldn't picture her grandparents' home without them; couldn't imagine what would be served there instead of the noodles with milk her grandmother used to put on the table year after year. Another thing: she couldn't begin to imagine how the meeting with her mother would go. Twenty years ago it had been *Bobe*, not her mother, who had run after the wagon pleading, "Write, children! For mercy's sake, write!"

Now it was Khane's mother, Gitl, who kept rushing to the Red Army commandant down the street, telegram in hand, begging his indulgence and asking yet again, "Are you sure the Kovno train won't, heaven forbid, be late?" She didn't rest, nor did she allow anyone else to. As Hershe, her husband, described it, "Since the telegram arrived, my wife stands on one foot, chews with one tooth and sleeps with one eye."

The oven blazed continually. The sponge cakes were done, high as top-hats. The *babkes*, rich in egg yolks and cream, were glazed and sprinkled with chopped nuts, cinnamon and sugar. The fruit flans, smooth and fluffy, were frosted over with powdered sugar. Gitl had decorated the honeycake with a goose and goslings made of cloves. The *teyglekh* were ready, the dough cut into pellets, cooked in honey, then flattened, sprinkled with ginger and cut into squares. There were also peppered flat rolls to go with the chopped liver.

Gitl had boiled beef, calf, chicken and turkey bones in the freshly-scoured copper pot. When Hershe tasted the thick broth and put the spoon down, it stuck to the plate. He couldn't contain himself,

"For pity's sake, who will ever finish this 'fountain of broth'?"

"If it doesn't get eaten, I'll pour it out. Such a guest, just imagine! Better you should fill the *kreplekh* and put them in the baking pans. Grease the pans, be generous! Don't be stingy! When they've tried one of my *kreplekh* in broth, they won't know where it disappeared!"

An onslaught of words followed as Gitl put the chopped liver on large platters, added a garnish of green onion, dill and the odd radish rose and sprinkled it with grated hardboiled egg. A ladle-full of unstrained goose fat, cracklings included, went over it all ….

"It'll swim away from you!" warned Hershe.

"So long as you remain beside me! Hand me the breast of veal!"

"Whoever wishes me ill should have such a paragon of a wife."

"*I* wish *my* good friends that their wives be spared that distinction," answered Gitl, piercing the chunks of veal. A stab, a garlic clove, another stab, a carrot, another jab, some parsley, spiced, topped with beaten egg, sprinkled with *khale* crumbs, encircled by bits of chicken and — into the oven.

"Don't slam the door!" she yelled at her daughter Mirke who'd just burst in, "everything in the oven will collapse ...."

"Mama, I'm dying of hunger!"

"Should I give you a piece of white meat? Take whatever you want and let me be! Better still, tell me, my dear daughter, where have you been?"

"Why ask when you already know?"

"Is that so!"

"Yes, it's so, Mama!"

"I'll speak to you later about it; right now, I have no time for you ...."

"Me neither," Mirke answered, grabbing a chicken breast and disappearing.

"Gitl, what do you want from her?"

"Hershe, I won't allow such a disruption in the family."

"Twenty years ago you wouldn't allow it either; so you were left the fool, clearly labelled."

"I have no strength to listen to you!"

"For listening you only need common sense."

"Then you'd have to have common sense, yourself .... Where are your eyes? She's a changed person. Does she have any idea who this Vladimir is?"

"Khanke didn't choose a Vladimir. Did that satisfy you?" Hershe asked, immediately regretted his words and fell silent. Gitl said nothing more. She just kept moving things around on the stove as if she hadn't heard him, but his words had cut deeply.

Finally, everything was done. Gitl contemplated the set tables, reorganizing the liquor bottles between the bowls of preserves. The large, translucent gooseberries were whole, yellow like polished amber; the dark red strawberries lay in their reddish syrup as if just picked.

But Gitl was no longer looking at the tables. Gitl was far, far away, holding Khanke's little hands as she took her first steps and her own mother, Peshe, was drawing a knife between the child's knitted booties chanting, "Run like a brook, grow like a weed, bring joy to all good people and delight to your father and mother."

Then Gitl saw Khanke in her hanging wicker cradle, trying to get her foot into her little mouth. "My hand had not yet written such terrible words to you, my child," thought Gitl. Yes, when Khanke had given birth to her own little girl, Gitl had written: "For all I care, you can lie there in Kovno's public ward and may your bastard be left an orphan. I want no part of it." Khanke probably wouldn't talk about it now, thought Gitl. But it was neither forgotten nor forgiven. Who knew how this visit would end?

Once again, Mirke ran in. Gitl looked at her and burst out, "It wouldn't hurt you to spruce up in your new dress for Khanke's arrival!"

"I'm on my way to the aerodrome, Mother!"

"Is Vladimir waiting for you?"

"Of course!"

"Happy is the believer!"

"I certainly can't derive any faith from *you*, Mother!"

"You'd do well to find out whether he hasn't left at least one slightly pregnant wife somewhere!"

"Don't you *dare* speak that way, Mother. I won't say one more word to you," Mirke yelled and disappeared.

"I beg you, Gitl, stop blowing against the wind."

"*You* feel a breeze, and you panic! I don't. Can't you see she's already cut herself off from us?"

"I've already told you: twenty years ago you accomplished nothing — do you think you will now?" asked Hershe. Then, noticing that Gitl was pale as the wall, he brought her a pillow, and said, "Lie down a bit. Enough yelling and commotion." But it wasn't meant to be. They hadn't even managed to lie down when Mirke blew in again, like a whirlwind.

"Are you asleep?"

"If you keep asking whether we're asleep, the dream'll be longer than the night. Why are you so flushed?"

"I want to tell you something, mother."

"And your father you don't include in your confidence?"

"Vladimir has just asked me ...."

"I understand ... . And what did you tell him?"

"I told him yes."

"So, then everything has already been said? It wouldn't have hurt for me to hear these glad tidings after Khanke's departure," cried Gitl, her trembling hands reaching for Hershe.

You might think that affection was lacking in Gitl's home because she was forever mocking and spewing words sharp as pepper. But should Mirke, heaven forbid, have a toothache, should Hershe come home later than expected, should a letter from the boys, now in Kovno, be delayed, Gitl would be beside herself. Seeing the state she was in now, Hershe took off her slippers, covered her and lay down beside her on the very edge of the sleeping bench.

The house was still. No-one heard Mirke tiptoe in and

take her raincoat. No-one saw the tall youth waiting for her near the house, nor how they merged for an instant before driving away to meet Khanke, the sister Mirke had only seen in photographs.

The moment Khanke got off the train at Datneve station, she caught sight of a girl looking for someone, a girl with her mother's blue eyes. She shouted, "Mirele, it's me!"

All the way back to town, the sisters were silent, unable to utter a word.

Gitl woke up the moment she heard Khanke's voice in the house. A wild cry escaped her, she stumbled on the threshold. Through a fog she saw a pair of outstretched arms and fell into them. Hershe quickly brought some water. No sooner had he wet her face than she was back in character, "This person has lost his mind; he's pouring water all over me! He's reviving me! You'd do better to offer Khanke something to eat."

Hershe was rescued when Khanke nestled into his beard. He felt it grow wet with her tears. They looked at each other, wordless. Mirke brought a glass of chicory which Khanke didn't touch. For a while they sat, then Gitl led Khanke into the parlour.

"Mother, what is this, a belated wedding celebration?" asked Khanke, staring at the laden tables.

"Wedding or not, for me this is a celebration!"

"Mother, you're as young as you ever were."

"Old is the one who doesn't remember her younger years, my child ...!"

"You're right, Mother, good; I'm sure you're wiser than you were."

"You didn't want the chicory, so take a *teygl*." So Khanke, lost in thought, chewed on a *teygl*.

"What are you thinking about?"

"Mother, I'm scared."

"Of whom my child?"

"I want to see *Bobe*'s house, but I shudder at the thought. Tell me what happened ...."

"When *Bobe* came back from the bathhouse, she didn't feel good, so *Zeyde* came to call me. I went in and there she lay, loveliness itself, except for a trace of foam at the corner of her mouth. 'Mother,' I said, 'what is it?' She motioned in *Zeyde*'s direction, so I understood that all was not well. My blood ran cold, but I asked, pretending to be calm, 'Shall I bring you a bit of cherry preserve?' She replied, 'Don't make a fool of me, Gitke. Bring the jug of cold milk from the pantry and bring a fresh *khale*!' *Zeyde* was crying. 'Peshe, God is with you. It's almost time to light the *Shabes* candles!' 'May you be well, my dear Elye. And you, Gitke, give me some cold milk with fresh *khale* and let me die sated ... .' Those were her last words."

It was quiet for some time, then Khane broke into the most frightful laughter, wiping her eyes and sobbing. She barely choked out, "Mama, have you really invited the entire who's who of the town?"

"I've invited no-one. They'll come on their own, once day breaks."

"Before anything else, rest a while; it's only five o'clock," said Hershe.

"Sleep! This man kills me! How do you like that?"

"Papa, what do you want from her? She'll catch up on her sleep when Khanke leaves, in a month's time," Mirke remarked.

"Mama, do you remember Dvoyre, Sore-Golde's daughter? How she used to lecture me when I came to borrow threepence? 'Little girl, go tell your mother that eating is only a habit. If you can't afford it, don't bake *khale*.' "

"Khanele, stop it! Since you're only a guest, Mama will feel free to turn your words around once you're gone."

"Nobody's asking you. You, go to Vladimir!"

"Mother, I don't know who Vladimir is, but Mirke is an adult. I beg you, please don't talk that way in front of me."

"And I beg *you* to act like a guest."

"That's not very hospitable," answered Khanke, clasping Gitl in her arms and so they stood for some time, pressed to one another.

Invitations had truly been unnecessary. It was a clear, warm *Shabes* morning. From eight o'clock on, women began arriving with pastries, cakes and cherry wine. They greeted guest and hosts, then left their gifts, promising to return later.

Gitl shone. Her long brown muslin dress fit as though moulded to her figure; her face was flushed and her blue eyes bright with happiness. Every little while, she'd throw a glance at Khanke as if to ask, "You're not ashamed of me, my daughter?"

Khane didn't take her eyes off her mother, thinking, "Now I know what kind of a mother I have; never mind what happened!" And the more she observed her mother, the more she felt her own good fortune in having come.

Enter Taybele the tinsmith, a woman skilled in her craft. The first to arrive empty-handed, she went right up to Gitl and said quietly, "Don't think ill of me; I must tell you what's in my heart. You were born in a silk shirt. You see your child before you and I envy you. For you I wish that she may forget everything that happened; may her love for you be as generous as the tears she has shed because of you."

There was an uncomfortable silence till Khanke

approached Taybele and, tearful, kissed her grey head and shrunken face. When the two had cried themselves out, Taybele turned to Gitl, "I want you at least to know that when my son Helmetske was on his death bed, it was Khanke who brought him eggs every day. That it didn't help wasn't her fault. Khanele, when you, God willing, go back to Moscow, I'll make you a coffeepot and some graters that will give you potato *latkes* that taste of seventh heaven. Is it really true: they say you write all kinds of stories?"

"I've just started."

"Doesn't matter, 'just started.' Take *my* life, for instance. *There's* something to write about."

"You just need to know how."

When Taybele had left, Gitl asked in wonder, "Khanke, do you really remember every little detail?"

"I remember. I remember a doctor being brought from Vilna and Taybele running through the streets yelling, 'Jews, have pity! My sixth child is going to join my husband, may he rest in peace. Don't let the doctor go till he cures my child!' And then I remember Helmetske's funeral and later, I remember Taybele's tears hissing as they fell on the soldering iron."

Mirke came in announcing, "Khanke! Honoured guests!" First to enter was Mume Malkele who seemed to have grown so much smaller that Khanke didn't immediately recognize her. Her white batiste blouse hung loose on her bony frame and her arms looked like dry clay poking out of the sleeves. Only her dark eyes had kept their fear and anguish as she looked at her husband, also a Hershe, who had just come in. Uncle Hershe pushed her aside, embraced Khanke and lightly brushed her face with his lips. Their daughter Blumke ran in and forced herself between them to hug her cousin. Both Hershes went outside to escape the fierce weeping that had broken out. Overcome, Mirke turned away. Leybke, Blumke's husband, a tall handsome man, stood frozen to the spot, tears running down his face. "Khanke, you bitter onion, you precious crown, at long last!" Blumke burst out.

Hershe came in, dried the cousins' faces with his large handkerchief and cried out, "Quiet! Not another tear will I allow. Let there be joy! Leybke, come, meet Khanke!"

"Let us kiss Khanke, my dear. You may not know me but there's a bond between us. Here you're much loved. Not a day goes by that you're not mentioned."

"Leybke, Blumke, Mother! Let's go to the table," Mirke called.

"Malkele, don't put on your sour act, give me that other piece of turkey and fill the glasses." Uncle Hershe had taken the celebration into his own hands.

They had drunk and they had eaten. Blumke's spirits rose; a delicate pink suffused her cheeks right to her tiny ears. She kept looking at Khanke and every little while asked questions, "Do you remember the river? Do you remember the corn-noodles?"

"I remember everything. How many children do you have?"

"Three girls."

"Little bats, who needs them?" said Uncle Hershe.

By the time all souls had been properly nourished, a gang of young people had arrived. It took Gitl quite a while to clarify for Khanke who was who. "Look Khanke, that's Srulke-Shaye the shingle-maker's son, dark and lively. Eats quickly and works fast. And this is Esterke, Dovid-Hirsh's daughter. Don't mind the pitiful picture she presents. You should see her knead a trough full of rye bread; a fire-brand, one of a kind! And this is Mordkhe's daughter Minke, she needs no advertising either." Gitl would have introduced everyone individually but Blumke wouldn't allow it.

"Enough, Auntie! Mirke, bring the gramophone!" Uncle Hershe was on his feet in an instant, he took off his jacket, raised his arms, and was off across the room, singing as he danced, "Ay, good sister, dear sister, when shall we meet again?" Singing with his eyes closed, soaring, stopping, gently stamping and clapping and suddenly, "Little bats, Blumke, Khanke, Mirke, here, to me!"

Gitl wove herself into the circle too and the young pushed her gently into its centre. For an instant she stood there, arms outstretched as if to bless the candles, then, pushing up her sleeves, she turned out her palms, lifted her long brown skirt and started off around the circle. She stopped on tiptoe before Khanke, came down on her heels, bowed and was gone again with quick short steps. It was a dance of forgiveness, of regret and of overwhelming joy. And when Khanke came slowly in measured steps towards her mother, made a wide turn, bent down and began to spin like a whirlwind around her mother's feet, Malkele began to cry.

The room grew quiet. So they took to eating again. Gitl brought in large platters piled with roasted veal brisket banked with sweet carrot pudding and large black prunes. The deep porcelain soup bowls had been refilled again and again with the thick, sticky gravy. The sweets untouched; untouched for the while.

"Blumke, Leybke, Malke, we're off! Don't stop us, Gitl, and you, Khanke, no offence. We must get to the mill! Khanke, take my advice: telegraph that man of yours to come here with the children. This is paradise! Carp the size of calves. You'll eat your fill, your children will put on flesh in the twinkling of an eye."

It was well into evening. Gitl and Khanke were alone for a minute. They looked at one another. Gitl kept moving her lips until she finally was able to say, "Tell me my child, why did you leave your first husband?"

"Mother, not now. There'll be time yet to talk our hearts out. And in any case, I can't comfort you because what I don't want to tell, I won't tell."

More people, more weeping, laughter, singing, dancing. It was after midnight when Mirke rushed in, "Nobody here?"

"Mother, Father and I are no-one?" asked Khanke.

"They didn't want to wait for you. What could I do? Glad you could make it even if it is after one o'clock," teased Gitl.

As if she hadn't heard, Mirke announced despairingly, "Vladimir had to fly out so suddenly."

"Where to? For how long?" asked Khanke.

"I don't know, and it seems to me, he didn't know either why the suddenness. The urgency ... something about it makes me very uneasy. Will you sleep with me, Khanke?"

"If you'll sleep without a quilt."

"I sleep on an air mattress that Vladimir gave me."

"And I'm not used to sleeping on air either. What I'd really like would be to sleep on hay. Do you remember, Papa?"

At daybreak Khanke came into the house carrying her bedclothes and wasn't surprised to find her father up.

"Papa, what's all that thundering?"

"I think it's manœuvres."

"You haven't been to bed yet, Papa?"

"I've got heartburn from all that fat food. I've already taken soda twice."

"I can't sleep either," Gitl called from the bedroom. "May it turn out for the best. Come to me, Khaninke!" Khanke went to her mother but there was more silence than talk.

It was broad daylight when Khanke got into the cart with her little suitcase. By then everyone knew. These were not manœuvres.

Now, when Khanke remembers those days, it seems to her that the lost, the loss, refuse to fade. Fate had contrived that she fully realize whom she had lost. Her mother's cry continues to ring in her ears: "Woe is us, Khanke! We haven't even had time to talk our hearts out."

TRANSLATED BY ETHEL RAICUS

Based on an earlier version by Shari Friedman and Roma Erlich

THROUGH THE EYES OF CHILDHOOD

Malka Lee

❦

The following excerpts, taken from Lee's autobiographic work Durkh kindershe oygn *[Through the Eyes of Childhood], follow Lee from her childhood in a Galician* shtetl *through her leavetaking from her home and family to her adjustments as a sixteen year old lonely immigrant in America in the Twenties. A typical portrait of the immigrant experience, these sketches also illustrate Lee's unfaltering dedication to her writing under circumstances that might have severely discouraged a less determined person.*

The first selection begins in a time and place where the reading and writing of secular material was frowned upon by the Jewish religious community. Traditionally, women were poorly educated and then only enough to read tkhines, *Yiddish prayers written exclusively for women, often by men. Lee's father, a Hasid, was a believer in this tradition.*

I HAVE NOW FINISHED three notebooks of poems. How did I ever manage to write them? It wasn't at a polished desk. I wrote them on my knee — not even aware that I was writing poetry. They created themselves; it was as though they came to life through my fingertips.

The words cried out from my wounded young heart, through the horrors of war, through the pain of those around me. Oh my poems, what were you to me in those days? You were the prayers through which I prayed during the gruesome days of the war.

Poems of mine, you freed me from death and despair. I have chosen you with reverent care, like pearls, for my treasured notebook. And I have filled my days and nights with you. You have cried and laughed; you have spoken to me in that subtle language of silent words.

You did not forsake me in my burning days of need. Like a nurse, you watched over me and nurtured me. You have been the bread and water of my thirsty young life. When I lay ill with typhus, you did not leave me; you were with me during those nightmarish nights. And when I first sat up in my sickbed, you stood around me. And in small shaky sentences, you laughed through me and sang from my heart. My poems, never forsake me, for you are the most precious treasure that no enemy can steal.

Only my father hated them, my words. How dare a Jewish daughter consort with such wickedness; she must have demons in her heart. A Jewish daughter must not make rhymes.

Perhaps because of this, I was my mother's joy. She saw in me her youthful, girlish dreams. My poems were her sunrise and sunset. Her fingers — which embroidered enchanted woods and human forms on canvas with silken threads — wrapped themselves in words through my poems ....

It was only my father who was ashamed of a daughter who created rhymes.

Early mornings, my mother would get up first to heat the oven. This morning, she kindled the wood. But the oven wouldn't start. She blew and blew, but still the fire wouldn't light. She pushed her hand in deep through the little door, until her hand touched the chimney — which was stuffed with paper. She pulled out the wrinkled papers and took a look. A darkness descended upon her. It was my poetry! My mother let out a shriek of horror in an alien voice.

As if the bed were suddenly ablaze, I jumped up and ran downstairs in my naked feet. I was no longer human; I was a wild thing. I saw wheels spinning before my eyes. I screamed until I spit up blood. My bothers and sister woke from their beds.

I'd suddenly gone crazy. I wanted to die. Without my poems, I didn't want to live anymore. My words lay torn and enfeebled. And who did it? My own father.

The whole house was in mourning. My mother and the children wept. Everyone was screaming and my poor wretched father stood frightened, trying to quiet me.

Only now did he understand what these poems meant to me. He gave me money to buy other notebooks. Everyone offered to help me rewrite my poems into new notebooks.

But I couldn't forgive him. He was now my worst enemy. He, my own father, wanted to destroy my creation, my poems.

I felt that I no longer belonged. I wanted to flee from here, to somewhere far, far away. Maybe to America, into the wide world where I could be free to sing and create. So that my heart could leap. Somewhere where no-one could stop me. I shouldn't need to hide my writing like a criminal, and guard against my own father ....

My mother understood me. These were her poems too. And my little sister Taybele brought new notebooks and sat down to recopy my poems. She glued the little pieces of torn paper together, wanting to make them whole again.

And my father took a prayerbook and, grieving before God, poured out his heart. May God help him to understand his own flesh and blood, his daughter. Perhaps God meant for her to write poetry.

I LEAVE FOR AMERICA*

A ticket of passage arrived from America, sent by Aunt Paula who had left our *shtetl* in time to avoid the dreadful war. It had been meant for my father, but my mother decided it was I who should go.

There was no future for me in our little village. My mother believed in my talent and understood my need to study. In our little town, I would waste away. The town's charred walls had begun to stifle me. Instead I was attracted to the faraway unknown, to a foreign land where I would be free to sing my poetry ... .

I would leave this little town. I dreamt of new unknown places that would reveal themselves to me. But how do you go away and leave your loved ones behind? How do you break the thread?

It was my mother, who had suffered so much for me, who persuaded me to leave. My mother didn't cry. Instead she sewed a small linen pillowcase for me and stuffed it with down. Then she sewed a sailor dress.

What did my mother think as she sewed the dress and sent her beloved child off into the unknown to a distant land? Perhaps she thought of a wedding dress for her daughter — a dress that she might never see. Of what did my mother think as she stuffed the little pillow? In a faraway land, would this pillow take the place of her mother-hands beneath my head?

*Translated by Ethel Raicus and Sarah Silberstein Swartz

As she knitted my socks, her tears blended into the yarn. Who could say of what a mother thinks when she sends her favourite daughter away? My mother bought me a woven straw basket in which to pack my notebooks of poetry.

The whole town envied me. Everyone would like to travel to America, and I was the luckiest girl in town.

The day of my departure drew closer. I travelled to Telmesz to say goodbye to my Grandfather Shloyme and Grandmother Rose and to the aunts and uncles who also lived there. My *Bobe* prepared a white bed, ceremonial-like, and I lay down to sleep. My *Zeyde* and *Bobe* sat down beside me, mourning as if I had died.

In my sleep, I imagined hearing my *Zeyde* pray. And when I opened my eyes in the middle of the night, my *Zeyde* was indeed still seated by my bed. "*Zeydenyu*," I said, "why don't you go to sleep? It's so late. I'm not dead, that you should mourn. Surely I'll come back from America."

But my *Zeyde* answered, "Yes, my child, God-willing, you will come back. But we will no longer be here. We are saying goodbye for the last time." Now I cried with my *Zeyde* and *Bobe*. In the morning, I went back home with an aching heart.

In my own town, the farewells had just begun. I said goodbye to the rooms of my home, to the streets in my town. Everything was dear to me and holy.

I went to the surrounding woods and climbed to the top of the hill, looking back at my childhood. How carefree I once had roamed here. For *Lag Boymer*, we children came here from *kheder* with bows and arrows. I flew like a bird down the hill into the valley. How joyfully I hid behind these ancient trees. The valley was in blossom with yellow dandelions; all was golden. We children picked flowers without knowing how lucky we were.

And now I sat looking down from the hill. The woods

were burned, the valleys gouged by the fires and bombs of war. Trees stood decapitated, their crowns consumed by fire. Here and there drifted a piece of some dead soldier's uniform. Crows flew low, picking at the ground with their beaks, cawing. A train passed breathlessly through the deep valley, twisting like a snake and disappearing with a shriek. Even the train was fleeing my town.

Why did I want to run? Was I not afflicted by the town's sorrow? No, I would not part from her! Let me be scourged like my scourged earth, tortured as she was tortured.

Below lay the entire town. There was a time when it dazzled, red brick against the sun, vivid as a peacock. Suns dipped themselves in sunsets in every window frame. Now it stood hump-backed in black catastrophe, walls damaged, chimneys like twisted necks, black, roofs swaying like gallows in the wind. Black smoke rose higher and higher from the river, wrapping the town in a twilight mist. The earth yawned damply. I arose and, walking towards the mist, was myself enveloped in a damp wind, as in a stream. It cooled my fevered cheeks that burned like a splintering firebrand from the town.

It was the last night before my departure. My mother — who could bear to look into her eyes? Tears lay in their sadness. She bit her lips in pain. On this last night, she would not show me her mute sorrow.

My chaste bed had been washed white by my mother's gentle hands. She heated a basin of water and put it near the bed. Soaping my feet, she said, "It seems only yesterday, my child, you were born and lay in your little tub ...." Meanwhile I stood in the basin, a sixteen-year-old, letting my mother bathe me. She wrapped me in a white sheet and said, "May you go to your groom, whom I may never see, as clean and pure as you are today. Through years of war, I protected your fair body, my daughter."

I didn't want to hear my mother; it was too painful. I lay down, threw back my head and pretended to sleep. And my mother sat and kissed my hair, kissed the comforter that covered me, kissed the pillows my head rested on and murmured, "I send you away like a lamb to a strange land. My child, may God protect you. My eyes will follow wherever you wander. When you lay ill with typhus, I pleaded for your life with our Patriarchs and won. Now I myself am sending you away."

It was dawn in my *shtetl*. Cocks crowed. The water carrier strode clumsily with empty cans on his yoke to draw water and deliver it. People began to gather at my house to say goodbye. My friend Mindl came in, planted herself at the window and shivered, despite her mother's large woolen shawl thrown over her convulsed shoulders.

I said goodbye to Taybele, my only sister, and to my little brothers. When I picked up Nutkele, the youngest, the two-year-old who was often in my care, the walls began to sway and the earth spun. My hands trembled.

I put a piece of chocolate between my teeth — our favourite game — and Nutkele bit it off with his little mouth. We kissed, our mouths mixed with sweet chocolate. Nutkele didn't know that this was our last goodbye.

In the street, the little orphans to whom I used to distribute bread during the war waited. They accompanied me to the train station, along with the others from the town.

At the station stood another black cloud of people, sad, bereft and hopeless. Every single one of them yearned to escape — no matter where. My father wept inconsolably. It was the first time I'd seen him cry like this.

I stood on the platform with the woven basket containing my entire fortune — my poetry, the pillow from my mother and a little book with relatives' addresses that people had given me.

The train chuffed; the wheels began to turn. A running form pursued us down the track: my mother with hands outstretched. Behind her ran my *Zeyde* Yosl. He raised his cane as if he wanted to delay the train for a moment. There was something he had forgotten to say ....

The noisy wheels drowned the voices of my home.

ON THE SHIP *ZEELAND*

From the outside, the ship *Zeeland* looked like an enchanted palace, a castle floating on the blue waves of the sea. The golden face of the sun reflected in the sea immersed itself and hid in the waves.

The *Zeeland* was divided into three levels and three classes. And down at the very bottom in the bowels of the ship was a fourth class for immigrants.

The company that sold the ticket to my aunt had not mentioned a fourth class. American aunts and uncles had paid in advance for what they thought would be decent accommodations for their relatives. Instead they packed us like herring into an underground abyss.

The women and girls were given quarters separate from the men. I was told to go down the spiral stairs — far, far below — to the cabin at the bottom of the ship. Near the entrance stood barrels of food, big sacks of potatoes and heavy iron rods. The cabin had no windows to look out at the sea. Huge fans producing a constant deafening noise provided the only ventilation. People felt sick from the smell of the rotting meat.

On both sides of the cabin stood rows of beds upon beds. And over each bed hung yet another bed. The passengers in the upper bunks almost touched the passengers below with the weight of their bodies.

Beds had been assigned according to designated numbers. I put my basket on a bottom bunk. Next to my bed, an elderly woman took her place and across from us rested a Polish mother and her daughter. Mother and daughter looked young, like sisters. On the upper bunks lay several middle-aged and elderly women. The older women had trouble getting in and out of their upper bunks.

On the first day, I went up the steps, looking for my cousin Elye who was on the other side of the ship with the male passengers. As I crawled through the rope ladders, I saw the fiery hell that enabled the ship to move. Half-naked men endlessly shovelled coal into the mouth of the furnace, making the lungs of the ship breathe and move. A terrible heat radiated from the innards of the ship and a stench rose.

When the ship had been at sea for a while, many of the passengers became seasick. I lay in my bed, listening to the women moan. Some couldn't even get out of their hammocks. They were dizzy and nauseated and begged for a drink. The women above vomited onto the bunks below. I was the only one who was well and able to help others with some water and slices of oranges which I had brought in my basket as a gift for my aunt.

The old women blessed me. God sent them an angel, they said. How could it be that their American children had arranged for them to travel in such a hell?

Meanwhile, the ship continued to hurl itself feverishly from side to side, as though it were suffering from typhus. When everyone finally fell asleep, I took out my notebook and wrote a poem about human pain, the roaring sea, a drunken ship with helpless passengers.

Out of nowhere, a lantern shone in my eyes, almost blinding me. The light danced in front of me, frightening me. Before I had time to look around, a giant was standing over me — the night watchman for our cabin from hell.

He grabbed my notebook and quickly thumbed through it. At that time, I wrote only in German, which he couldn't understand. He asked me if I were spying on the ship, making secret notes. My hand trembled with fear. I wanted to hide my notebook from him. He threatened to tell the captain of the ship about my writing and they would send me back from where I came. When he left, I lay on my bed with eyes open, trying to control my tears, my heart pounding with fear.

The next day, I went on deck again to look for Elye and found him in pain with a swollen cheek. He had developed a terrible toothache. I told him nothing about what had happened during the night.

When I returned for dinner to my purgatorial cabin with its nauseating smells, I began to fear the night and the figure of the watchman. He had looked like a gangster or a prize fighter with his large face, pig-like nose and small mouse-like eyes. I lay down in my bunk beside the elderly woman.

As soon as the lights went out, I heard the watchman's heavy, foreboding footsteps coming in our direction. He sidled over to where the mother and daughter lay. I heard laughter and whispering in the dark cabin. I pulled the covers over my eyes, so as not to witness the shame of the mother and daughter with the brazen watchman ....

At sunrise, I went on deck with my notebook of poems. In the light of day, my persecutor would not dare frighten me. I wrapped a blue chiffon scarf around my hair and held on to the railing, looking down at the ocean waves. Sky above, sea below, the ship cutting the waves, flags fluttering, smoke rising from the steam pipes. My heart sang. My notebook beckoned me and I wrote:

> The sun kisses the water breasts of the sea
> And the sea blushes with embarrassment....

Sailors came on deck with hoses and began to wash the deck. Their sprays of water smiled at me with sparkling eyes. Such lovely boys with faces ruddy, blooming from the wind. I ran down the spiral steps, happy with my new poem.

Below in my cabin, the passengers sat at a long table made of planks eating their breakfast. They sat like prisoners with tin cups. I was very hungry and joined them. But I couldn't look in the direction of the mother and daughter who were now suspicious of me. I knew their nighttime secret and they looked at me with anxiety.

At night, I again felt the fiery eye of the watchman's lantern. My heart started to hammer with fear. I sat up in bed and tried to get my elderly neighbour's attention. The watchman came over to me asking to see my notebook. Again, he threatened to report me, telling me they would send me back because I wrote revolutionary secrets in my notebook. I didn't reply. Even after he left, I couldn't sleep, imagining how they would separate me from the other passengers and send me back on the same ship.

The *Zeeland* slowly floated over the stormy sea and the nights stretched out like eternity. But the daytime was mine. Every morning I greeted the dawn with a poem, my song on paper. I soared like an eagle on deck. Sky and sea, two blue eternities, blended into each other. The sun, like a fiery heart, embraced them, melding them together....

A few days before our landing, I decided to tear out the patriotic poems I had written when I joined a small circle of girls and boys who called themselves *Shomrim*. At that time, we were reading Theodore Herzl's *Jewish Nation* in German and my friend Mindl and I had dreamt of our own Jewish homeland where our people would return and everyone would work together. I was worried that perhaps these poems about a free land might be construed as revolutionary. So I decided to tear them out of my notebook and throw them into the sea. Every page I tore out of my notebook felt like a fistful of hair from my own head, so painful ....

Suddenly, someone grabbed my hand and said in a soothing voice, "Too bad fish don't read poetry."

Before me stood a man with a head of white hair and a kind, gentle face. He introduced himself as a professor of anthropology who had travelled around the world collecting antiques and works of art. He had noticed me from his first-class cabin as I wrote in my notebook every morning and decided to befriend me before our ship landed in New York. And now here I was, throwing my poems into the sea to the hungry fish so that they too could read poetry.

I was so shocked, words failed me. Only when he reassured me and I began to trust the honesty in his good-natured eyes did I tell him why I wanted to throw my poems into the sea. I explained about the night watchman who followed me and threatened me.

The kind stranger was moved and comforted me. In order to ease my terror, he contacted the captain of the ship, who transferred me to another section of the boat.

Throughout the remainder of our days at sea, my protector kept an eye out for me. Each time he saw me, he brought me a new book to read and told me stories about his past ocean voyages.

An epidemic broke out in fourth class and the passengers were put into quarantine. My friend told me that our ship could not land at the designated port. The first class passengers would disembark in lifeboats and the remainder of the passengers would remain quarantined on the ship. Before he left, my mentor gave me the address of his villa in New York. He also asked for the address of my aunt with whom I would be living and promised to visit. Then he said goodbye, telling me that he hoped someday to read my poetry in a book in America.

The first-class passengers disembarked onto lifeboats and our ship moved on to anchor at an island near Boston. Here they rounded us up like herds of sheep and let us out on hanging bridges. Nuns in black and nurses in white counted the women and the men separately. Then they pushed us into a large hall, made us stand in a long line and gave each of us an empty bag. Each person was instructed to undress and place all our clothing into the bags to be disinfected.

The women quickly undressed and put their belongings into the bags. We were left naked as Eve. Each person was given a number. When the nurse noticed that I was embarrassed to undress, she jumped on me like a vixen and spoke very rudely, pulling my underwear from me. And before I had time to look around, they pushed me forward in line and a man in a white smock sprayed me with a liquid chemical which went into my eyes, my hair and on all parts of my naked body.

We went through the disinfection process as though it were a lime kiln. Then they led us to another large hall where they gave us each a blanket in which to wrap ourselves. After a while, we were asked for our number and in exchange were each handed our own bag of disinfected clothing.

I pulled my dress out of the bag. My mother's embroidered sailor collar had shrunk into a wrinkled rag. I began to cry like a little child and showed the supervisor what had been done to my beautiful dress. How could I meet my aunt in America in such a rag of a dress?

A young sailor standing guard with a gun came towards me. In a friendly manner, he promised to bring me an iron after he got off duty from his job. He kept his word. In exchange he wanted my address in New York to set up a date with me.

Here on the island, ships intersected and signalled each other with flags, but I didn't understand the language of the flags. Albatrosses swept over the waves and my eyes counted the waves swimming towards the shores of New York.

When no more infected passengers were discovered, they put us in small boats and took us to a train station from which the trains would bring us to our New York destination.

WELCOME TO NEW YORK

We all left the island and got into a comfortable warm train, headed for New York.

I looked out from the well-lit train carrying us through the night. Inside, there was great joy amongst the young immigrants who were travelling through the new land. They hoped to transform their lives of sorrow in Europe into more joyful, creative days. Nurses dressed in white from the Red Cross came in to distribute bread, white as snow, from white paper bags.

White bread, so many small slices of fresh, white bread for all of us. My eyes lit up with hunger. Was this a dream? I reached out my hand and the friendly face of the nurse looked at me, as she handed me the white velvety bread with yellow cheese.

Fresh white bread — my first thought was not to taste it, but to bring it to my aunt in New York as a gift. I opened my basket, hid the bread inside and closed the basket. Then I spread myself comfortably across the plush seat and looked out into the night, as small, solitary lights danced in the darkness ... .

Suddenly, I was engulfed in a shower of illumination. It was the city of a million lights: New York! Brilliant stones were scattered and took root in the night's darkness. All the passengers rose spontaneously and sang "*Hatikvah*," as they greeted the "golden land" with song.

We disembarked from the train and were led into a large terminal, where relatives embraced the immigrants and everyone wept with joy.

No-one called my name. I looked for my aunt in the crowd. I sat myself down beside my basket and inspected the face of each new person who entered ....Could *this* be my aunt and uncle? But no-one came for me.

We were a group of six girls abandoned in the station, whose relatives had not yet come to claim us. Finally, a representative from HIAS (the Hebrew Immigrant Aid Society) arrived, gathered us together and put us all in a taxi. We were taken to a HIAS office until our relatives would come for us.

We spent the night at HIAS and after breakfast we were taken to an old mansion, a house with many rooms. We six girls walked back and forth amongst the old antiques, looking out the window impatiently, waiting for our relatives to appear. Time passed and still no-one arrived ....

Suddenly one of the girls in the group, a spinsterly type, said, "Do you know where we are? This must be a brothel. It's a lie that someone will come for us. We have been deceived!"

Out of fear, we broke into a chorus of weeping. And before anyone could stop me, I grabbed my basket and fled down the circular staircase from the third floor. As I rushed down the stairs, I saw a tall man. I stopped and my pleading eyes turned to him for help, begging him to save me from being put in a brothel.

The stranger looked at me with bright eyes, and asked, "What is your name, child?" I told him my name and he answered, "I am your uncle and I've come to take you home. Your Aunt Paula is waiting for you. Because of a misunderstanding in arrangements, we weren't at the train station to meet you."

I hugged him as if he were my father and cried for joy, thanking God this was not a brothel, but a house where HIAS brought families together. My uncle took my basket and a HIAS representative accompanied us home.

The subway was filled with people, girls with painted lips, women and men who chewed and dozed simultaneously. The train travelled through underground tunnels — and still they dozed. I thought: There is so much to see through these windows and they sleep through it all! Here, for the first time in my life, I saw Black men and women. I had only seen them before in pictures from geographic magazines and now I couldn't take my eyes off them.

I imagined my uncle was seven feet tall. One of his eyes was obscured by a thin film of skin. He was American-born and had fallen in love with my aunt when she worked as a governess for his family. He was good-natured and sincere.

We approached Prospect Avenue. The streets were muddy with melting snow, the brick buildings dirty and gray. We arrived at my aunt's apartment with its four immaculate rooms. In the middle of one room stood a new piano and her handsome son who had just turned thirteen. He had flaming red cheeks and huge black-cherry eyes.

My Aunt Paula beamed. The house smelled of fresh baking and the table was set with the best of everything. She showed me to the front room, which had a folding bed. At night, I could open it up and that was where I would sleep.

She pulled off my dress and the black plush coat in which I'd travelled, opened the garbage chute and threw everything down. Don't worry, she told me, tomorrow she would buy me new clothes from head to foot. I thought to myself: My lovely black coat shouldn't be thrown out and my mother's dress that she had worked so hard to make for me — my little sister would be thrilled to wear it. I wanted to send it all back home.

My aunt saw the straw basket and asked, "What is in *that*?" I opened it and she saw the white bread that had by this time dried out. Again, she opened the garbage chute and out it went. Next she eyed the notebooks that contained my poems. "What else have you dragged with you from Europe?" I told my aunt that these were my poems. "What? Rhymes?" she asked in wonder. "Who needs rhymes from Europe? In America you can't make a living from rhymes. You have to work." And she was ready to open the garbage chute again and throw out the basket with the rhymes — my poems.

At that point, my good uncle got involved. "Paula, why do you bother with the rhymes? Better give her something to eat. America is a great land of opportunity. Something might yet become of her ... ."

My aunt led me into the bathroom and put me into a fragrant bath. After I got out, she said to my uncle, "See, Louie, she is my brother's child. See her complexion? Just like my brother."

My aunt spoke to me in a motherly way as she handed me her skirt and blouse and a big pair of shoes. " A girl of sixteen," she exclaimed, "is already a *kale moyd*. She shouldn't be wearing her hair loose and curly." With this pronouncement, she pulled my long hair back and pinned it up in a bun. When I looked into the mirror, I hardly recognized myself. I looked like an adult.

We sat down at the festive table and I gulped down six rolls. I ate and ate, and still I couldn't fill myself. I felt as though I could never make up for all those hungry years of my past.

Suddenly the doorbell rang. The neighbours had arrived to examine my aunt's "niece" — that's what they called me. And from the neighbours' faces shone friendliness and welcome.

After the meal, my aunt told me she already had a groom for me. A bookkeeper with a new car. He worked at my uncle's factory and wanted to marry only a European girl. "But be patient. Tomorrow we'll go shopping for new clothes from head to toe. And then we'll introduce you to him ... ."

Saturday, we went shopping. We walked on Broadway and I observed the throngs of people, people of all races who came together, as in a dance. I also saw the large, magnificent shopwindows. My aunt bought me a dress, a coat and pointed tan shoes. And I came out of the store a real American.

Then we walked on the avenues, where pretty, slim girls with round hatboxes passed us by. My aunt pointed them out and commented on their bad reputations. They were models. She said, "Here in New York, a girl should not walk alone on Second Avenue because there's a bum at every step ...."

I asked my aunt what Second Avenue was. She answered, "Even though you were educated in Vienna, you are truly a greenhorn!" I told my aunt that in Vienna we hadn't learned about Second Avenue. She continued to lecture me, "In America, everyone must work." She had already found me a job; it was waiting for me in a basement on Prospect Avenue. I would be sewing buttons and pressing shirts.

I knew from her letters that my uncle owned an ice cream factory. I didn't quite understand why she had found me a job pressing shirts in a basement.

We returned home. My aunt stuffed me with rolls again and still my hunger was not satisfied. And a strange longing for my mother fell upon me. My mother always let me travel alone on trains and never talked to me about morals. She knew she could trust her child; she knew I would do no wrong. With silent looks, we always understood each other. And here, at every step, my aunt taught me American morals.

On Sunday, the bookkeeper, a sallow bachelor with a new

car, came to visit. And he invited me to join him for a ride —
so he said. I didn't feel comfortable sitting next to him in the
front seat of his new automobile. But my aunt gave me a sharp
look and I joined him in his car as if it were a prison sentence.

As we drove past several streets, the bookkeeper put his
arm around me and pinched me. I was shocked, disgusted by
his behaviour. I wanted him to turn around and return to my
aunt's house.

But the bookkeeper was already sure he wanted me. My
aunt had made promises and he had not been disappointed.
The photograph of me, which my aunt had shown him, was a
mere shadow compared to the reality. And again he put his
paw on my knee. I was nauseated by his words and felt sick to
my stomach. I told him to take me home because I felt ill.
And when he took me back to my aunt's house, he sat down
for a while before leaving.

Later, my aunt wanted to know everything he said. Did he
declare his love? Yes, aunt, here in America you proclaim your
love with rude hands. Where I come from one wouldn't dare ....
And for the first time, I was rebellious and told my aunt that I
would never again go out for a drive with this bookkeeper.

MY FIRST JOB

In the dim cellar there were two rooms, their windows half-
hidden underground. The upper half looked out onto a naked
grey wall. Three older women sat at a long table and sewed
second-hand shirts. Illuminated by three electric lamps, the
women's faces looked pale and wrinkled. The women
reversed the shirts' torn collars and sewed them back on.

My aunt brought me to the cellar for my first job. They put
me at a long ironing board to press the old mended shirts with
their turned collars and to sew back on the torn-off buttons.

On the walk to work, I saw the morning crowd of men and women. Everyone rushed to the subway platform, while I, heartsick, went down into the cellar to press the shirts with a large steam iron. My white, still childish hands smoothed out the sweat-stained shirts to press them.

Noon hour. While everyone sat down to eat a sandwich, I continued standing and ironing, waiting for the boss to tell me to sit down. When he finally did, I looked up and my gaze collided with the stone wall which hid the sun from me.

After I came home from work in the evening, I helped my aunt with the dishes and rushed off to evening classes to learn the English language. At night school, a new horizon had opened for me. Young women and men, all newly arrived from Europe, occupied the benches and diligently learned the English language, the language of the land.

At the end of the week, the boss handed me an envelope. I counted my first earnings — fourteen dollars. And I believed I was the richest person in America.

I brought my pay to my aunt. She deducted five dollars for my room and board. And she suggested I save the rest to send to my parents.

One day, I met a relative and when we got into conversation, he told me he didn't like the job my aunt had set up for me. He recommended me to a friend of his, a manufacturer who owned a clothing factory.

I left my job to become a "draper" in the heart of a New York factory. I liked my new work very much. I fitted the colourful organza garments on lovely mannequin forms which looked alive. In baskets lay basted pink and blue pieces of fabric; I pinned the pieces together. From these pieces, I created whole garments as I pinned them on the mannequin.

I began to imagine the mannequin was alive, that warm blood flowed through her veins. And she began to move ... .

No, this was not a waxen mannequin. She could feel the flutter of the pink organza dress and wanted to dance. She became part of me. The mannequin and I — together we felt the rustling of the silken dress on our body.

Without warning, I sensed two pointed wolf-like eyes observing me. Next to me stood the supervisor. He was angry and cursed at me, "See what you've done! You've stained the garment with blood!"

I stood guilty and ashamed. My fantasy had carried me away in a heady dance, and I had pierced my finger with the pins and spoiled the mannequin's garment.

At the end of the week, they paid me eighteen dollars and the supervisor told me to look for a new job.

LONGING FOR HOME AND MOTHER

I was the apple of my mother's eye. Her letters wept over me. My mother wrote: "Every day I set the table and forget that you, my child, are no longer at home. I put out a plate for you and the plate remains empty. Oh, what I wouldn't give to see you with my own eyes. You were always the crown of my home. And when you went away, I was left without a crown....

"My longing for you looms large. I read over and over each piece of paper with the poems you left behind and hold them close to my heart .... At night, after a hard day at work in the country, your father comes home and we both sit near the lamp. I take the warm pieces of paper from near my heart and read the poems to your father. You do remember how your father used to sing on *Shabes* with the rabbi? Well, believe me child, when I look into your father's face, I see the same transcendent expression shining from inside him. He doesn't speak. Instead he sings quietly into the night, the rabbi's same *nign*."

After reading such letters from my mother, I poured out new poems to her from my yearning heart. Each poem was written not in ink, but in tears. But I never sent them because I didn't want her to know how deeply I missed her.

Instead, I found myself here in an orderly home with costly furniture where no-one dared to take a step that might, heaven forbid, damage the highly polished floor of my aunt's immaculate apartment.

All my mother's letters were first opened by my aunt. As soon as I came back from work, she waved my mother's letter in my face. Why hadn't I written home, she demanded to know.

She didn't believe that I *had* written home and no explanation or pleading on my part could convince her otherwise. The letters would probably arrive soon, I explained. But my aunt's anger ignited into a flame and she almost swallowed me with her reproachful words.

One day, I left for work with my head throbbing. I felt as if the ground were swimming under my feet. I now worked in a factory where little combs were packed into small white boxes. Young girls sat at tables and sorted the sparkling combs shimmering with rhinestones.

My head was spinning and the combs seemed to float in front of my eyes. The girls seemed to be holding paddles in their hands, swinging them back and forth. I myself was swaying as if I were in a ship. The combs soared into the air like a flock of birds.

The manager came over to me and touched my forehead. I looked at her through foggy eyes. She was sure I had a high fever and instructed me to go home and get right into bed.

I barely made it into my aunt's apartment. My tongue felt heavy as a tank. As soon as I opened the door, my aunt greeted me with a shout, waving another letter from my mother in my face.

I cried in front of my aunt, swearing that I had already written home, and had even enclosed five dollars from my earnings in the envelope.

But my words didn't help. She ran to my bed where I kept my basket of poems, pulled the basket out from under the bed and told me to leave her house immediately with my rhymes. They were the reason I didn't write home. And she threw my basket out the front door. My head was now pounding; I was very sick. In my despair, I felt drawn towards the open window. Maybe it would be better if I were dead. Then I would no longer have to listen to my aunt's disparaging words.

But as I approached the window, my mother's face appeared before me. No, I couldn't do this to her. No, I would not die just because of my aunt. I would rise above it all and see my mother again.

I ran out the front door and sat on my basket outside the door. Quietly, like my silent poems, I wept over my miserable life, my bitter destiny. Suddenly I saw my uncle's silhouette. He looked at me sitting on my basket, crying. He lifted me into his arms and helped me back into the apartment.

He admonished my aunt, "You should be ashamed, throwing out your brother's child! Look how she's burning up; she's ill. Woman, where is your fear of God?"

He immediately set up my folding bed and helped me into it. My aunt came to me and asked me to open my mouth. She shrieked, "Look at her throat! Surely she has diphtheria. How can we allow her to sleep in the same room as our son? He'll surely catch her illness!"

After that, I heard no more. I remember my uncle sat with me all night long, applying cold compresses to my throat. He gave me aspirins and never took off his day clothes.

In the morning, I felt a little better. Neighbours came in and these strangers' hands helped to heal me. Their sympathy comforted me. My aunt was good to me again and constantly put something in my mouth.

It was at that time that I wrote my mother a letter about how good my aunt had been to me — just like a second mother. The wide ocean that had separated me from my mother carried my letter to her. But my mother's heart must have sensed that between the lines lay the tears of the lonely, isolated child she would never see again.

KHANALE

I didn't know her from the old country. She lived in Shortkov, while I lived in Monastrikh. She was a child of the rabbis' court and I was a child of the war, an uprooted child.

Our grandfathers were brothers. Her grandfather was the spiritual leader and *gabe*, caretaker of the Shortkover rabbis known to all *khasidim* in Galicia. And my grandfather Reb Yosl Dovidl was a noted talmudic scholar and a pauper.

Khanale came to my aunt's home to visit me, her green-horn cousin. I saw her in full bloom, with her red cheeks and blue eyes and lovely ringing laughter. I sat hunched over, frightened, yearning, dreaming and very dispirited.

Several months had gone by since my arrival in the "golden land" and now she had decided to visit me. And right away she asked to see my poetry.

My poems still lay in my basket underneath the bed, but now they had become like a curse. My aunt still wrangled with me over them. And here was a cousin who asked to see my poetry. I hesitated, but she insisted. Shyly, I dragged the basket out from under the bed and handed her a notebook filled with poems written in German.

I opened to the first poem that caught my eye. It was called "The Third One." In our *shtetl*, a Jew had been murdered by a Pole in broad daylight. The Jew had been sitting in the market, selling apples. Without warning, the Pole hit him in the head, killing him instantly. The murderer spilled the basket of apples and, cursing all Jews, left the market.

The murdered Jew had been the only wage-earner for his sick wife and six small children. After the murder, all the Jews in the village trembled with fear, while the murderer remained free.

The young people of the town decided to establish a fund for the widow and her orphans. They organized a ball in a partially burnt-out barn. All the young people from the *shtetl* came to the dance and I was among them. Dancing a circle dance, I saw the dead man dancing with us. He was "the third one" in our dance.

Later, I read my poem aloud in our town and a shower of money was collected for the unfortunate family.

Today, I read the same poem aloud for Khanale. There were tears in her eyes. She hugged and kissed me and suggested I immediately send the poem to the newspaper *Der tog*.

At that time, I hadn't read any Yiddish papers and didn't even know what she meant by "*Der tog*." I asked her if *Der tog* published in German. She answered no, but she thought they might translate my poem into Yiddish. In fact, she was convinced of this and told me to write a letter and address it to the editor Glants-Leyeles.

I liked Khanale's words, as well as her looks. And I immediately felt that my aunt did not exemplify the spirit of America after all. There was also Khanale who understood my soul. I didn't need to tell her anything; she already knew what I thought and what I felt. She bid me farewell, saying her husband Levin would come to pick me up sometime soon.

My whole frame of mind changed. At night I took out several nature poems and sent them to the address Khanale had left for me.

How surprised I was when, a few day later, I received a letter from *Der tog* signed Glants-Leyeles. And he wrote: "Dear Miss, we received your poems. You have much talent. I would like to meet with you. We hope you will write in Yiddish because *Der tog* is a Yiddish newspaper. I look forward to much future pleasure from our acquaintance. Come visit our newspaper office sometime."

Weeks passed. I was too timid to visit the office and the writers. In the meantime, another relative from my father's side dropped by to see me — Hersh-Mendl Hirsh, an elderly, intellectual, refined man; a person well-read in Yiddish literature. And he too asked to see my poetry.

So I showed him my letter from *Der tog* and he suggested that, in heaven's name, I not hesitate to go to *Der tog*. Only one thing I shouldn't mention: that I was born in Galicia. Here in America, Galicianers were not liked.

I looked at him in wonder, thinking: By us in Galicia, there are such good, honest, lovely Jews. Why should they be disliked? And I decided I would go to *Der tog* to pick up my German poems and talk to the writers.

Meanwhile, Khanale could not rest. She sent her husband Levin to bring me to their home. In the warm atmosphere of their home, out of sheer happiness and love, I wrote new poems.

One fine day, I travelled down to East Broadway. With shaky, timid steps, I made my way up to the newspaper office and asked for Glants-Leyeles. Glants-Leyeles came to greet me, looking at me with two lilac-coloured eyes and extending his warm hand.

And how wonderfully they all greeted me. Jewish colleagues welcomed me with open arms. They all knew my poems, the very poems I had come to pick up.

I didn't deny that I came from Galicia. I also told him I studied in Vienna for several years and had full command of the German language. I spoke with Glants-Leyeles about the German classics: Heine, Goethe, Schiller, and about my favourite poet Rainer Maria Rilke.

Again, Glants-Leyeles told me to write in Yiddish. Then *Der tog* would print my poems.

Glants-Leyeles accompanied me to the door to say good-bye. I took my package of German poems, knowing that I would return with Yiddish ones.

The street sang beneath my steps. People came towards me, strangers, and I thought: Oh, dear people, some day I will sing you my song — which now lies dormant within me like a spring of water seeking a way to spout forth the most beautiful of rainbow colours — in the language of my mother and my father, in the language of the Galician home where my cradle once stood.

Oh people, look at me! You don't know me, but some day you will read me. I am the mountain carrying within itself a spring of unsung songs. I will sing out your sorrow and your joy. I will blend together my Galician blue sky with the sunny sky of America.

Strangers, bless me and wait for me. I have come to be and to sing. Amen.

TRANSLATED BY SARAH SILBERSTEIN SWARTZ

UNCHANGED

Yente Serdatzky

❦

Yente Serdatzky's story takes place in the Jewish radical and progressive political milieu in which she spent her own life. She wrote about women workers and activists who hoped to achieve political and sexual freedom, but too often ended up disillusioned, poor and alone. She illustrated in her stories the inequities between men and women and class divisions, even in the new idealistic movements which promised to support equality of every kind.

This story begins with the sensuality and hopes of youth in revolutionary Europe (circa 1905) and ends with disillusionment as the protagonist becomes embittered and contemptuous of what she considers impoverished American culture. The protagonist addresses herself to writers looking for a subject, thereby objectifying herself and adding to the multiple ambiguities of the story.

YOU SAY THAT I haven't changed. My acquaintances say so too. Their venomous words freeze the blood in my veins ... . They begrudge everything, often snapping, "All that pessimism just for a man." Last year, when I wanted to die, they watched my every step to keep me from doing it. Now that I want to live, they won't allow that either ... misguided creatures!

Are you saying I now interest you? Well, of course I do. Writers in search of subject matter look for characters. A year ago, gloomy, barely able to drag my feet, I wasn't "material" for you ... . "As if life doesn't have enough of these," you say, "haven't they poisoned the air enough?"

Shall I tell you about my life? My past? Specific periods in my life? Well, human existence is all very boring. But, I'll start like a writer.

Period number one: A summer night, a wedding in the village, I'm seventeen years old, my blond hair is loose and tied with a blue ribbon. A blue summer dress clings to my slender body. My face aflame, my eyes, blue like the dress, luminous. I soar, I dance.

A red band on the eastern horizon shines through the window. I grow tired and quietly leave the house. A bit further along is a grassy spot with a couple of trees. I lie down in the grass, lean my head against a tree trunk and fall asleep. But not for long. I feel a flash of light and open my eyes. They're bright and clear, and my heart ... well, I ask you. Let's not talk about "heart"! How tedious the words "heart and soul" in modern talk and writing ... . With clear eyes I see the sun unbraiding from the russet sky (even that is a cliché), the green field is flecked with gold, the village houses are like chunks of fire, the nearby lake a wine goblet. My hair is blown by a breeze and rainbow-coloured by the sun. The wind makes my blue dress billow, revealing the white of a starched petticoat ....

But that's not all ... not far from the lake on a large boulder sits Avrom, staring at me ... and he looks so strange ... so reverential. Aha, you'll likely find all kinds of comparisons: "He looks like an enchanted knight gazing at a dreaming goddess" and so on and so on.

Ha, ha! Avrom is the bridegroom's brother, a boy of about nineteen, tall, pale and very handsome. He gets up and slowly comes towards me. A ray of sun catches his hair. Lord, how beautiful he is! So, you'd like to know more?

Period number two: A large city, enormous houses, wide streets, public gardens, shops with large windows displaying an endless variety of all the good things in life. The streets are teeming: people from everywhere, decked out, shining, in their best. It holds little interest for me.

I live with three other girls in a garret. We study, we're preparing. For what? I really don't know. We already have four diplomas: one from high school, one for massage, one for administering inoculations, one for midwifery, and now, we're preparing for hairdressing. We wear misshapen shoes, shapeless hats, tattered dresses. A gas burner sits on a wooden crate in our room. Milk and bread are the greatest extravagance ....

I'm twenty-four now, I already have wrinkles on my forehead, around my mouth; short-sighted, I wear pince-nez. Avrom long ago faded into a "dream." He left for America to avoid induction, and married there. I scurry through the same few streets every day, but I see the life around in a fog. My head is full of textbooks and tutorials that I'm forever giving. The students are thick-skulled, their brains suspended in fat. I eat my heart out; my heart has withered and often the pain is piercing.

Well! Period number three: I'm twenty-seven. The same city, stormy days. I've been in the movement a couple of years now. I don't do anything momentous. I'm in the sanitation section. Great events don't take place in our city. For every garnet-ring there are twenty hands .... Isn't that interesting! I go to demonstrations with ambivalence. The workers stick together; they sense I'm from another class. And the intellectuals gravitate towards the workers, particularly the women among them ... I march with others like myself ... well, that's human nature ....

The "storm" subsides. Apathy sets in. Sunflowers burst from every little corner; girls in bloom sprout as from the earth .... I am enveloped in darkness. An eerie fire sears my vision.

The fourth period: I'm on this side of the ocean, drawn

here by Avrom. I didn't want to disrupt his family life, heaven forbid. I wanted only to glimpse at a shadow of my former happiness. And perhaps ... who knows? Who can penetrate the hidden corners of the human heart ... ! Avrom is "well off." Fat and handsome, he has a fat, beautiful wife, five fat, healthy children and a thriving business. Not a nerve trembled when he saw me. His nerves awash in fat as my happiness drowns in fat ....

I have no friends here, nor close acquaintances. A few girls from our "cell" work and study here; they dream of becoming "noyses" ....

I can't even learn the language. I'm stuffed to the gills with study. I can't work either, but I have to.

I wake when it's still dark. My clothes are the ones I brought from the old country, my shoes worn out. I slog three blocks through rain and snow to the tram, my lonely lunch under my arm. I'm uncomfortable in the shop. My small hands are unsuited to the work and my nerves give me no rest. I produce very little and in the evening, I come back broken. I spend very little time in my room: the Missus is busy with little children and the Mister goes to meetings every night.

I belong to no organization here. Fed up with them. There are lots of books on my windowsill but I can't read them. As if I haven't read enough! Every day I grab a couple of newspapers. Some days I seem to discover treasures in them, consume even the advertisements ... and other times, I leaf nervously through one paper after another tossing them one by one to the ground.

I have few acquaintances and even these few avoid me. No wonder: their zest for life vanishes when they look at me.

But who owes me anything? Who actually denied me a rich, beautiful, golden past? I hold no-one responsible; expect nothing of anyone.

When you're young, there comes a moment to seize your fortune by the beard. Miss that moment, and it's lost ....

Suddenly, my few girlfriends begin to drop by morning and evening. They whisper secretively with my Missus ... they've guessed my thoughts .... Ha, can they really hold me back?

The thought of suicide came to me like an old friend. Somehow, it seemed that I'd been living with it for years. I don't believe you literary types who think you can penetrate the insides of a suicide; you prattle mountains on the subject. I felt only dreadful fatigue, the strongest desire for rest. I wasn't even romantically inclined; I didn't deck my room with flowers nor dress myself in bridal clothes — as depicted in your novels. I hadn't combed my hair for days, hadn't taken off my shoes. The room, cluttered with books and newspapers, was neither swept nor tidied. My dress was still damp from the rain; I just dropped on the bed as I was. But not before I had carefully sealed all the cracks and turned on the gas.

And now the fifth period: They pried open the door and rescued me. After that, relatives turned up. One brought me a present, a dress; the other, a suit; the third, a blouse. And suddenly, I acquired girlfriends. They sprouted like mushrooms. And, listen to this: boyfriends too ... ha, ha! And he, my current one, was among them.

Now, as you see, my room is decorated with white curtains and the "deadly" gas has a milk-glass shade that spreads a lovely glow. We live together. I am arrayed in my relatives' gifts.

I glow, you say. Well, of course. He's young and handsome. Tender and refined. I am his wife, his goddess, his ideal. He loves me with the purity and innocence of first love. His kisses would revive a corpse. His embraces .... You detect the shadow of sadness in my eyes? Well of course. One step beyond our happiness gapes the dreadful maw of disaster. Soon I'll again have to reach for the gas. This time, tragedy will come from my own circle. They didn't expect this: that he would fall in love with me, and so passionately ....

And now they all dislike me. Everyone dislikes the unfortunate, but the fortunate they dislike even more .... It seems I owe everyone something, particularly the girls. I, the pessimist, faded, no longer young, ought not to appropriate such a handsome young man.

This wouldn't bother me either; true happiness is beyond such trivia. But they crawl like worms into my very being; no sooner have they finished their supper than one by one they arrive. They fill my small room to suffocation. They smoke, they chatter; a sea of platitudes chokes the air. And should he touch me, they eye both of us with venom, scorn. They probe and criticize and hold forth and sit there half the night ....

Their main topics are love, "variety," and so on. He's still so young ... he's often lost in thought .... He hasn't really lived yet .... And I! Oh, I'm so far from him ... and so afraid of his awakening.

It's almost six o'clock ... he's coming soon .... Go in good health; happiness is brief and tremulous ... fearful of a stranger's eye ....

After all, it's not as though you are my friends. Let me be. Leave me alone with my small happiness ...!

TRANSLATED BY FRIEDA FORMAN AND ETHEL RAICUS

A DANCER

Celia Dropkin

❦

*"A Dancer" is the story of a woman who retreats into a
private dream world because domesticity offers her no
chance of fulfillment or happiness. It also represents, in its
articulation of the protagonist's affection for and consciousness of her own body, a rare moment in Yiddish fiction. It
is through the body that Gysia expresses her longing for
creative expression — but only in dream can she soar.
When the border between dream and reality collapses,
tragedy results.*

AT HOME THEY CALLED HER "dummy" and other names like
that because she was always so quiet and still, never stirring
when she was called. When she was nine years old, she went
to school and began calling herself Gysia. She remained
silent, motionless and without expression during her first
years at school. The school mistress, who suffered from
migraines and couldn't stand classroom noise, praised Gysia
to the skies for her ability to be still.

One May, when Gysia was twelve years old, her quiet
demeanor snapped. She had been sitting at home at the big
wooden table, studying for her examinations. The distant
scent of lilac drifted through the open window when the
dressmaker arrived to measure Gysia for a new brown
school-dress.

When the dressmaker left, Gysia remained standing at the
full-length mirror. She was in no hurry to get dressed. Gysia

saw herself in the mirror in the white, ruffled slip, her thin, bare white arms and dainty feet, and suddenly she leaped into a wild gallop around the table. She looked like a colt one chases but can't catch. Sparks flew from her eyes which had been so dull and expressionless. With strange impetuosity, she spun and whirled round the table. The house virtually shook and the crystal drops of the chandelier tinkled melodiously. No-one was at home but the servant girl, who stood at the door open-mouthed, her eyes fearful. She had never seen Gysia like this.

Another year went by and two round little mounds appeared on Gysia's chest. The white petticoat with the embroidered camisole no longer fit and a new one which laced in the front had to be made. Gysia couldn't resist looking down to catch a glimpse at the beautiful, curving rise under her blouse. Changing blouses and watching how the fresh folds of cloth laid themselves over her shapely length was a special joy to Gysia, a joy that made her move as if to a musical beat. At the same time, she would admire her dainty feet.

At school, during recess, Gysia would often burst into peals of laughter. Once the schoolmistress reproached her angrily, saying, "I didn't expect this from you!"

When Gysia turned sixteen she was taken to Warsaw. There, for the first time, she bought the kind of shoes she really wanted, not like the ones her mother usually bought. These were dainty shoes, red in colour. The salesman told her that an actress, a dancer, had left them behind and he was selling them now at half price. They were perfect for Gysia and suited her highly arched, well-turned feet (although she did get a corn on the small toe of her left foot). In Warsaw, Gysia saw an opera, "Carmen," for the first time. From that time on and for many years thereafter, in moments of joy and blood-tingling excitement, she would raise her hands and feet, just as Carmen had done. The Carmen who appeared on stage was a stout prima donna. Gysia felt she could dance the role of Carmen better.

At eighteen, Gysia married the tall and handsome young man who had fallen in love with her when she danced in the red shoes at her sister's wedding. Gysia wanted to have a child just like her sister, who had come home to her parents to give birth. Soon afterwards, Gysia's husband left for America. When she was left behind in that Polish *shtetl*, alone with a baby at her breast, she suddenly sensed that she had neglected something unique about which neither her husband nor anyone else would want to know. She felt this even more strongly after she weaned the child.

Gysia's body was agile, young and slender, her legs slim and lively. It was not of her body she was now thinking but of a melody within herself singing to the rhythm of her body and to the summer life around her; summer in that small Polish *shtetl* where woods and fields were only a few steps from her street. Clouds danced in circles overhead, trees bent their green shoots over her and grasses curled at her feet.

Gysia felt the dance of nature all around her, felt the dancer within her awaken. More than once she tried to express her longings to the rhythm of dance. When no-one was around she was rhythmic and expressive. However, she knew that to become a dancer you had to study. So Gysia began to dream that instead of travelling to her husband in America, she'd leave the child with her parents and run off to Warsaw and enroll in dance school. She would pay for these lessons with the money her husband sent her for the fare to America .... But Gysia did not do this. The child's father was waiting for them in America. So there she went.

All, all was over the moment Gysia's feet touched the ground in New York! Her husband worked hard to earn a living for her and their child while she toiled to raise, nourish and build a home for the family. But that struggle, together with the alien bit of sky between the tall buildings, clipped Gysia's wings. She became pregnant with a second child, then a third. With every pregnancy she became rounder at the hips and shoulders. A pair of thick blue veins bulged here and there through the white skin of her legs. She stopped admiring her body, didn't even want to look at it any more, not even through the transparent crystal green of the water in which she bathed.

Gysia's years dragged on, sometimes better, sometimes worse, with growing children, four in all. At thirty-nine, Gysia's body was already quite heavy; the skin on her face beginning to sag. Only the eyes retained the same opaque sheen. At celebrations Gysia rarely danced, but she didn't take her eyes off the young feet gliding by on the floor. Several times in her life, Gysia had attended recitals by famous dancers. Her pleasure at seeing these dancers bordered on ecstasy, yet she didn't envy them. It never occurred to her to imagine how she'd feel if she were to lift herself up ever so lightly off the ground and spin like a top. Though she lived in a world of house, husband and children, her heart would sometimes beat strangely when she saw people dancing; would beat as if in premonition, as if trying to recall something ... something dear to her.

The momentary pleasure of watching dancers and couples gliding by did not raise for a moment the curtain on that strange magic that sleep brought her. Whenever she saw dancers and dancing couples, she tried to recall this magic, but without success. She wouldn't have called it a dream because it was repeated time and again so naturally, as though she had come to a familiar house and discovered a well-remembered object there. This magic was a world unto itself and didn't want to reveal itself to drab reality.

Gysia was never able to remember this strange dream, which she kept dreaming again and again. She used to wake up feeling she had not dreamt at all. It was magic but this magic was so natural to her, so easy, so pleasant. It was a very simple matter. Gysia would lightly, oh so lightly, like a feather, lift one foot after the other. Faster than a gliding bird, she would soar and hold a position, a dancer frozen in a pose. It was no trick. She did it so simply, so easily, just like a bird. Sometimes she saw herself surrounded by her women friends who were also trying to do the same thing but, unfortunately, they didn't know how. She, Gysia, did it almost without being aware; felt a strange spirituality, a sweet serenity pervade her. No effort, no ecstasy, no superfluous joy — she felt like a bird lifting herself over a field of corn or over a tall forest.

In her magic, Gysia was nevertheless human. She understood with human intelligence that she was accomplishing something with this ability to lift herself at will ever higher than an ordinary person, even though it was so easy. Soaring into the air for several moments was no more to Gysia than smoking a cigarette was to her neighbour. A lot easier. Gysia didn't even have to spread her arms like a bird with outstretched wings when it takes off, or like a dancer before a leap. She simply took off again and again and yet again. So easily, so gracefully, so effortlessly. Her entire body felt beautiful, in harmony; the movements of her legs like Anna Pavlova's, her entire being swaying in rhythm like Isadora Duncan.

She was dressed as always when she finished her housework. A simple black or blue silk dress. Gysia remembered that the last time, she had worn the blue crêpe with the white ruffles. She had been with her friends and wanted to demonstrate her artistry, had wondered why no-one present could do the same. She was filled with quiet, good-natured pride.

It was a magical world that had separated itself from the real world and kept itself hidden and secret, the proof being that Gysia could never recall the dream when she awoke. Other dreams she did manage to remember, but nothing about that magical lifting off from the earth could she consider merely a dream. It was so real to her, so strangely real, that when her magic world suddenly revealed itself to the cold light of day, Gysia did not turn a hair in wonder. She simply could not think of it as a dream.

Gysia was now alert. It was just past the evening meal and she was clearing away the dishes, when she stopped to glance at the newspaper lying on the table. Her eye was caught by a headline about a famous dancer who had just died. She immediately began to read it. It said that he simply floated in the air whenever he danced. Gysia was wearing the blue crêpe dress with white ruffles. For the first time when awake, she was suddenly able to remember that it was in this very dress that she had lifted herself several feet off the ground. For the very first time, she was able to recall that she could float through the air.

Gysia wondered why the newspaper was making such a fuss about this dancer. Was dancing in the air such an art? How many times had she herself done the very same thing? She simply lifted herself upward! The newspaper was silent about this; no tickets were sold to see her perform. With a mocking smile she tossed the newspaper aside, quietly rose from her chair and slowly went into the kitchen to be alone. She stretched, stretched again, tried to lift both feet. Why couldn't she do it? What had happened to her? She became frightened. Her heart beat strangely. Her feet spun in the air, begging her heavy body for help. She wouldn't believe that she was incapable of doing it.

She went into the living-room. Her husband was reading the newspaper. "Have you read it yet?" Gysia asked him, making an effort to remain calm.

"What?" he asked, not raising his eyes from the news-paper.

"Such a trifle they consider art," she added scornfully, "see for yourself ...."

She lifted herself up and lunged forward. Her husband's face was hidden by the newspaper but he heard the dull thud and threw down the paper. He saw Gysia, strange, lost, her pale face covered in beads of sweat; she looked so drawn, so different.

"What happened?" he asked anxiously.

"I can't understand it," she replied disconsolately. "I can't do it any more."

"What do you want to do? Who asks you to work so hard?" her husband asked angrily.

"You don't understand. I used to be able to do it."

"What's the matter with you? Should I call the doctor?"

Gysia sensed terrible danger. She began to understand with shuddering clarity that she was confusing reality with dream, but this awareness lasted but a moment. Just as earlier she had been unable to remember her dream, now she could not remember reality. With the instinct of an animal, she felt that she must now be wary of ordinary people; they wouldn't understand her. When her husband again asked anxiously, "What's the matter with you?" she answered with a conspiratorial expression, "Probably something I dreamt" but she knew it was far from a dream. She really was a great dancer, but tragedy had overtaken her. She was cursed, she could no longer do it. Her husband wouldn't possibly understand; she would tell him nothing. Even if she had dreamt it, he didn't want to understand and he said, "How can a person dream such things working around the house? You were talking to me just now. You just asked me something." He noticed that she became terribly upset by his words.

"Go on, go to sleep, maybe you'll sleep off all these dreams after all," he said in a worried voice. He heaved a deep sigh as she went off to her room. "All we need is more troubles!"

Gysia took it into her head that she had to regain the art of soaring into the air. "I'm too heavy," she thought to herself, "that's why I can't dance through the air any more." She virtually stopped eating and went about in a gloomy state. When no-one else was around she would try to glide off a bench. Each time she fell forward clumsily, bruising herself. Once, she was even laid up for an entire week with a sprained ankle. She had seen a stranger whom her husband called "doctor" near her several times already. This person tried to engage her in conversation but she stubbornly remained silent. She dared not talk about her great artistry which was now cursed. Once her daughter saw her standing on the window-ledge facing into the room. She stood there like some mournful bird wanting to warm itself and fly into the room. Although the window was closed, her daughter screamed in terror. From that time on, Gysia was carefully watched.

Many months have now passed since Gysia entered the sanatorium. The curse of being unable to dance, to soar, has been lifted from her. Quietly she floats with a benign smile on her parched lips. Her body, unnaturally thin, seems to float in the air. Impetuously, she tears herself from the spot and barely lifts her feet. She raises her head in ecstasy as a smile plays on her withered lips.

TRANSLATED BY SHIRLEY KUMOVE

AT A PICNIC

Miriam Raskin

❦

The protagonist of this story had been a member of the Bund in czarist Russia. Like most other Jews, she came to North America to escape the pogroms and persecution of the regime. In America thousands of Jews continued to devote their lives to the goals of the Bund, working and organizing within the trade union and progressive political movements. For the most part, however, the children of these Jewish immigrants, like those of the protagonist, moved into business and the professions, dramatically changing the character of Jewish class structure in North America.

THAT MORNING SADIE hadn't slept since dawn. When she pushed the curtain on her window aside she saw the sun rising red and her heart gladdened.

"A great day for a picnic!"

For Sadie, a socialist picnic was a holiday better than any other. Sadie was proud that in the old country she had been part of the heroic past of the *Bund*. Then she had been known as Zeldke the dressmaker, the first to do dangerous underground work and the first to sing at holidays; so too her late husband Arontshik the gaiter-maker. Heroic and courageous in those great struggles, his name was known in all of Berezin and in all the towns around Minsk.

Nowadays Sadie was forever busy with the work she brought home from the shop to support her household and her three children. She had a hard life, Sadie, but drew strength from the firm heartfelt belief that in the society of the future people would not have to suffer so much.

On the day of the picnic Sadie was in a holiday mood from early morning. She made her house beautiful for the holiday, dusting the photographs on the walls, the innocent faces of boys and girls standing in heroic poses; among them Karl Marx with his rabbi's beard and clear face. Sadie stared at her pictures. It seemed to her that through them she was united with her ideals and with the memory of her husband.

Sadie herself then seemed happy. Her pale, tired face was serious and devout, and in the dark depths of her eyes a spark glowed.

Her three sons, all of whom attended college, were good-naturedly patronizing but proud of their mother. The youngest son lovingly lectured her.

"You'd do better to rest up on a Sunday, Ma!"

Sadie sadly nodded her head. Her heart quietly ached. Those sons of hers, her own flesh and blood, she would do anything for them; she would have them educated so they would grow up important people. But they were so Americanized, not the least bit "class conscious."

In difficult moments, when hardship touched their young lives and they lost courage, Sadie taught them not to surrender, not to give in.

"Imagine how it was for me at your age. We were hungry and we were put in jail ... in the old country ...."

They didn't answer, Sadie's sons, but exchanged glances silently. Her lessons didn't stick. And this hurt her very much. The field that led to the picnic grounds was green and bright. Throngs of people were converging on the field from all sides and all directions.

A socialist picnic is like a great migration. From the Bronx and from Brooklyn whole families set out on the journey, their movements imprinted with the feverish pace of New York and the shop. People carried huge bags of food in hairy hands, sleeves pushed up, everyone lively and animated. The July sun played overhead and the gang laughingly exchanged banter.

"Say *landsman*! Say there, hard worker!"

"Stop — what's the hurry? This isn't piece-work."

Sadie kept pace with everyone else. They were her kind of people, one big family. She heard the friendly conversation and the laughter, and it was sweet music to her ears. And as one thinks one's own thoughts listening to good music, so Sadie took stock of herself, seeing her youth, her husband Arontshik the gaiter-maker, thinking about her children and her whole life.

"Hello, Sadie!" she would hear every few minutes and would turn hastily and answer merrily, "What kind of *Sadie* am I to you? *Zeldke* is my name, did you already forget!"

She felt thrilled to see her dear old friends Dvoyrele the lanky one, Bertshik the tailor and Avreml the scribe. In this country Dvoyrele had grown fat, and Bertshik very much wanted to speak only English to Sadie; Avreml the scribe had learned here in America to be a union leader and had become very pompous. But in Sadie's eyes they hadn't changed a bit. She still remembered their features as they had been in the past.

"You see? Uncle Sam's country!" she said to them, smiling knowingly.

The holiday was already in full swing in the big shady park. Like tribes of common ancestry, the celebrants divided according to their town or group. At the tables the loud, lively conversation was accompanied by a sandwich and a tasty beer. Someone was already involved in a heated dispute;

someone else had already set up a choir to sing proletarian songs.

Sadie and her old friend Tsaytl the sock maker stood to the side leaning against a tree and pouring out their hearts to each other about all the long years that had passed. Tsaytl had become in this country a bourgeoise who called herself Celia Kaufman, but she was still drawn to her warm old friends.

"Tsaytele darling, if I would start telling you ... ," Sadie said in a singsong voice. "You know my Arontshik *olevasholem* ...."

The traditional "*olevasholem*" slipped out unwittingly and Sadie immediately hid her mouth with two fingers.

Now Sadie talked about her children, holding her friend tightly by the sleeve.

"The oldest, the doctor, has a golden heart, may he only be well. And the other, he will soon be a lawyer and is still involved in sports. Sports, only sports, what else? He's not at all class conscious," Sadie finished somewhat sadly.

Tsaytl quickly responded with great authority.

"He's probably growing up to be an American *dope* already!"

But Sadie would not allow anyone to think badly of her children.

"Well, let it be, Tsaytl, he'll still have time to come to his senses. Let him play a while longer. The good life we ourselves had with *our* parents ...!"

"*Nu*, and the youngest?" her friend wanted to know.

"Kling-klong, kling-klong." Sadie in the meanwhile caught a tune coming from another corner of the park and recognized the proletarian song immediately.

"You mean the youngest?" she continued the interrupted conversation. And her face lit up in a special way. "May he live long. An artist, that's what he is. Plays the violin; that's what he plays."

"Is that so?"

"What else? You can certainly believe me: it's murder to pay for the lessons every time."

"Why didn't you make at least one of your sons a worker?"

"You listen to me, they are growing up to be only professionals," Sadie pronounced with special pride.

The sun was nearing the horizon and the whole park rejoiced with life and human noise. Sadie was sitting among a group of her friends, her face enraptured, eyes half-closed. She was singing. In her hand she held a yellow-paged booklet with all the songs they used to sing in the movement.

"*Akh, ti dolya moya dolya!*"

Her voice trembled with great emotion, and it seemed as if the song were part of her own life.

A crowd gathered around her: handsome grey heads, seasoned old fighters joined in the chorus with their strong bass voices. And it was as though they were singing out some faraway secret desires, some longing for beautiful times, for their youth ... .

And Sadie, surrounded by such people, was overwhelmed with joy. She felt protected against all the evils of the world by a strong wall.

The singing was often interrupted. Someone would throw in a familiar saying. Someone else would answer with a juicy joke. The bygone movement, the *Bund* in the old country, immediately came to mind. Sadie remained seated, pensive, to hold on to that wonderful time.

Just as Jews read from the *hagode* every year at *Peysekh* at the table, so everyone who ever belonged to the *Bund* knows how to tell beautiful stories about it, without ever tiring of them.

There were in the crowd former leaders of the *Bund*; wise, learned heads, a youthful fire still in their eyes, and Sadie listened to their conversation with respect. She herself was silent like a simple Jew in the presence of scholars. She sat, her hands folded, mute joy in her heart. But all her senses participated in their conversation, and her face was aglow.

That wonderful evening songs rose from all corners of the park. And among them the youth with their exuberant new revolutionary songs. But as she listened to those new songs, Sadie did not find any to her taste. She looked at her old friends again and with fear in her heart thought: What will happen to the world when this strong old army will, God forbid, die out?

It was late at night and the picnic was almost over. People said goodbye to each other as they hurried home. Very few people were left in the park. But Sadie liked to stay to the end. She had to see everyone, to exchange a word with everyone. She felt a kind of sweet sadness in her heart, like a pious Jew at the end of *Shabes* ....

Sadie walked through the field to the train station almost alone. Her friends dispersed in all directions but this didn't bother Sadie. She was overflowing with what she had just experienced.

In the subway Sadie sat completely alone. Her face was flushed, her hat slipped to the back of her neck. Strangers looked at her but Sadie was oblivious to everything around her. She rocked to the rhythm of the moving train, her thoughts far away. And she saw now before her her wonderful youth and her husband Arontshik the gaiter-maker, and she thought about her house and about her children and about her whole rich, unusual life.

TRANSLATED BY HENIA REINHARTZ

THE ROAD OF NO RETURN

Rachel Korn

❦

Among the many atrocities perpetrated during the Holocaust, one particularly tormenting and vicious involved the process of self-selection. Nazis regularly demanded that families themselves choose one of their own to be sent away, often to certain death. This method guaranteed that everyone became a victim.

"The Road of No Return" is set in an occupied town in Galicia. Rachel Korn, a survivor herself, writes of a family's dilemma and resulting shame when forced into the betrayal of one of its members.

BY MORNING the whole city had heard about the new edict, but in Hersh-Lazar Sokol's household everyone pretended they knew nothing. And just like on any other day, Beyle lit the stove and began to cook the family's ghetto portion of grits and half-rotten potatoes. And just like on any other day, she set the table with seven plates and seven spoons laid out in a double row. The double row was to ward off the evil spirits lurking outside.

Every few minutes she ran to the door, and with a corner of her apron wiped the steam from its glass windowpane and looked down to the street. On that autumn day of 1942 there wasn't a Jew to be seen in that Galician village, except for a

Jewish policeman with a bundle of documents under his arm who would pass by and disappear in the street that led to the office of the *Yudenrat.*

"Father hasn't come back yet," Beyle muttered, more to herself than to the others. Her aged mother-in-law, who was sitting near the kitchen sorting plucked feathers into a patched bag, turned and asked, "What's that you're saying Beyle?"

"Nothing, *Shviger.*"

All at once there was a commotion in the corner where the two youngest children were playing. Dovidl was pulling a doll out of Sorke's hands and waving a stick at her. "When I order you to hand over the baby you must obey! Otherwise, I'll take you away too, and you'll be beaten into the bargain."

Beyle ran over to the children. "What's all this uproar about — what's going on here?"

"Mother, he's hitting me!" Sorke burst out.

"Let go of her this minute!" Beyle ordered. But eight year old Dovidl wouldn't let go, and kept on tugging at his sister's doll.

"We're playing the game of cursing, and in cursing, there's no mother around. In this game you must obey the police! If she won't hand over her baby then both she and the baby will have to go! See, here's my rifle," and he pointed to the stick.

"Tfu, may your game moulder and smoulder in some wretched wilderness! Throw away the stick this instant! And come here! Some game you've invented for yourselves!"

"But Mother, you saw what happened to our neighbour Malke, and to Shmerke-Yoysef's son? The police took her away along with her child — don't you remember?

"In my house I won't allow such games, you hear? Such a big boy and he understands nothing! Go, go to your brother Lipe."

Whenever Beyle couldn't handle Dovidl she would turn

him over to her oldest son. Lipe was the only one Dovidl would listen to.

Lipe was sitting at the table in the next room, writing. He neither turned around nor uttered a single word. His mother came in and stood at his back waiting for him to help her rein in her unruly young one. Dovidl too was waiting. He had become suddenly quiet and was staring eagerly at his older brother. The pen in Lipe's hand moved quickly across the blank paper as if it were hurrying towards some inevitable goal where Lipe was only an accessory and the instrument of someone else's will.

Beyle's ears, always alert to the smallest sound, now heard an odd rustling like the swish of silk. Turning towards the sound she saw the open wardrobe, and between its doors her daughter Mirl taking out her dresses and trying them on one by one in front of the mirror.

"What bleak holiday are you celebrating today?"

"Oh Mother, I just felt like trying on my dresses."

Beyle gave her a searching glance as if she were some newly-arrived stranger. For the last two years, living with constant anxiety and fear, she had begun to think of her children as a precious charge she must protect from all outside threat and danger. And in that same instant she recognized that Mirl, her fourteen year old daughter, had suddenly grown up and ripened into a young woman. Mirl's thin childish shoulders were now softly curved as if waiting to take on the burden of new and mysterious longings. Her brown gazelle's eyes were filled with a womanly acceptance of fate.

And as if she owed this burgeoning daughter something she could never repay, Beyle, like a bankrupt debtor, sat down and gave herself up to a wail of grief. Her bottled-up fear and dread of the unavoidable future now found its way through some obscure channel inside her, releasing a storm of tears.

Beyle began to rock to and fro, her head in her arms, sobbing all the while as if her breast were being torn to pieces inside her.

The two children tiptoed into the kitchen and began to nose around like two kittens among the pots and pans. Sorke returned and pulled Mirl away from the clothes cupboard, "Come, let's stick a fork into the potatoes and see if they're done."

Dovidl ran to the door. "I'm going outside to find out what's taking Father so long."

Beyle was startled out of her trance. "Don't dare step out of this house! Do you want to cause, God forbid, a catastrophe?"

The dragging sound of feet was now heard on the stairs, climbing each stair slowly one at a time. Lipe folded his writing in his breast pocket and ran to open the outside door, which had been kept locked and bolted since the arrival of the Germans.

Father and son confronted each other. The son's eyes were full of questions, demanding to know what the father had learned and what, for the time being, would have to be kept hidden from the others.

The father bowed his head as if he himself were guilty for what was now happening, guilty for having taken a wife and for having brought children into the world — a wife and children he could no longer protect.

It took only one look at her husband for Beyle to realize there was no point in asking him anything.

The lines in Hersh-Lazar's face had grown deeper. They were etched in greyness, as if they had absorbed all the dust and debris of the street. His nose seemed to have grown longer and was as sharp as that of a corpse, while his usually neat and tidy dark beard was unkempt and dishevelled.

" — Will you wash your hands now, Hersh-Lazar?"

"Yes, at once, and we'll sit down to eat."

They ate in silence. No-one paid attention to what and how much each spoonful held. They swallowed their food half-chewed. Even the children, already used to uncertainty and fear, felt a disaster was about to happen but dared not ask what. Something ominous was in the air.

Whenever a spoon accidentally struck the edge of a plate and made it ring they were all startled, and looked reproach-fully away. Of them all, only the grandmother concentrated on her food as she brought each spoonful to her toothless gums.

The first to rise from the table was Hersh-Lazar. Wiping his moustache with the back of his hand, he began to pace back and forth with maddening regularity. When Beyle start-ed to clear the table he signalled her — "Don't bother, Beyle."

She let her hands fall; they had suddenly become too heavy and she stood in front of her husband blocking his way and trying to stop him pacing the room.

"Have you heard anything more? Is it true what people are saying?"

"True, all true, Beyle." Her husband's voice sounded hoarse and muffled as if a thorn were stuck in his throat. "Placards are posted everywhere — on all the buildings and fences. Every family must send one of its members within two hours. Do you realize what that means? Each family must choose its own victim. One of us must go, otherwise all of us will be taken. All of us, without exception! And," he added ironically, "the Germans are allowing us free choice!"

They were all stunned but no-one was surprised. You could expect anything from the Germans. Each one studied the others. Who, who would go? Go to the place from which there is no return?

Abruptly a wave of estrangement overwhelmed them. Each one could already see the victim in the other. Each one felt the enmity of the others. Who would be chosen and who would do the choosing? With what measure should they be measured, on what scales should they be weighed in order to decide who must die now, and who deserved to stay alive, at least for now?

"— In that case," Lipe spoke with unusual calm without looking at the bowed heads. " In that case ... " and he stopped in mid-sentence as if the weight of his just-now-uttered words were too heavy for their quaking limbs to bear.

"In that case ..." all of them sat down. They all tried to find the lowest, most insignificant chair as if they intended to sit *shive* for their own inner selves.

Beyle seized the two youngest as if she could hide them in her own two hands, or build walls around them which no enemy could breach.

The grown-ups had begun to calculate the years each had already lived and the years still promised. They added up the lines in every face and counted the gnarled veins on the back of every hand.

The father mustn't go, that was clear. He was the provider, the breadwinner. And the mother, definitely not. What would become of the children without her? As for Lipe, what had he tasted of life in his four-and-twenty years, the last two darkened by the German occupation? Let him consider carefully. Maybe he should quickly steal away and be done with it. His mother would wail and tear her hair, his father would agonize while saying *kadesh*, and Dovidl would miss him day and night without understanding why his Lipe had disappeared.

But at first they would all breathe easier because he would have released them from the need to mourn their own lost souls.

In his mind Lipe was already bidding them all adieu. Tomorrow he would be gone. Everything would remain just as it was except that he would no longer be among them. He would no longer see the sun, the sky, or the old clock on the bureau. He touched his breast pocket and removed his watch and the money he kept there, and unobserved, pushed them underneath the big clock, folding a few bank notes into the pages he had been writing. It was a letter to Elke; his last letter. He would have to find a Polish messenger since it was forbidden to receive letters from the ghetto. Elke was living on the other side as a Pole with false aryan papers, and she had recently let him know that she was preparing similar papers for him, complete with seals and signatures. Together they would go to one of the big cities where it would be easier to hide and lose themselves in the Polish crowds.

Was there anyone who should go in his place? What about the grandmother, his old *bobe*? As Lipe's glance searched for the grandmother it met his parents' eyes. They had already added up her years, years that had fallen as gradually as leaves from a tree in autumn, leaving its trunk naked and vulnerable. But no-one dared utter such thoughts aloud, no-one dared to say "go" or to become the judge of her last few ragged years. As their eyes ate into her, the old lady began to droop and hunker down into her chair, as if she would have liked to dissolve and become part of the chair. She wanted to become so rooted in the bit of ground under her that no-one would ever be able to dig her out. In that moment the senses of the others became suddenly keener, and more sensitive. Each one's thoughts lay open to the others in these moments of heightened perception. Only the grandmother's thoughts remained closed to them, as closed as her half-blind extinguished eyes. She had sealed all the avenues to her inmost self in order to ward off this prelude to death. She suddenly felt isolated in the circle of her family — beside the son she had given birth to and cared for, beside her own flesh and blood. Even her son's eyes sought her out, and pointed to her. And because of it she would resist with all the strength of her being. There was no-one to take her part, no-one to give her a loving look across the wall of separation. When you know you will be missed, it is easier to die.

They imagine it's less difficult for old people to die. Maybe so. But only if death comes in its proper time and place, in your own bed. But to go forth and meet death willingly, carrying your bundle of worn-out bones! Quiet, hold everything, she's not ready yet — she still has to go back over her life, she still has to remember it once more from the beginning, starting with the time she was a child in her mother's house. She too had been a child just like her son and grandchildren. She too had sat on her mother's lap just like Sorke on Beyle's; "Mother, Mother," she murmured through blue lips as if she would call her back from the world of the dead. "Mother," she called, just as she used to do in her childhood when she was afraid of being spanked. She had almost forgotten what her mother looked like — her features had faded, and were rusted with time. Two big tears rolled from her closed eyes and fell into the net of wrinkles covering her face.

And later — she pictured herself as a bride. She had only seen her bridegroom David once, at the time of the betrothal. Even then, all her dreams were centred on him. When they began preparing her wedding clothes she had insisted on the best of everything, on the most costly materials. She chose an iridescent blue silk shot through with roses woven into the cloth. She had wanted to please her bridegroom. Her wedding dress had hung in the cupboard until recently. She hadn't let anyone touch it. It was only during the last few months that she had let them make it over for Mirl, because Mirl looks like her. When she looks at Mirl she sees herself as a girl.

The clock struck once and then twice. Everyone suddenly came to life. Soon, soon. Until now they had all been waiting for something to happen. Some miracle. And now there was less than an hour left.

Mirl drew herself up to her full height. She whipped her coat off its hanger and stood in the middle of the room.

"I'm leaving."

All heads turned.

She stood there in the made-over iridescent silk dress she had forgotten to take off when her mother scolded her for trying it on. Or perhaps she just enjoyed wearing it. Whether the dress made her look older and more grown-up, or whether it was the stubborn expression on her face, it seemed to everyone that Mirl had grown taller in the past few hours.

"Where — what kind of going?" This from her father with his red-rimmed bloodshot eyes.

"You know very well where .... Goodbye everybody." And she was at the door.

With a single leap her father was beside her, holding her sleeve.

"Get back this minute. If you don't there'll be trouble! Do you hear?"

As Mirl struggled with her father there was a sharp whistling noise as the ancient silk of her sleeve split and tore.

Everyone looked on but no-one moved, neither to stop the father, nor to help Mirl. With one hand Hersh-Lazar was holding Mirl, and with the other he was undoing his belt.

No-one understood what was happening. Was their father intending to beat Mirl now of all times? His favourite child against whom he had never before raised a hand? The one for whom he always bought special gifts — for her rather than for the two youngest? It could only be due to the confusion and turmoil they all felt, the kind they had suppressed with all their might. Now it had grown and festered in their father like a boil that ripens and finally bursts.

At last he had the belt in his hand and was twirling it above Mirl's head like a lasso. He lowered it over her shoulders then slid it down to her waist and tightened it as if she were a stook of wheat in a field. He tested the belt several times to see if it was tight enough. Only then did he grasp the loose end, and, dragging Mirl like a trussed-up calf, he led her to the table and fastened the belt to the table's leg post. Tying a knot at the other end he pulled the belt through the buckle with his teeth, then he wiped his forehead and sat down with his hands on his knees and drew a few harsh choppy breaths.

Mirl was on her knees leaning against the table leg where her father had left her. She was motionless, completely drained by the scene of the last few minutes. For the first time in her young life she had aspired to something brave — let it be death — so what? She had gone forth to meet it like a bride her bridegroom. From early morning she had been preparing for this gesture. And now she had been shamed and humiliated. And her father, her darling father, who knew her better than anyone else, including her mother — was the one who had shamed her. He wouldn't let her make her sacrifice. It was all very well, it seems, for Isaac to be sacrificed, but not for her. And his father, Abraham was himself the one who brought him — he had taken him by the hand knowing full well what God demanded. And here, all of them — yes, she saw it, she knew, all of them wanted the grandmother to go. Did grandmother have the strength to drag herself to far-away places? And what was the sacrifice of an old person worth, since the old person would have to die soon anyway?

For the first time in her life Mirl felt a deep hatred for her father. She tried angrily to free herself so she could at least stand up, but she had forgotten about the belt which now cut more and more into her body. She fell back and lay stretched out across the threshold, her head buried in her arms.

A band of light from the window came to rest at her feet. As the light fell on her the iridescent blue silk interwoven with rose-coloured flowers shone with new life. The room had grown silent again, except for the buzzing of a single fly as it searched for a quiet spot to have its last wintry sleep.

All heads were bowed. Let whatever was to happen, happen. Let the parting be dictated by some external force, by fate. And if all of them had to go instead of just one, then so be it. If God above willed it, if he could let it happen, they would accept it gladly.

Only the ticking of the clock divided the silence as its hands moved inexorably towards the appointed hour.

Abruptly the father turned; all eyes followed the direction of his glance. The grandmother's chair was empty. Everyone was so absorbed in his own thoughts that no-one had noticed her going. Where had she gone? How did she leave the house so quietly that no-one had heard her? Not one of them had heard her. It must have happened only a few minutes ago.

Everyone's eyes now searched the corners of the room. Suddenly a shadow appeared on the glass pane of the door that led to the vestibule. As the shadow came closer it gradually filled the entire window. All eyes followed it — yes it was the grandmother in her old black cape, the one she wore on holidays. Under one arm she carried a small pouch with her prayer book, while with the other arm she slowly unfastened the chain on the outer door. Soon the door closed and swung back on its hinges.

None of them left their places. Not one of them called her back. All remained seated, frozen into place. Only their heads moved and bowed lower and lower as if their rightful place lay there at their feet with the dirt and dust of the threshold.

TRANSLATED BY MIRIAM WADDINGTON

ON SAINT KATERINE'S DAY

Lili Berger

❦

Hundreds of thousands of Jewish children were murdered in the Holocaust. As the war escalated in the early Forties and Jews were sent to ghettos, and to work and death camps, parents tried every imaginable way to save their children. Many gave them away for hiding, hoping to come back for them after the war. Children were taken to convents. Some Christian families were willing to risk their own lives to save a child, others were bribed and still others turned over the children to the authorities while keeping the remuneration.

The hidden children were usually raised as Christians. Those who were given away as babies did not remember their parents after the war and often were reluctant to leave the only family they knew. If no mother or father survived, the child's background was withheld. Today, particularly in Eastern Europe, thousands of middle-aged adults know nothing of their true parentage or religion. Writer Lili Berger tells a not uncommon story of a teenage girl who discovers an identity hidden from her for fifteen years.

"FROM '42 TO '57 IS FIFTEEN ... and one is sixteen ... no, it doesn't add up, perhaps it was later, she said 'from '42,' then I'd be .... She also said 'perhaps almost two,' I would now be

... the years are probably also fabricated, everything, every-thing is false ... ."

The more Katerine calculated, the more entangled she became and the more numerous her doubts. Straining her memory, she tried to remember things, events, experiences; in her head everything became a jumble; everything now appeared strange. Things that once seemed simple, natural, were now suspect. "Why didn't I catch on at the time? Why was I such a foolish idiot? Why did I let them pull the wool over my eyes?"

She saw her saddened face in the wall mirror opposite. The thought ran through her mind that she was now entirely other. She rose from her chair, went over to the old, worn mirror, sought her former, familiar likeness there, regarded her face — the hair, eyes, nose — as though they were not her own, as though they had, within the last few hours, been pulled over her own former face. She drew her thick hair back with both hands, looked at her face with surprise as if it were a stranger's, then wearily dropped her hands. Her face was once more framed in a cascade of black curly hair.

How often had she heard, "What beautiful hair!" They always smiled when they complemented her beautiful hair, complemented and smiled enigmatically. "Why did I not catch on? Why was I such a foolish cow?"

"You don't have to wave your hair, you have naturally curly hair," Marilla used to say to her.

"Would *you* like hair like this?" she had asked her best friend.

"No," she'd answered shyly, "yours is right for ... for your face, right for you. For me ... ours is better."

That's how Marilla had spoken at the time but she had paid no attention, she soon forgot about it. Katerine never thought that her hair, her face, were different. Now she looked at the mirror and she seemed to be someone else; she felt her eyes beginning to fill with tears, something stuck in her throat; she held back from crying, questions swirling in her head, a cluster of questions: "Who am I? Who? Why do they say that I'm .... Would they make it up? And my mother, how did they ...."

"Katerine, Katerine, of all things, playing in front of the mirror? I thought you weren't home. What's the matter with you? Has something happened?"

Katerine didn't hear her mother come in from work, she hadn't heated the mid-day meal her mother had prepared that morning before going to the office. Head lowered, she followed her mother into the kitchen and saw a box of cakes and a bunch of chrysanthemums; she looked away, they went unappreciated, now none of this belonged to her ....

"Dear God, it's your saint's day and you look like you've seen a ghost. Did you quarrel with someone? Have you been to see Sister Katerine yet?"

"I've been ...."

"Put the flowers in the water, they're for you; aren't you at all pleased?"

"No .... Yes, I'm pleased ...."

"I see you're not ... probably something happened in class, probably you forgot to prepare something —" her mother probed.

"No, no," Katerine answered with a contrary scowl.

"What then? What happened? Why so down at the mouth?"

"I want ... I must speak with you, I must ... ," Katerine stammered in a voice not her own.

Fifty year old Magdalena Vrublevska, a former teacher, now an office worker, turned from the kitchen perplexed, looked at her daughter and, after a short pause, asked, "Just to 'speak' with me? Is that a reason for such a face? And of all days, today? On your saint's day?"

"I must, today, now ... I must."

"At this very moment? Will it run away? Lunch is ready, sit down, eat; you haven't even put the flowers in water, you're not yourself ... give me a smile, come on. Come, let's eat."

"I won't eat, I'm not hungry."

Her mother sat down, pretending not to concern herself with her daughter's whims; "It'll pass, then she'll sit down on her own and eat; at that age she won't be able to stay hungry for long." But Katerine didn't sit at the table. She went to her room, once again stood before the mirror and scrutinized her face. Everything in the room looked changed; hundreds of questions once again sprang to mind. No, she wouldn't be fooled any longer. This time she would have to find out everything, everything, everything, and today before the day was out .... .

Katerine Vrublevska had thick black curly hair, large, dark velvet eyes, a pale, dreamy, longish face and was fifteen years old.

Her classmates described her skin colour as "café au lait." She knew she was a beauty, how could she not know since they always told her so. Among her school-friends she looked like an exotic rose by some chance growing amidst wild flowers. Ever since she could remember she had been called "black beauty," and when her Uncle Karol, a pharmacist from Warsaw, came to visit, he brought gifts for the "pretty gypsy." Uncle Karol loved her dearly, her aunt did too, but now their love seemed so strange to Katerine, so distant, even her mother's love. Why did she hide it from her? Everyone knew, but she didn't. That's why Fat Theresa felt free to make fun of her. Probably everyone, everyone was laughing at her; she had understood nothing, now she understood very well, now she remembered everything. Sundays, at church, she would feel them looking at her strangely. "Because you are a beauty," her mother would tell her. Not true, it was because of something else, all of them, all of them were always looking at her; she had never guessed, was never suspicious. Now she knew, this morning she finally understood everything, now she remembered how they would sometimes say to her, "You're different, somehow." Why hadn't she caught on? She probably wouldn't have caught on, even now, if it weren't for Fat Theresa, that red-faced girl always blurted out what others wouldn't say, she'd often dropped hints.

What did Theresa have against her? She never did her any harm — on the contrary, while others ridiculed her, disliked her, imitated her duck's waddle, Katerine wouldn't. That one was so silly and fat as a barrel, her face puffy, red as a beet; learning was hard for her, she couldn't absorb it. But was it Theresa's fault? Wouldn't she have wanted to be pretty and clever? Katerine had always sympathized with her, had never done her any wrong, and still Theresa never had a good word for her, only barbs, insinuations, always resentment, until finally Theresa had blurted out,

"You shouldn't bring flowers to Sister Katerine! It's not your place! It has nothing to do with you!"

"Why not with me?"

"Because ... because ... you're a Jew!"

"You're one yourself!" Katerine answered impulsively and immediately regretted it. Everyone laughed and Fat Theresa with the red face laughed the loudest of all, gasping with laughter, jeering.

"Who's a Jew? Me or her?" the fat girl asked triumphantly and again burst out with mocking laughter.

That laughter had cut and stung Katerine like a whip. She fled, escaping their laughter, found her way to the convent which wasn't far from the forest. She didn't feel the cold wind on her face, walked quickly, almost running, as though pursued by their laughter. The flowers' wrapping came apart, she paid no attention. Every year she brought flowers to Sister on her saint's day, it had always been a pleasure for her. Now she arrived at the convent out of breath, distraught, and nervously rang the bell. When Sister Katerine appeared at the door, she fell into her arms weeping.

"My child, what happened to you? You're crying on such a day? On the day of our patron saint? Tell me, what happened to you?"

" They ... they ... said that it's not my saint's day, Saint Katerine's Day, that ... it doesn't belong to me, that ... that I'm a Jew."

"Don't listen to such foolish talk, my child. People like to smear others, they don't have God in their hearts, they fill their time with evil talk...."

"Why do they think I'm a ... ? Why? I ask you, tell me, I want to know why, I want to know what I am." Katerine pleaded tearfully.

"What are you ? You're a good Christian, a Christian for a long time now, since 1942. You were probably a year old, certainly not two; foolishness ... not worth talking about, people love to babble —" the nun held herself back, sorry that she'd said this much.

"Once ... was I a Jew once?" Katerine persisted with a new question and her eyes, full of tears, begged for an answer.

"You're a good Christian like your mother. Go, my child, go home, I'm busy now, it's our name day. Remember, today you mustn't cry; on Saint Katerine's Day, one doesn't cry; a great day, she was a great saint. Thank you for the flowers; you always remember, you're a good Christian ... go home, my child ...."

The way home from the convent could be shortened by going through a small field, then across a little bridge over the stream. Katerine didn't like that path; this time she took the back road, walking quickly, gasping for air, overwhelmed. Only at home did she calm down a bit, began to make sense of Sister's vague words, counting the years, remembering various insinuations, overheard conversations about Jewish children protected in convents. She did know something about these things but never gave it much thought, had read several books about how those people perished. Her mother wouldn't let her read such books; "You'll get sick, you mustn't read that." Now she understood why her mother had taken *Maria's Farewell* from her hands, why her mother always avoided questions, didn't answer, squirming exactly the way Sister Katerine had. She wouldn't put up with it any longer; she would have to find everything out, figure it all out herself, and she'd force her mother, her mother would have to tell her the truth, she'd beg with tears, she would have to know today, today her mother would have to ....

"I thought you were lying down, but here you are sitting staring; you said you had a headache, so why are you fretting?"

Her mother's voice interrupted Katerine's thoughts. She let her finish, raised her head, and looked at her mother suspiciously, the way you look at a stranger whose closed face you want to decipher, but she was immediately ashamed of herself and lowered her head.

"What's wrong, daughter? I can tell that something's happened; tell your mother; you've always told me everything.

You trust your mother after all; tell the truth; you've never held back from me."

"And you, mother, have never withheld anything from me? Told the truth?"

"I think ... why should I hide, when you ask, if it's appropriate, I tell you ... but what kind of talk is this, my daughter? You're not speaking nicely to your mother," said Magdalena tenderly and with wily humour.

"I want to know ... I want to know ... who I am; they said that ... that I'm a Jew, everyone, everyone knows it, they look at me ...."

Magdalena Vrublevska turned pale, held on to the bed railing with both hands. It was suddenly difficult for her to remain standing. Slowly she sat down beside her daughter, sat mute as though the power of speech had been taken from her, and then she quietly answered,

"You accept all this gossip and take it seriously, fuss over every foolishness ...."

"I want to know who I am," Katerine interrupted her. "I want to know the truth!" By now she was shouting.

"Who drummed such thoughts into your head?" her mother tried raising her voice.

"Everyone, everyone knows; Sister Katerine also told me a while ago that I'm ... no, Sister also didn't want to tell me everything, didn't want to answer ... put me off with — " Katerine burst into tears, holding her face in both hands and sobbing. Magdalena moved closer to her, holding her, pressing her against herself, trying to convince her in a soft, shaking voice,

"Who are you? You're my daughter, my whole life. I love you as you love me, your mother. Why pay attention to ... ? Why? Why listen to foolish prattle?"

"I want to know ... I must know. Tell me the truth! Tell me!"

"Fine, I will ... tomorrow. First, calm down, my foolish child. Come and eat, my little fool."

"To you I'm still a child, a 'little fool.' I want you to tell me everything right now!" And Katerine burst into even more violent weeping.

"So, good, let it be, but stop crying. That's why I didn't want to tell you in the first place. You make a fuss about any little trifle. I beg you, daughter, there's nothing to cry about. Promise me, my child, that you won't exaggerate things. You're a grown girl now, and crying is unbecoming. Is life so bad for us?"

Magdalena caught her breath, silent for a while, thinking of how to go on with this painful conversation with her daughter.

"If you want, I'll tell everything. But it mustn't change anything between us. What can it possibly mean to us? Isn't that so? Do you promise me, daughter dear?"

Katerine nodded and blurted through her tears, "I promise, but tell me everything; tell me the whole truth."

Mother and daughter sat clinging to one another. Katerine, sobbing quietly from time to time, dried her eyes. Magdalena Vrublevska was silent for some time. What she had feared of late had come to pass. Katerine was an intelligent girl, but so sensitive; she felt everything so intensely. Now she could no longer pull the wool over her eyes. She must tell her the truth, but how? She had thought about it many times; in her imagination, that daybreak reappeared. She covered her eyes with her hands, steeled herself, and began,

"I adopted you, Sister Katerine probably told you that. You were tiny, really tiny; you were with Sister Katerine. I adopted you and from that time on you've been my daughter and I your mother."

"From the beginning, start at the beginning. Where did Sister Katerine get me? Tell me, tell me from the beginning, everything, everything, I beg of you."

Magdalena remained silent, her face clouded over. She clasped her daughter more tightly to herself, stroking her hair, and then began again.

"It was in 1942, dawn, still dark. They were being driven on this road, the back road that leads to the forest; they passed close to our house. I lay in bed shaking as if I had a fever. The wailing and howling was unbearable, wailing and howling, then an echo of gunshot, then — silence. There was no question of sleep after that; my heart was heavy, in my ears the wailing rang but outside it was as silent as the graveyard. Suddenly, I heard whimpering, like a sick kitten, then something like the choked cry of a baby. I got out of bed to listen at the door. Everything was quiet; I stood there a few minutes and went back to bed.

"It was daylight at last but the town was lifeless; people were still afraid to go out. It was a Sunday; no-one went to work, they stayed indoors. It was very stuffy and I wanted some air, so I carefully opened the front shutter and stuck my head out and ... a parcel at the door, some sort of strange parcel, a kind of bundle. I panicked; we were afraid of everything. I closed the window but, recalling the whimpering earlier on, I opened the door a crack. The bundle stirred. I looked around to see whether anyone was watching, pulled the bundle in and untied it ... a child ... seemingly smothered; the sop had fallen out of the little mouth. I put my ear to the child; it was breathing. I took it out of the knotted little quilt; it looked frail. It occurred to me to pour warm, sweet water into the little mouth; it wasn't long before it began to cry, first quite softly, then louder and louder. Oh my God, a catastrophe! Then I really panicked; such a risk, everyone knew I was a widow, alone; my child had died three years earlier, and here a child, and one so dark, my God. I quickly stopped your mouth with the sop; packed it with wet sugar. I was so terrified that it would cry; I was almost out of my mind with fright, what to do with the child? It was then that I remembered Sister Katerine, she was so compassionate and wise, gave good advice; she wouldn't refuse. I dressed quickly, put the child into the vegetable basket, packing the sop with wet sugar, covered the basket with an old towel, put the flowers from the vase on top, as well as some vegetables I had prepared to take to the convent on Sunday. Fortunately you didn't cry, you were hungry and sucked on the sugar. When Sister Katerine removed your clothing to bathe you a note fell out of your little right sock: 'Merciful people, save this child; God will reward you.' Then the name. Date of birth wasn't given, probably forgotten. Sister Katerine fed you, then made out a certificate of baptism. It was Saint Katerine's Day, just like today; you were given her name and I was forbidden to come to see you, just as well. After that, difficult times befell me."

Magdalena Vrublevska stopped as though the telling had exhausted her and looking at Katerine saw her strange expression: the girl was staring straight ahead, mouth open, not a muscle in her face moving, as though everything had frozen from shock. Magdalena waited for her to respond, then could wait no longer. "My child, should I go on to the end?" Katerine only nodded and two full, round tears rolled down from her dark eyes. Magdalena, now hurrying to finish, spoke in chaotic, unfinished sentences.

"Told myself that if I survived, you'd be my child; my little girl died, God sent an unfortunate child, had to wait. After the war my situation was difficult, had to come back to myself; thanks to Uncle Karol, he helped me a lot, always loved you; according to the baptismal certificate, you were four years old. Sister Katerine led me to a dark little girl and, pointing to me, said to her, 'This is your mother, a good mother, you must love her ... .' Since then, I have been so happy; grew to love you like my own child, what's the difference? You really are my own child, my only daughter. I was so ... ."

The words stuck in her throat, choking. Both were silent now, their heartbeats could be heard in the stillness. Magdalena became alarmed at Katerine's silence and said,

"You see, my child, I've told everything, hidden nothing; you know everything now."

"Not everything yet."

"What more do you want to know?"

"What was my name?"

"Miriam. Miriam Zack."

"And my parents?"

"Sister Katerine may know."

"The note, my note? I want to see ... ."

"I'll ask Sister, perhaps she has it, perhaps ... . But be patient, better I go myself, it's more fitting."

"And family? Relatives? Do I have someone ... ?"

"How can we know that? You have ... me, Uncle Karol, Auntie, aren't we your family ? Am I not a mother to you and you a daughter to me?"

"Yes, yes, you are, of course you are, but — " and Katerine broke into tears again.

Shortly after Saint Katerine's Day, mother and daughter together composed and mailed the following notice to the Red Cross, Missing Relatives Division: "Miriam Zack, daughter of Leyzer and Rivke Zack from the city of T., seeks relatives, wherever they may be, within the country or abroad. Reply."

TRANSLATED BY FRIEDA FORMAN AND ETHEL RAICUS

CORRESPONDENTS

Blume Lempel

❧

Set in the present in New York City, "Correspondents" is a series of associations and flashbacks. It was published in 1992 in Yidishe kultur [Yiddish Culture] and is unique in its elliptical style and its allusions to contemporary lesbian life.

The narrator recalls figures from her life in pre-Holocaust eastern Poland. After the Hitler-Stalin pact in August 1939, this region came under the rule of the Soviets. But in June 1941, Hitler broke his agreement, invaded the Soviet Union, and began the Jewish genocide in this area.

THE MOMENT I FINISHED the letter to the girl with the black hair and hungry eyes, I tore it up.

We had met in a library. She happened to have checked out the very same book I had just returned.

"It'll give you a lot of pleasure," I said suddenly.

"Really? How do you know?" she asked and laughed.

"I don't. I just have a feeling."

We left together and walked through the streets. She told me she wrote poetry, not for publication, "but for myself." I looked at her more closely — very closely — and had the feeling I was seeing myself in the distant past. Something in what she chose and chose not to say resonated like an evening echo in a forest.

Her voice heavy with unfulfilled longing caressed and at the same time repelled me. I felt myself engulfed by a spring breeze heavy with the scent of mint. My clothes suddenly felt tight. The seams burst and released the garment which I had concealed from the outside world as if I were ashamed of who I was.

There was no way I could explain all this in a letter. I also couldn't tell her that I saw her as a rose infested with slithering worms. I felt I first needed to clarify this aversion to myself. Only after I realized that this too was impossible did I tear up the letter and write her another — not about her, but about someone else.

In the letter I told her that a while back I had taken the subway from Brooklyn to New York. I held my little boy in my arms. I don't know where or why I was travelling. It was a summer afternoon. There weren't many passengers in the car. A young man got on one of the stations and took a seat near me. He was carrying a violin, maybe even a violoncello, wrapped in a blue silk cover with a gold zipper. The zipper touched my knee accidentally. I raised my eyes and saw how the violin or the violoncello beneath the blue silk was shaped like a dancer waiting for her cue for her first step. Or perhaps it was the power of the young man's eyes which looked into mine and awakened octaves from a hundred-year sleep. I don't know how long I held his gaze, but when I turned my head towards the window through which the dark tunnel looked in, two hot tears fell from my eyes.

Usually I'm not the type who cries. The last Jewish destruction had sealed the well of my tears. The summer after Liberation, I couldn't talk to people. I shared my sorrow with a felled tree which peered at me over my neighbour's fence. I became close with a cat who had lost her newborn kittens. A murderous tom had gouged their throats and left them on the threshold of her den. The cat didn't shed any tears. She just followed the tracks of the murderer, only sought revenge. She didn't touch the milk I put out for her. When I tried to pet her, she clawed me.

What the cat did to me, I did to my friends. I didn't want, nor could I tolerate, any comfort. I just wanted to remain mute, or to scream the same cries that come from a violin or violoncello ... .

Seated this way near the young man, the violin between us, I saw another violin under another sky in another time. The symphony of that other violin has remained unfinished.

With his violin under his arm, he stood on the bottom step of the panting Express. The violin wept as we exchanged our last kiss. He kept waving his handkerchief for a long time. The wheels began to turn. A rain beat down. For three days and two nights the train wheels sang the Song of Songs to me: "I love you. I love you." All the way from Lemberg to Paris and the Gare du Nord.

After the *Shoah*, I couldn't conceive of these three words. I avoided all musical sounds. I would stop up my ears against the songs of street singers who milked tears from passersby over their betrayed loves. The love which had forced us to separate was betrayed by the world: the world that knew but pretended it did not know when it burned, systematically exterminated, not hundreds, not thousands, but an entire people to the beat of Beethoven's Ninth.

Music, which had once lifted me to heavenly heights, had fallen, together with the ash of burned bodies, into the abyss where snakes swarm and lizards laugh. For many years, I avoided the sounds of strings. Now, the young man on the seat near me, the one with a violin wrapped in blue silk, filled me with fear. Every time my foot accidentally touched the silk, the instrument groaned.

I turned my head away, pressed my forehead against the cold pane. In the black tunnel on the other side of the window, I saw not the young man, but the aristocratic image of Arnove. She was the wife of Dr. Oyerhan, the only woman in our *shtetl* who could play the violin. She had no dealings with our women. She was on friendly terms with the gentry and visited Count Szeminiski's home. She had even been a beauty queen at a strictly Christian aristocratic ball.

Summer evenings we could hear her violin through the open windows of her palace. Her dog stood guard lest, God forbid, anyone would set foot inside the fenced-in flower garden. Dr. Oyerhan would come to *shul* once a year to say *yisker*. She never set foot inside *shul*. People doubted that she was even a Jew. But the murderers without horns, without drums, the descendants of Goethe, Mozart, Kant — they knew better. When they drove the last Jews of the *shtetl* to the market place, she was among them. She didn't cry or scream. True to her self-created personality, she played her role to the bitter end. Her husband the doctor was already dead. She had no children. The gentry with whom she'd been friendly had been exiled by the Soviets. All that she had left was the violin.

She was leaning against the ramp, the violin under her blue silk kimono, her hair loose, her face pale. Her skin was drawn, transparent like that of a porcelain statue. The plush slippers on her bare feet were soiled with the dung of the animals which we brought to the fairs. Suddenly she swept back her hair, raised her head, took up her violin and, posed as if she were getting ready to play, drew closer to the officer with the black swastika on his arm. "Gracious sir," she said in her best Viennese accent, "spare me the shame."

The officer looked her over, up and down. His eyes paused on the violin. "Close your eyes," he ordered. And with one bullet, he granted her wish.

The young man sitting on the seat near me kept his head down. Without looking directly, I observed how his lips moved. I thought that perhaps he was keeping time to the music that emanated from beneath the blue silk cover. His head brushed over the divider between us. I felt his lips on my hand. "Madonna, Madonna," he whispered and drowned the rest in a foreign language.

As soon as the train stopped, I got out. Standing on the other side of the door, I turned my head to the window where he had been sitting. But he was no longer there ....

The girl with the black hair and hungry eyes read the letter and answered as follows: "As you know, I write poetry for my own pleasure. For whose benefit are you running around in circles? What are you claiming, that life repeats itself? You take one step forward and immediately you're back in the *shtetl*, back to 'once upon a time.' The whole gamble of life is nothing but one banal repetition. Fortunately not without some variations.

"I am now attached to a young woman. It's an extraordinary experience. Think about it, my dear.

"I'm enclosing the address of our club. It has many lost souls. You're a person who makes an impression. I'm certain that you'll find there the right note for this life-performance ... ."

I tore up her letter. I wanted to burn it on the spot. But the word "burn" awakens in me holy images. So I tore her letter into very tiny, tiny pieces.

TRANSLATED BY IRENA KLEPFISZ

EDGIA'S REVENGE

Chava Rosenfarb

❧

"Edgia's Revenge" takes the concentration camp experiences of its characters as the starting point for an examination of their post-Holocaust lives. After the Second World War, survivors of the nazi Holocaust began arriving in Canada, despite the country's restrictive immigration policy. A large number of these survivors settled in Montreal, which is the setting for "Edgia's Revenge."

Kapos were concentration camp inmates who had been put in charge of their fellow inmates by the nazis. This led to their morally ambiguous position in the community of survivors after the war.

EVER SINCE EDGIA DISAPPEARED beyond the horizon of my life, the desire to put an end to myself has grown stronger within me. This is Edgia's victory over me, her definitive act of vengeance. I am ready to submit, ready to surrender to the perverse law which still seems to rule over the psyches of those survivors whose souls remain trapped in the concentration camps, and who will never break free. I refer to the law which says that for every life saved another must be sacrificed. The account must tally. For having saved Edgia's life I must put an end to my own, if not today then tomorrow, if not tomorrow, then twenty or thirty years from now.

At the same time I feel a need to resolve for myself the conundrum that Edgia represents in my life. I mean my life after the war, because in the camps there were no conundrums, and all complications of the soul resolved themselves by themselves, or were thrown overboard like so much extra ballast. In the camps only one question mattered — how to survive another hour, another day.

But how can I indulge in ruminations about my life in the camps, when even today my hand is incapable of writing the words "concentration camp" without trembling? It is incomprehensible to me, it is silly and ludicrous, that even now, just as I am about to unlock the gate to eternity and free myself of all entrapments, I should still fall prey to the fear of my memories from there. For this reason I must limit myself in this account to touching on only the most necessary points.

Just now, as I wrote the words "the gate to eternity," my hand did not shake. That's not surprising. How many times have I peered through that gate? I do so even now and will continue to do so — until I myself pass through. But my indifference in the face of eternity is not a consequence of habit. One may grow accustomed to gazing at the gates of nonexistence in order to watch how others pass through — or are driven through. Don't modern intellectuals, who were never there, speak about the banality of evil? The annihilation of others may be banal, but when it's a question of one's own personal one-time-only demise, then banality vanishes and so does indifference. I am no exception. On the contrary. My own salvaged life is precious to me. I have paid a higher price for it than other survivors did for theirs. I have paid for it with my conscience. From this stems the sang-froid with which I approach this particular subject.

My voluntary passage through the eternal gate has become for me a categorical imperative, a final summing up. In order for a sum to tally there can be only one correct answer; no ifs or maybes. Edgia's disappearance from my life has once and for all brought this fact home to me. The revulsion I feel for my precious life has finally conquered the revulsion I feel for death.

I first got the idea of supplying myself with sleeping pills in the very first weeks after my liberation from the camp. As soon as the German guards disappeared from behind the barbed wire fence, I fled the camp. I then drifted from one end to the other of that devastated German countryside, trying to escape from myself and from others, regardless of whether they were the conquerors or the conquered. The sight of a human face disgusted me. But with the passing of time loneliness set up such a howling inside me that I could no longer endure it, and I attached myself to a group of former concentration camp inmates who were wandering from one camp to another in search of relatives. They had come from the English Zone, and not one of them was a native of my hometown. I myself had no relatives to find, but I trailed along with them, because I was overcome by panic at the thought of being alone, and because I hoped that with them or through them I would discover the quickest way out of Germany.

It was a bright spring day. Along with my group of wanderers I was sitting on the edge of an unploughed field near the highway. The normal means of transportation had not yet been restored, so we waited for a military truck to come along and give us a lift. After a while such a truck drove up. The American driver jumped out of his seat, dropped the back flap of his vehicle, and we climbed up. And here unexpectedly we came upon another former camp inmate sleeping on the floorboards of the truck. The noise of our clattering aboard woke him. He jumped to his feet, took our measure with a quick glance, and retreated to the furthest corner of the truck. As soon as we started to move, he turned his back, and caught hold of the vibrating sides. We moved closer, anxious to question him about which camp he was from, where he was heading, and what information he had.

Just at that moment, one of my group cried out, "I know him! He was a *kapo* in my camp! We called him Romek the Executioner!" He pointed a bony index finger at the stranger's face, as if he were aiming to poke out his eyes.

A moment later, the stranger lay stretched across the swaying floorboards of the truck, as my companions unloaded the burden of their pain-filled hearts on his prostrate body with kicks and jabs, cursing and yelling all the while. The stranger made no attempt to defend or shield himself. He endured the blows with muffled groans from between compressed lips. Perhaps he desired these blows, craving the ritual purification that such a beating would confer, in the hope that having paid the price, he too would have the right to enjoy his freedom?

I was so disturbed by the beating that I felt each blow as if it were landing on me. But I had been even more shaken by that first cry of "I know him! He's a *kapo*." The cry reverberated in my ears and would not die away. That must be the worst — the shock of being recognized, the inner trembling at the sight of a pointing finger. The mere thought of this took my breath away.

What happened afterwards to Romek the Executioner I do not know. As soon as we came to the next town, some of the group dragged him to a military police station. I took advantage of the confusion to steal away from my companions.

Somehow I managed to make it to Munich, where I sought the advice of a compassionate, terribly naive and ignorant UNRRA doctor. I went to see him because I was suffering from insomnia, and begged him for sleeping pills. "It's no wonder, my child, that you can't sleep," he said, affectionately patting my shoulder. "After all that you've lived through, you must be having nightmares even in the daytime when you are wide awake." How could I explain that I wanted the pills not only to squelch the nightmares evoked by my past, but also to squelch the nightmares inspired by my present-day, wonderful, dearly bought life.

And so I escaped from Germany in my one and only civilian dress, which I had managed to "organize" for myself out of a German house. But in my knapsack I carried the twenty-five sleeping pills which the good doctor had given me. These pills were the only possessions that I brought with me to Canada from the European continent. They took the place of my parents, my grandparents, my sixteen-year-old brother and my ten-year-old sister, my darling Maniusha. They took the place of all my aunts, uncles, and cousins, of my hometown, my childhood, my early adolescence, and my first and only love. Sleeping pills became my life — and my death. And now they have become my only road back to innocence.

Throughout all the years that I carried the pills around with me, I found strength in the promise I had made to myself that should the day ever come when someone recognized me and pointed a finger at me, I would turn to my brightly coloured, bead-like saviours. I told myself that it was my prerogative to set the limits of my post-Liberation hell, and that I had no intention of letting others decide the boundaries for me. If I was to be devoured by guilt then let me be the one to measure its immensity and the extent to which I had earned it. Because I am not the true culprit. What happened would have happened even without my assistance. I did not add a single drop to the cup of poison. I just kept order among the imbibers.

If there was such a thing as a good *kapo*, then that is what I was. The only reason that the inmates of the women's camp called me Black Rella was because I have black hair, dark eyes and dark skin. I am not a murderer, I do not even have a violent nature, although I did beat people and I suppose you could say that I had a hand in murder. I grew up in a cultured middle-class home. I had good manners. I liked people. I enjoyed life. And I loved my little sister Maniusha, to whom I was a second mother, since our own mother was sickly. I took pleasure in the long sun-drenched days of our summer vacations, and delighted in the mild caressing evenings at our country house, when we all sat on the verandah and Maniusha recited children's poems. I loved poetry with a passion.

In the camps I saw my entire family float heavenward with the smoke from the crematorium chimneys. I wanted to save myself. I was nineteen years old. I wanted to survive. I didn't choose the means by which to do it. There were no choices to be made. Everything depended on luck. The means chose me. Perhaps, in my dazed state, I was helped by blind instinct. But instinct is itself the slave of luck. It doesn't always function as it should.

It was the second week of my incarceration in the camp. I hardly knew what was happening to me. A sandy smoky phantasmagoria whirled ceaselessly before my eyes: whistles, shouts, the barking of dogs, barracks, chimneys — and faces. Faces like stones, stones like faces revolved before my eyes like the dislodged cobbles of a disintegrating pavement. From pre-dawn twilight until late into the evening the five hundred women of my barrack loaded stones onto lorries and transported them from one place to another. Even though I was tortured by hunger, I still felt vigorous. Hard labour had not yet broken my spirit. But I had another kind of trouble to torment me. In my lost former life — as close as yesterday and yet as distant as a dream — I had been vain of my statuesque figure and my healthy, well-developed body. Now my height became my greatest curse. It was not possible to hide or melt into the crowd. Whenever we marched in columns, I stuck out like an exclamation mark, which provoked in our guards an irresistible urge to smack me down to size. I suppose that my height irritated them because it disturbed the symmetry, the perfect harmony of the world which they had created.

Never before had anyone raised a hand against me. Now I endured more slaps and kicks than any one of the other marchers. Those slaps and kicks were the worst. I could not bear them. I was convinced that neither weakness nor hunger would destroy me — but those blows could. (Maybe this was why I was later so generous in meting out my own kicks and slaps to the girls under my supervision.)

In this way my life in the camp dragged on, until the moment came when my despair prompted me to risk my neck on a gamble. I risked my life in order to save my life. I turned my very visibility to my advantage, as I did my proficient German. The language of my home had been Polish, but we had had a German cook. I also learned German in high school. I was just beginning to appreciate the true glory of German poetry, when the war broke out. *Mach deine Rechnung mit dem Himmel, Vogt.* "Settle your account with heaven, Vogt," Schiller's William Tell said to his oppressor. I settled my personal account with heaven one bleak dawn before sunrise as we were marching in our columns past the men's camp on our way to work. Usually I tried to place myself in the middle of the row, which consisted of five women, in order not to be quite so conspicuous. But this time I walked on the outside of my line of five, the closest to the barbed wire fence which surrounded the men's camp.

I knew that the shaven-headed *kapo* Albert, our overseer, would be waiting for us at the gate. Our column of women marched past him with eyes lowered and heads bent. According to camp rules, it was forbidden to so much as glance in the direction of the men's camp. I alone did not obey the order. I drew myself up to my full height and when my eyes met Albert's I beamed my most bewitching smile in his direction, then took a chance on greeting him with my perfectly accented *guten Morgen*.

Albert wore a green triangle on his striped suit, which meant that he was classified as a criminal. And he was German, a heartless brute who could strangle his victims with his bare hands. Not only was he incapable of smiling, but he could not even manage a facial expression that resembled a smile, and I am certain that in all that valley of death he had never once encountered a smile like mine. In the dark before dawn I could sense how deeply my chutzpah had shocked him.

That same bleak pre-dawn he came up to me at our work place. He caught hold of my arm, and without saying a word, dragged me to the far end of the sand field which surrounded us. There, behind a shack, stood a mountain of broken lorries, one stacked on top of the other. I was certain that he was about to kill me. He pushed me into an overturned lorry, and there he took me.

This was how Albert became my first man. I, who had been brought up to be so shy with men! The first great love of my life had had to be satisfied with stolen kisses on dark boulevards and in shady parks. But with Albert I forsook inhibition. In return, he saw to it that I should become a *Stubendienst*, a supervisor in my barracks, and then an auxiliary *kapo*, and after six months in the camp I was made a full *kapo*. That was lucky, because I was pregnant. As a *kapo* I could move about freely, and Albert could arrange things so that I was soon rid of my problem. Albert — my Teutonic god! He could do with me what he pleased. When he told me for the first time, *Ich liebe dich*, while the smoke of the crematoria burrowed into my nostrils, my heart nearly stopped beating. Did not such words, spoken in an upside-down world, have exactly the opposite meaning? Might this not mean that he was ready to do away with me?

My god Albert knew well enough that he was committing *Rassenschande*. But this amused him and added fuel to his hellish love for me. He even promised to marry me as soon as the war was over. I stroked his shaved head, and wondered if my god, the monster Albert, had ever been a child, had ever been dandled on a mother's knee, had ever absorbed even one drop of the milk of human kindness. Such a thing did not seem possible. My god Albert impregnated my soul with a demon which I did not dare exorcise because it guaranteed every single day of my life. Thanks to that demon I evolved into the person that I became. I was proud of my Albert, I was proud of my position in the kingdom of death. In the camps, the word *kapo* elicited the kind of awe reserved in ancient times for the priests and priestesses who guarded the sacred flame.

The women inmates sucked up to me. If I said a kind word, it was music to their ears. It made them feel more secure about the next few hours of their lives. They quarrelled among themselves as to who should wash my underwear and clean my shoes. They trembled at each disdainful motion of my hand, and anxiously read and interpreted every expression of my face. I, who before the war had blushed to hear language that was even remotely risqué, now became positively prolific in inventing entries for a lexicon of obscenities. I, who before the war had spoken the Polish language in the most elegant and refined tones, now took a wild pleasure in ranting like a bitch. And I, who once thought that my hands had been created for nothing but tenderness and caresses, now kept them clenched in rocklike fists, the better to pound them against hunched skeletal backs — and I did this with pleasure, with genuine sensual delight, orgiastically.

The newly born demon within me gave me a sense of freedom in the midst of slavery, a sense that one day of life was an eternity, that the concentration camp was the universe, and that there were no roads leading away from this point. Of course, we spoke and dreamed of real freedom, but no-one really believed in it. The smoke rising day and night from the chimneys confirmed the finality of existence. It drugged my fear, intoxicated my senses, and made me wanton. All the restraints of civilized human conduct fell away from me. I had the impression of wandering about as if the skin had been peeled from my body and I was left to revel in an orgy of the most primitive impulses. The borderline between what is and what is not vanished, and the dividing line that distinguishes man from beast similarly disappeared. If an ember of humanity still glowed within me it was no more than a spark.

But why am I tearing my hair trying to describe things which cannot be described? I had no intention of going off on this tangent. Even so, I must emphasize that it is false to think that not every one could have been a *kapo*. It is a lie. In that world from which I miraculously escaped, every single person had the potential to be a brute, a thug, a murderer. When it comes to fighting for one's own life, moral laws cease to exist. You may ask, were there really no exceptions? To this I answer, of course there were — fools who risked their own skins in order to preserve God's image in their hearts. But I was not one of them. I did not want to put my life at risk.

Charitably, my memory has failed to preserve the face of Albert, my concentration camp god. All that I remember of him is the grey shadow of his shaven head which looked as if it were covered with ashes from the chimneys.

My tragedy after the war stemmed from the fact that I could neither unburden my heart to anyone, nor ignore the weight of the sins which I carried within. I agree with the modern psychologists, who claim such deep understanding as they dig into the psyches of the survivors, when they say that each survivor is afflicted by an immense feeling of guilt for the simple fact of having survived. If this is true, then what should be the extent of my guilt-feeling? The trouble is that it is not so much guilt that I feel as it is disgust, an all-embracing disgust — mostly for myself — accompanied by a peculiar anxiety, a strange dread of the word *kapo*. The word has been stamped on my soul like the mark of Cain. I shudder whenever I hear someone speak it. This is why I ran away to this remote corner of the world, hoping that the frost which is native to this land would freeze the word into oblivion, or that the snow would erase it. I was mistaken. And the paradoxical result has been that I have remained passionately attached to life, while constantly flirting with death, all the while waiting for the moment when someone would exclaim: "I know you! You were a *kapo*!"

This same suicidal impulse has kept me attached to Edgia. It was from her that I expected to hear the accusation.

It was during a roll call for selection in the camp. Edgia — I didn't know her name then — was on her last legs. Most likely she was afraid that she would be picked out of her row and sent for "scrap," as we called those who were selected for the crematoria. She did not respond to the roll call, but hid in the mud between the broom box and the latrine. A silly place to hide. If not I, then some other *kapo* would have found her. In my search for those who evaded roll call, it was not long before I discovered her there. She crouched in the black mud like a submerged sack of bones, while the bristly hair which had begun to sprout on her shaven head stood up like wires. Her face was as dark as the mud.

I grabbed her by the collar of her ragged dress. She fell forward onto all fours, and this was how I dragged her along like a recalcitrant dog.

"Have pity," she whimpered, and dug her thin hands into the loose soil. I jerked her from the spot. But at that moment my eyes met her pleading gaze. Her dirty face, small and shrunken, was blotted from my sight and all I could see were those eyes. I felt as if I were drowning in them, as if I were being sucked into an abyss. I saw the eyes of my little sister Maniusha looking at me imploringly as the SS man tore her from my arms.

I continued to pull Edgia after me. "No ... no ... ," she squealed hysterically. I hit her a few times, and ordered her to stand up. Then I wrapped my arm around her head, blocking her mouth with my hand. In this manner I dragged her into my barrack through the back way, and into the corner that I occupied behind a curtain made from a blanket. I pushed her under my bunk — not a great place to hide either, but there was nothing better — and ran out of the barrack. By the time I got back to roll call, they were already leading away the group of "chosen" girls.

I returned to my barrack, and looked under the bunk. Edgia was no longer there. I did not know her number, nor her name; I did not know who she was, nor where she came from. I never saw her again inside the camp. Most likely she deliberately kept out of my way.

The smell of war's end hung in the air, and I sensed that my end too was drawing near. I began to fear what the Germans might do to us in the last moments, and to fear as well what the prisoners might do to the *kapos* if we survived our liberation.

On one of those last days, I was sent out to the train station. I was supposed to assist with the loading of a transport of women who had been assigned to work at another camp, maybe one of those camps where the crematorium no longer functioned. I envied these women. In spite of all my good fortune I considered that they were luckier than I was, because I had to remain behind.

I helped to pack the women into the roofless cattle cars, and that is how I suddenly saw Edgia clumsily trying to climb into a wagon. I grabbed her arm. She stared at me with a pair of frightened mousy eyes as if she were looking at the Angel of Death. "Where are they taking us?" she gasped.

I did not answer, but hissed into her ear. "Swear to me this very minute, that if we manage to get out, and we happen to meet somewhere else in this world, you will never breathe a word to anyone that I was a *kapo*."

She remained frozen to the spot, one foot dangling in the air. My request must have struck her as idiotic. And, in fact, it was idiotic. Several hundred other women inmates knew that I was a *kapo*. I suspect that all I really wanted at that moment was one last look at Edgia, the beneficiary of my one and only heroic act in the camps.

As I stared at her I had the impression that at any moment

her face might dissolve into a smile. "And must I also not reveal that you saved my life?" she asked, as it seemed to me then, with false humility.

"Not that either. Swear it! Swear by your life!"

"I swear by my life, if that is still worth something. Where are they taking us?" she asked again as she pulled her other leg into the wagon.

I could not bear the gnawing at my heart brought on by the sight of her, so without answering I ran off, and busied myself herding the other women into the boxcars.

Not long afterwards, we were liberated. At one stroke I was freed from the Germans and from my god Albert. Instead, I fell captive to my conscience and to the perpetual fear that somebody would recognize me.

As I said, I was happy to emigrate to Canada, which I considered a land "far from God and from people" — by which I meant former concentration camp inmates — where I would be unlikely ever to be confronted by an accusing finger. In fact, when I first landed, I was one of the few survivors to have reached these shores. Later I realized that I had only been among the first swallows. Soon the others started to arrive in their thousands. The entire American continent swarmed with them. Commemorations, memorial evenings, remembrance ceremonies were attended by masses of people. Books began to appear on the subject of the Holocaust, all of them providing detailed descriptions of the tragedy. There were so many books that they filled entire libraries. But nobody tried to get to the bottom of the particular tragedy of the Jewish *kapos*.

I did not read these books. I knew more than they could ever tell. I did not go to the various commemorations and memorial evenings. I needed no-one to remind me of what had happened. I remembered on my own and only too well. Even if I had been tempted to attend a Holocaust memorial, I could not have given in to the urge for fear that someone might recognize me.

As soon as I arrived in Montreal, I went to work in a factory, and in the evenings I diligently studied English. With the first money I earned, I went to a plastic surgeon and asked him to remove the tattooed number from my forearm. I did not see the point of advertising where I had been. Of course I knew that it was easier to remove the tattoo from my skin than to erase the mark of Cain from my soul. But what went on in my soul had the advantage of not being visible. Outwardly I inhabited a new skin, a new identity, which could disguise whatever I found convenient to disguise.

Because I was afraid of being alone, I tried to make contact with the local Jews, but we had no common language. They knew almost nothing about the Holocaust. What they did know they did not understand. I was drawn to my own kind of people, in fact to those very people whom I should have been avoiding like the plague. And so I made friends with other new immigrants. A few of these I suspected of having been *kapos*, but most of the others had survived the war on the aryan side in Poland, and after the war had made their way to Germany, where they feathered their nests by profiteering and trading in black-market merchandise. When the occupation forces began to wrest some order out of the chaos of a devastated Germany, my friends found themselves with nothing more to do, so they came here. I soon realized that what tied me to these people mattered less than what separated me from them. They were vulgar moneybags with base appetites. I longed for culture. I needed it as a bridge to throw across the abyss of my war years and link me to my home and my happy childhood. I needed culture as a form of purification.

It was at this time that I really began to suffer from insomnia. During the course of the day I wandered about as if I were drunk. I found myself inhabiting two worlds at the same time, tormented by all kinds of visions and hallucinations. In the faces of people who passed me in the street, I saw the features of camp inmates. Every chimney of every factory seemed to me to be the chimney of the crematorium. In every dog that ran past me, I recognized the German shepherds and Doberman pinschers of the camps who had been taught to savour human flesh. The sight of any man in uniform — a policeman, a fireman — brought the SS to my mind. And if I happened to be travelling by train and the whistle blew, I imagined that I was again travelling with my loved ones in the cattle car, drawing ever nearer to the station of the concentration camp.

The worst of it was when I saw myself in my flashbacks repeatedly striking someone who resembled one or another of the women I had known in the camp. I would see my hand go up and down, up and down, like the hand of an automaton. I went about with an ache in the muscle of my right arm, as if I had been carrying a heavy weight. The palm of my hand burned. I had to quickly rid myself of these afflictions because they endangered my work at the factory — and what was just as important, my learning to write English. I found it difficult to hold a pen in my hand.

For these reasons I became a frequent visitor at the doctor's office. With a tactful little smile on his face, the doctor informed me that I was suffering from pernicious hypochondria which was not amenable to treatment. But since the sleeping pills which I had brought with me from Germany had long since run out, he kept me supplied with more. They helped me very little, because I took them so sparingly. I had to be careful of maintaining a sufficient supply of pills against the eventual hour of my reckoning. Having my little stash of pills made me feel more secure.

And in order to feel still more secure, I became obsessed with beautiful clothes. I had an urge to be constantly changing my garments, rearranging my appearance, but my earnings did not permit me the luxury of a constant change of clothing. It was the summer of 1950. I heard that HIAS was distributing used clothes for newly arrived immigrants. It was clear to me that a second-hand dress donated by a wealthy Montreal woman would look better on me than some cheap rag that I could afford to buy on my own, especially since I had a good figure and even cheap clothing looked expensive and elegant on me. Yes, I looked good, despite my nightmares. I was like the proverbial apple, beautiful and healthy on the outside, wormy and rotten inside.

So one day I paid a visit to the HIAS storerooms. I walked into a room full of racks of clothing. There were dresses, suits, skirts and blouses, all tightly packed together. The sight made me dizzy. I pounced on each full rack, moving rapidly from one to another, and this was how my restless gaze came to fall on the figure of a familiar-looking woman as she too rummaged among the clothes racks. My heart stopped. My first impulse was to get away, but my feet refused to move. I could not take my eyes off the woman's profile. The face of that monster Albert had been erased from my memory, but Edgia's face, which I had glimpsed only twice in my life, I remembered so well that it was not difficult for me to recognize her, despite her altered appearance. Although her complexion still had a sallow hue, her profile was rounded and her hair was of normal length. I felt myself drawn to her face — the face of my own kindness.

I broke away from the spot where I was standing and threw myself at her. I pulled her into a corner. The yellowish cast of her face turned white as chalk; her head sank down between her shoulders, just as it had during the scene of our first encounter near the camp latrine. She acted as if her life were still in my hands, but this time we were both trembling with anxiety.

"Do you recognize me?" I asked her.

"Yes, I recognize you," she stammered.

"And do you remember that thanks to me you are still alive?"

"Yes, I remember."

It annoyed me that even now she refrained from thanking me. All of a sudden, my voice assumed the shrill harsh note of my camp days. "I hope you also remember the vow that you swore to me then."

She nodded, turned away from me, and with trembling hands resumed rummaging among the dresses on the neighbouring rack, her head sunk between her shoulders. She hastily pulled a dress from a hanger and stuffed it into her bag. I realized that she was about to leave. I felt compelled to follow. I must not let her get away. I must keep my eye on her. I caught up to her and blurted out, "I've forgotten your name."

"I remember yours," she answered. "You are Black Rella."

"What's your name?" I insisted.

She told me her name. I ventured to ask for her address. To my astonishment she gave it to me, almost eagerly. Most likely she wanted to keep an eye on me too. Maybe she felt as drawn to me as I did to her.

I visited Edgia uninvited. I visited her again, and then again, and in this way I became a frequent guest at her home. She introduced me to her husband Lolek, a handsome blond man, unusually amiable and extroverted. Edgia proudly told me that he had been a partisan and had survived the war years somewhere in the forests of Lithuania. This was one of the rare occasions when Edgia mentioned the war during our habitually awkward conversations. As a rule we talked about insignificant daily matters and never touched on our shared experiences, not even remotely. As for Lolek, I felt immediately at ease in his company. We were on the same wavelength. He was a cultured man with good manners, and I was very eager that he should think well of me. I needed to win his confidence in order to find out whether Edgia had not by chance been babbling the truth about me.

Edgia and Lolek introduced me to their circle of friends, who were all my kind of people, immigrants from Europe, cultured and intelligent. Fortunately none of them had been incarcerated in my camp. I was drawn to them like a moth to flame. The group's frequent get-togethers resulted in my seeing more of Edgia than either of us really desired. We were both trapped in a situation which we had created ourselves but which we chose to regard as something that could not be changed.

And that is how I became Edgia's omnipresent representative from the past, and she mine. I was her living nightmare and she was mine. She symbolized my one and only moment of humanity, of kindness, and I — her moment of humiliation. I reminded her of the time when she had crawled on all fours and pleaded for her life. She reminded me of how I had raised myself to the level of self-sacrifice. In this manner, we became bound to one another in a singular friendship — our reward and punishment for having survived.

The first ten years of my life in Canada were financially difficult for me, but intellectually I accomplished a great deal. I mastered the English language. The only thing that upset me was my European accent. My teacher good-naturedly teased me with the assurance that I would never lose the accent, so I had better make peace with it. But for me this was not a laughing matter. The accent prevented me from becoming a new person.

Some time later, I opened a small ladies clothes shop, and as if to spite myself, I called it in French, "*La boutique européen.*" My European accent contributed to the continental ambience of the shop, which in turn appealed to the predilections of my customers. This made me realize how attractive Europeanness could be when it appeared in a non-European setting. My boutique grew even more successful a few years later, when I graduated from an evening school for dress design. After that, I prospered to such an extent that my clientele included some of the wealthiest and most socially prominent women in Montreal. The result was that my financial worries evaporated, but not my discomfort with my accent, which remained an attribute I would gladly have done without.

My new circle of friends also made great financial advances. They too were in the process of fitting themselves into new identities. Like Lolek, none of them had any intention of crying over the past. We were, all of us, determined to be positively inclined towards life, and we prided ourselves on looking forward, not back.

Our group of friends — and this was especially true of the women — took particular pleasure in getting together at Edgia and Lolek's apartment on Esplanade Avenue, even though it was more modestly furnished than that of any one else in the group. Socializing at Lolek and Edgia's place had the great advantage that there the women could relax. Not only did they not have to cook in their own homes, but they were also freed from the obligation of helping the hostess serve or clear the table. At these gatherings even the pretense of rising in order to help Edgia was superfluous. Dear Lolek's unusual amiability and hospitality expressed itself also in this — he issued a decree that no woman besides Edgia was allowed into the kitchen.

"Stay where you are!" he commanded in the barking tone of a theatrical general, snapping at any woman who attempted to help Edgia. And if one of us, just for the fun of it, did approach the kitchen with a tray full of dirty dishes, Lolek would block the door with outstretched arms, as if he were heroically guarding the entrance to a fortress. "*No pasaran!*" he would declare, playfully shaking his head as he sent the tray and its bearer back to the table. Or he would personally steer the miscreant back to her seat, his arm thrown over her shoulder in good-comradely fashion, as he added, "Really it's not necessary. Edgia and I would be insulted. Edgia does it all with the greatest pleasure."

If, on the other hand, Lolek and Edgia paid one of us a visit, it did not take long before Lolek began winking meaningfully at his wife. The result was that her contribution to the success of the evening was to take over the hostess's duties in the kitchen. Edgia did not even take up an extra seat.

I don't mean to suggest that the members of my circle of friends were not supportive or helpful to one another. On the contrary. There was a warmth and caring in their relationships which is rarely found among groups of friends born in this country. The group was a substitute for our closest family. But as far as Edgia was concerned, it was somehow not possible to have any serious regard for her. And it was Lolek, Edgia's wonderful husband, under whose spell we had all fallen, who saw to it that we should have no qualms about our treatment of Edgia.

Only once do I remember Edgia's name being mentioned at one of our gatherings. We were all a little tipsy and jolly, so we decided to play a word game. At that point, Pavel, the most reserved and quiet member of our group, suddenly asked, "Why don't we call in Edgia to join us?"

We all exchanged looks, and then, with a slight undertone of assumed guilt mixed with irony we called out, "Edgia, where are you? Come and join us!"

Edgia's head peeked out from behind the kitchen door, and her thin lips stretched into a pathetic half-smile. "Go ahead and play. It doesn't matter about me."

And this was the truth about Edgia. She did not matter. (Except, of course, in the special way in which she mattered to me.) Even among her closest friends, she was of no significance. With her characteristic pathetic little smile she served us so deftly at table that we hardly noticed when and how she did it. We turned to her with mechanical civility when we needed something from the kitchen, when there was a knife or a fork missing, or when we wanted another cup of coffee. We often became excited and thirsty from our heated discussions on the subjects of modern art or literature — subjects which were as distant from Edgia's concerns as day is from night, and which further caused us to forget that there was an Edgia in the world at all.

I would not say that Edgia was a fool or an idiot, or even that she was ugly. Far from it. But there was something in her manner which cancelled her out. She belonged to that type of woman who blends into her surroundings like an object to which the eye grows quickly accustomed and stops noticing. She was there and yet not there. It did not matter if what she had to say was clever or stupid. Nobody was curious about what she had to say. Her words swam past a listener's ears and dissolved in the air as if she had said nothing. Nor did anybody care whether she was beautiful or ugly. The pallor of her frightened mousy face, the delicacy of her profile and her opaque absent gaze ensured that the eyes of others would glide past her as if she were a void. She left no impression.

In addition she made herself appear smaller than she really was. Thin, slightly stooped, she always carried her head tucked in between her raised shoulders as if she were afraid that something might at any moment fall on her head. Even the tattooed number on her left arm seemed paler and more crooked than any other such number I ever saw. When I once advised her to have the number removed, she threw back her head in sudden anger and exclaimed "Not that! Never!"

Her shadow never darkened the doorway of a beauty parlour and her hair, which was the colour of mud — as though she had dyed it for life in the mud behind the camp latrine where we met for the first time — dangled negligently from her head, stiff, dull, and brittle. Long unkempt bangs covered her entire forehead to the eyebrows, as if she wished to hide her already-small face behind a curtain of hair. She dressed without taste —although neatly — in dirty-looking clothes of indefinite shape, as if in that way too she were trying to erase her presence from the eyes of others.

I behaved towards her as the others did, taking care not to betray the role which she had played in my life. I was convinced that she expected such behaviour from me. We were satisfied with one another. Basically, the way she looked pleased me. She looked just as I wanted her to look. I liked her very much. I told her so once, when we were alone.

"I like you very much too, Rella," she replied with a comical little sigh.

Just as Edgia counted for very little in our circle of friends, so her husband Lolek counted for a great deal. In my opinion it was only on his account that Edgia was even tolerated in our circle. The friends accepted her as if she were just a flaw in Lolek's character, a blemish on his personality. This made him, the hero of the partisans, appear more human in our eyes, nourishing both our respect and our compassion for him. There was no doubt in my mind that if Edgia had been single, as I was, she would never have been accepted by our group of friends. The group was very selective about who was allowed to join. We considered ourselves to be the intellectual elite among the new immigrants. If we decided to include somebody in our company that somebody had to be capable of making a stimulating intellectual contribution.

We were immersed up to our ears in modern culture and its achievements. Most of us had lost the last vestiges of religious belief in the camps, and since we required some form of faith to hold on to after the liberation, we seized on the idea of modern culture and allowed that to take the place of religion in our lives. This was the luminous bridge which we threw across the dark abyss of barbarous savagery that had once swallowed us. For this reason there were no greedier, more avid readers of the most recently published books than we were. We threw ourselves at every bestseller as soon as it appeared on the bestseller lists. We ran to all the modern and post-modern experimental performances. We enthused over pop-art and op-art. We even had a few marijuana-smoking sessions when that became fashionable. We practiced Hatha-Yoga and regularly visited a guru in his ashram in the Laurentians.

In our zeal we tried to effect a spiritual escape not only from the outmoded Jewish *shtetl* but also from the Jewish mentality that had once inhabited the East European metropolis. If culture symbolized a bridge, it had to be a bridge that led away from the past, no matter how sweet the memories that still bound us to our childhood and youth. We were frightened of the dampening effects that such memories could have on our present positive attitude towards life. We wanted no part of the past. We were dying to be in tune with the progressiveness of modern times. We wanted to absorb everything new that had been created since the Second World War. By inhaling the winds of change we tried to fit ourselves into the present, to incorporate ourselves into modern society, to be energetic and optimistic, at least on the surface. It was the surface that mattered and nothing else. What remained crippled and wounded within each of us was nobody else's business; it was a burden which we had to carry on our own.

The women of my circle were by no means less avid in their intellectual hunger than the men. We were modern women in the full sense of the word. And I would venture to assert that just as women are generally more devout than men, so our greed for culture was even stronger than that of the men (not counting Lolek). When you come right down to it, men's interests tend generally towards business and politics. For them, literary discussions or going to the theatre were no more than weekend pastimes. But the women, especially those who stayed at home keeping house and raising children, felt acutely the dulling effects of being constantly imprisoned in their homes. Neither politics nor business offered them any spiritual sustenance. So, for them, culture became a breath of fresh air. No, more than that — it provided a forum where they could indulge their inclination to devotion, even to fanaticism. As for me, who had no husband and no children, my passion for culture was another means of jumping out of my skin and obliterating the nightmare of my sins.

Pavel, the cynic in our group, took pleasure in labelling us sarcastically "culture vultures." He would call us this in Yiddish. In the group, we generally spoke either Polish or English, and it shocked us whenever, out of the blue, he burst out with one of his vulgar Yiddish expressions, in order to give spice to his critical opinion of us.

Pavel was a pharmacist. He came from Lithuania, but he had studied in Warsaw. He spoke Polish well and his English was as good as mine, if not better, because his accent was not as pronounced as mine. He was a man of middle height, broad-shouldered and heavy-set. He had a round child's face and a pair of deep blue eyes, which when viewed behind his thickly rimmed glasses seemed even larger and bluer than they actually were. The childlike innocence of his appearance belied his personality. He was an unhappy, bitter man, stingy with words, and without a spark of joie de vivre. I disliked him intensely. The mere fact of his unaccented English would have been reason enough for my dislike, but he was also a thorn in my side because of his penetrating gaze. His stubborn silences irritated me no less than the sickening philosophy of life which he preached on the rare occasions when he did speak up. True, his sarcastic remarks often found their mark, but precisely for this reason, they seemed tactless and offensive. Pavel resembled Edgia in having no burning passion for the achievements of modern culture.

But then it was not he, but Lolek, who was our spiritual guide. Lolek surpassed us all in his enthusiasm for everything that was new and stimulating. Like the other men in our group he was preoccupied with politics, but in contrast to the others, who did nothing but talk, Lolek was engagé and an activist. A humanist to the bone, he marched in all demonstrations and attended all rallies called in support of individual rights and freedoms.

Lolek was the heart and soul of our circle, its compelling force — even though his English was much worse than ours, worse even than Edgia's. He lacked the patience to acquire a thorough grounding in the language. Perhaps he had no ear for languages. His sentence structure was catastrophic, his choice of words horrendous, his idiomatic expressions unrecognizable. In later years he stopped speaking any language as it should be spoken. He mixed so many Anglicisms into his ungrammatical Polish that it sounded like a new dialect altogether. But, after all, what did it matter? The important thing was that we understood him perfectly well.

He was not only our inspirer, but also our chief animator, book provider and ticket buyer, a connoisseur of what was "in" and what was "out," our resident expert on contemporary sexual mores. Unlike the other men in our circle, he never discussed business, as if this were a topic that was beneath his notice. And he was in fact beneath the others in business affairs, which is to say that in financial terms he was a failure, and in comparison to the others, a virtual pauper.

He owned a small leather goods shop where he manufactured purses. Edgia, when she was not too sick, helped him with the bookkeeping, and performed the functions of an all-purpose errand-girl. Whereas the others in our group had long since moved into comfortable new homes in other parts of town, Lolek and Edgia were still stuck on Esplanade in the district of the Mountain, as we Jews called the neighbourhood near Mount Royal. This was the part of town where we greenhorns had settled just after our arrival in Canada.

According to Pavel our group was even more snobbish with regard to financial status than it was with regard to cultural status. Despite this, the sorry state of Lolek's pocketbook did nothing to diminish his prestige among us — a clear proof of the magnetism of his personality. He earned our respect for his idealism and contempt of material values, a respect which did not interfere with our own enjoyment of the things that money could buy.

We very nearly idolized Lolek. And to tell the truth, we preferred it when he came to see us without Edgia. When this happened we really were all on the same wave-length, although someone always asked him with feigned concern, "Where is Edgia?"

He would wave his hand dismissively: "She's not feeling her best today."

Edgia often did not feel her best. She suffered from migraine, stomach cramps, bellyaches, and all kinds of neuralgia. She was also prone to accidents. One day she slipped on the stairs to her door, another day she burned herself; one day she cut her finger, another day she fell and bruised her knee.

Another time when I asked Lolek where Edgia was, he shrugged, "You know Edgia. This won't interest her."

The "this" was usually a lecture about the most recent discoveries in sexual research, or an experimental film, or an exhibit of modern painting, or a concert of electronic music, or a nightclub, or even a day-trip to the guru in his ashram in the Laurentians.

I found Lolek's appearance and comportment, in fact the style of his masculinity in general, very much to my taste. He had a fine, interesting face with a high forehead. After a time he took to adorning his cheeks with trimmed sideburns as was then the fashion. When his hairline began to recede, he compensated by skillfully combing the long hair from the side of his head over the bald spots to form bangs, and by growing a mane of thick blond hair at the back of the head, which curled charmingly around his neck. He was not too tall, but he wore shoes with elevated heels which gave the impression of agreeable height. He dressed stylishly in shirts with open collars, a silken ascot of oriental design tied under his chin. Often he wore tightly fitted jeans, and in summer he wore tight shorts beneath a shirt kept unbuttoned to reveal his hairy chest. Around his neck he wore a gilded chain or a velvet ribbon from which dangled a miniature Maori idol—a symbol of fertility and a good luck charm. He was not overweight like the other men of our group whose middles, after a time, began to look like mobile bagel stands, the rings of fat stacked on top of one another. Lolek looked much younger than any of them.

One day, about ten years after I first met Lolek, I happened to be sitting — much against my will — next to Pavel in a car into which we had all squeezed for a drive to the theatre. Lolek was at the wheel. Pressed against my stubbornly silent neighbour, I tried to alleviate my discomfort by teasing him out of his reserve with a little verbal pinprick.

"It's hard to breathe in your company, my dear Pavel," I said, smiling at him. "If Lolek were sitting beside me I might have more air."

"No doubt about that," Pavel answered, with a glint in his blue eyes. "After all, Lolek is nothing but air."

"What do you mean by that?" I retorted, feeling offended for Lolek.

"Nothing more than what I said. I just wanted to explain to you why you would be so much more comfortable if you sat next to Lolek."

"I would be more comfortable because he is slim and you are as round as a barrel."

"Forgive me for that. I will do my best never again to be seated next to you."

I did not want him to take offence. I wanted to live in peace with all my friends, even with Pavel. "Don't take me so seriously," I said in a mollifying tone, as I patted his hand. "I only wanted to suggest that you might do well to lose a little weight." And in order to change the subject, and since Lolek was always on my mind, and I was very curious about every detail of his life, I broke my resolve never to mention the past, and took the opportunity to ask Pavel for information. "Tell me, Pavel," I whispered in his ear, "you know Lolek from the old country, don't you? When did you actually find out about his participation in the Resistance?"

Pavel did not answer, so I repeated the question. He fixed his deep blue eyes on me, while seeming to weigh his answer. Finally, he whispered back in my ear, "I knew it all the time, from the very beginning; that is, if participating in the Resistance means sitting in a hiding place and not being caught."

I was stunned by Pavel's words. I could barely fathom what he was trying to tell me, but that he intended to blacken Lolek's name was perfectly clear. So I exploded: "Who needs enemies with friends like you? Couldn't you have invented a more plausible lie than that about your most devoted friend?"

"He really is a devoted friend. And believe it or not, I am devoted to him too. But that doesn't change the fact that I was the one who supplied him with money and food while he was in hiding."

"So you're trying to say that you were the hero, not he?"

"Hero, my foot! My heroism consisted of the fact that I looked like an aryan and so could move about more freely and not be recognized as a Jew."

"But Lolek also looks like an aryan. He's blond after all."

"True, but he has brown Jewish eyes, while my eyes are blue."

"Edgia surely knows the truth about Lolek better than you do. She never stops babbling about his bravery."

"She needs to believe it. It makes her feel like a partner to his courage."

"So why don't you open her eyes for her and tell her your lying truth? Why don't you tell it to all of us? Why don't you confront Lolek with this particular truth?"

"You must be joking! Why should I do such a thing? Whom does he hurt? Whether or not he was actually a partisan, he still fought for his life tooth and nail, and he has had more than his share of suffering. He needs to feel that he is important and virile. Where is the harm in that? I would never have answered your question about him, if I hadn't wanted to make you see Lolek in a more realistic light — for Edgia's sake. Your innocent flirtation with her husband must cause her pain. She is so sensitive, and she has suffered so much!"

I ignored his remark and asked angrily, "But how can you be close to someone who is such a fake?"

Once again Pavel fixed his deep blue eyes on me. "He and Edgia are the closest people in the world to me. But I worry more about Edgia than about Lolek. She cannot seem to get back on her feet, and no superficial distractions are of any help. And Lolek himself is certainly no help. But since I can't do anything for them, I have to content myself with just keeping an eye on them, which I do also out of curiosity to see what effect this so-called normal life can have on two people who have miraculously escaped from hell."

I did not react to his words. I was too bewildered and distraught.

In the course of the next few days I mulled over what Pavel had said. Despite the shock his words had given me, they did not really manage to penetrate my consciousness. I was incapable of seeing Lolek in any light other than the one in which I had always seen him, and my feelings for him remained unchanged. It did not take long before Pavel's words began to seem like nothing more than tasteless gossip that I had picked up in some indistinct place, and they dissolved into such a haze that I managed to convince myself I had never heard them. Once again I saw in Lolek the former partisan hero and wonderful human being, the same dear friend, affectionate and loyal.

It made a woman feel good to be seen with Lolek in a restaurant or at the theatre. He did in fact often go out with us, his women friends, usually to places where the other men had no interest in going. I have no idea what he did with the other women after a theatre performance or dinner downtown, but when he went out with me he usually ended the evening by coming up to my apartment for "a cup of coffee."

I considered myself a liberated woman, although before the war I would have been called an old maid. During the war I had lost my first and only love. Then that monster Albert had come into my life and robbed me forever of the wish to live with a man. His *Ich liebe dich* murdered my belief in romantic love. I never married — not because I had no opportunities, and not because I had completely rid myself of romantic illusions, but because I did not want to have any children, so what would be the point? True, I would have liked to carry on the hereditary line of my family, but I was haunted by the fear that I might bring potential *kapos* into the world — that's how neurotic I was! My sexual encounters with men gave me little pleasure, but my loneliness would not permit me to give them up. My heart was rent by a million anxieties; terrifying hallucinations tormented me throughout the day. My sins pursued me and instead of diminishing seemed to grow to colossal proportions. I had the impression that the moment of reckoning lay in wait for me around every corner. Most often it seemed to peer at me from the eyes of children, especially from the eyes of ten-year-old girls on their way to or from school. My sleepless nights were steeped in horror. And when sleep would not come, and I tossed and turned on my bed, I ached for the proximity of another human being and yearned to feel the touch of warm skin against my skin.

Lolek looked up to me with respect and admiration. "You are the only one of us," he would compliment me, "who has completely freed herself from our spiritual ghetto." He raved about my excellent English, my up-to-date expressions, and my fashionable style of dressing. My chameleon-like qualities pleased him no end. In him I had an enthusiastic admirer and attendant. It required no more than a wink from me for him to run and fetch whatever my caprice dictated. He was always at my disposal. Time was never an issue. He managed to get away from his shop for hours at a time, leaving Edgia, whom he had trained, to mind the business.

Since Lolek and I were not indifferent to each other, the coffee-drinking at my apartment often dragged on until late at night. Becoming lovers was no more than a natural step in the development of our friendship. Lolek reawakened in me the distant memory of the poetic charm, the warmth, and heartfelt tenderness that had accompanied my first lost love. But no emotional scenes were ever played out between us, no jealous keeping of accounts, no reproaches, as often happens between two people who are as intimate with one another as we were. If Lolek ever unwittingly hurt my feelings, I forced myself to ignore the pain. My romance with him was my greatest treasure.

Lolek and I believed that we had no reason to be ashamed or to hide our conduct from our friends — or even from

Edgia. As far as I was concerned, I did not see why I should be circumspect with Edgia, and this was not because she was so unaware of what was going on around her, or because I was afraid of hurting her feelings. Such niceties did not even occur to me, since I seldom thought of her as a full-blooded person, but saw her instead as the symbol of my essential goodness. When it did occur to me to acknowledge her humanity, it was only to consider that she was more fortunate than I. Lolek put himself out for her. He would not abandon her, and it was to her that he actually belonged. I was jealous of her. So the reason I was not careful to hide my affair from Edgia had another source: I already knew for certain that Lolek knew nothing of what had happened between Edgia and me in the camp. He did not even know that we had been in the same camp together. I kept silent whenever our group's conversation turned to those times. I never so much as mentioned the name of my camp, and if I was asked where I had been incarcerated, I always answered vaguely, "Oh, it was near some Bavarian village."

I was grateful to Edgia for not betraying me. She, who was otherwise so weak and helpless, displayed an odd strength of character in this instance. Because of this, and because of my feelings for Lolek, I felt even more attached to her. This was why I considered it my duty to do nothing behind her back.

I will not claim that this was easy for me. Vestiges of the old sexual morality still clung to me, and they made me feel sick with guilt, a guilt which merged with my other powerful feelings of sinfulness. As a result, it became clear to me that my behaviour was no more than another form of flirtation with death. I realized that I was playing games with Edgia in order to provoke her into accusing me. That was why my frankness with her required a great deal of courage.

As for our friends, they reacted to Lolek and me as we

anticipated, and made no comment. Our group was made up of couples who had gotten married after the war, some for the second time. Most of these couples clung to each other and were very devoted. But only one or two of them were really well-matched. So I was convinced that the majority of our friends admired Lolek and me for daring to put into practice those freedoms which we preached in conversation.

Only Pavel, the silent and embittered one — embittered possibly more against himself than against us — would occasionally direct venomous remarks at Lolek and me. But that didn't matter, because Pavel did not spare the rest of the group either. He believed that we were a bunch of phonies, that we were not genuine or authentic in our feelings and behavior, that we were dilettantes who succumbed to foolish enthusiasms for every new fad — and all because we were afraid to face the truth. And that truth was that we felt alien in this new world, that we were so caught up with modernity because we found it so frightening.

But we were accustomed to Pavel's needling. His game was to cut everyone down to size, himself included. He too dragged behind him the baggage of the past. During the war, while he had been so preoccupied with caring for others who were confined to their hiding places, his wife and child had been captured, and he never saw them again. Throughout all the years, he never lost the feeling that he had been responsible for their deaths. Fortunately, he had Sylvia, his attractive, vivacious second wife. She would insist that he accompany her to our get-togethers. She held us in great esteem, and we, in turn, were proud to have her in our midst. She had come to Canada just before the outbreak of the war, but we considered her native-born, a genuine Canadian. Pavel did not appreciate her. He made her life difficult. More than once Sylvia complained about him to our group, how he sadistically tormented her with the reminiscences of his first wife and child, and with his habit of constant self-accusation.

But although we ignored Pavel's sarcastic remarks in the same way as we ignored whatever Edgia had to say, Pavel was by no means a masculine version of Edgia. First of all, he had had a university education, which we, whose university had been the concentration camps, envied. Secondly, although he lacked enthusiasm for current fashions, he nevertheless knew what was going on in the world. Moreover, he was capable of great kindness to others without making too much of a fuss. This I had to admit, despite my personal antipathy towards him. For instance, I knew from Lolek that it was Pavel who kept an eye on Edgia's health problems and that he did so in such a way that neither Edgia nor Lolek felt uncomfortable about it. This was why I felt a cold respect for Pavel at the same time as I disliked and avoided him.

And if Pavel was correct in his opinion of us, so what? Was not his opinion, especially about Lolek and me, basically superficial? How deeply, after all, could he peer into our souls? What did Pavel know about the real me, or the real Lolek, for that matter? The human tragedy — or better said, the human tragicomedy — harbours the sad truth that who-ever nourishes a viper in his bosom and consumes a daily dose of poison is blind to the fact that his neighbour nourish-es a similar viper and also subsists on a diet of poison.

Pavel did not know, nor did he suspect that Lolek and I were like two drowning people who cling to each other. Even if this clinging makes the two sink faster into the whirlpool, at least it gives them the momentary illusion that they have found a support and are saving themselves. What did I, apparently strong-minded as I was, hard and shielded as I was, possess in this world besides my salvaged lonely neurotic life, a life which demanded so urgently to be lived and which forced me to seize with gratitude and without scruple upon every grain of pleasure that fell across my arid path? And Lolek, who loved life so enthusiastically and joyfully — did he not have days of deep depression?

Whenever I felt indisposed or in a bad mood, Lolek would call me ten times a day to find out how I was doing. In the evenings, he would come over and stay with me. If something similar happened to Lolek, and he fell into one of his depressions, I reciprocated with the same solicitude.

If I called his home and Edgia picked up the phone, she would exclaim with exaggerated friendliness, "Oh it's you! How are you, Rella?" And without waiting for an answer, she would add, "Just a second. I'll give you Lolek straight away."

When Lolek got on the phone, I would tease him. "You see," I would say. "Your Edgia gives you to me." As I said this, the receiver in my hand would grow strangely heavy. Calling Lolek at home, when my call had nothing to do with our group, always made me uneasy.

One time when Lolek was in a deep depression and had no energy to leave home, I felt it my duty to visit him in his apartment on Esplanade Avenue. As I made my way there, I could feel my heart fluttering with joy and apprehension. I asked myself how Edgia would receive me.

A Montreal-style winding wooden staircase led directly from the street to the second-floor apartment where Lolek and Edgia lived and where our group's get-togethers so often took place. The apartment was long and dark. Only the living room possessed a large wide window with a panoramic view, a view which gave out on a large sports field in the foreground and Mount Royal topped by its cross behind. The furniture in the apartment was the same that Lolek and

Edgia had acquired in the early years after their arrival in Montreal. The passage of time had burrowed holes into the upholstery of the sofas and armchairs, sucked the vibrant colour out of the curtains and left them an indeterminate hue. But the rooms were neat, arranged with modest means yet in good taste. I had no doubt that Lolek had had a hand in creating this agreeable effect.

Edgia received me with a shy half-smile. She offered me a glass of tea, put some refreshments on the coffee table, and Lolek and I sat down, or to put it more accurately, sank into the deep sofa with the broken springs under the seat. I eagerly launched into a conversation, trying to cheer Lolek with my chatter about all kinds of cultural events, while Edgia served us. She forgot to bring lemon for the tea, an omission which Lolek politely brought to her attention in a silken tone of voice.

She clapped her hand to her cheek and exclaimed, "How absent-minded I am! It's coming right away!"

When she returned with the lemon, Lolek good-humoredly remarked in her presence, "Edgia lives on the moon."

Edgia nodded her head in agreement. "Yes, I have a weakness for astronomy."

Lolek winked at me meaningfully. We waited for Edgia to disappear into the kitchen and take with her the black tomcat which rubbed sensuously against her thin, rather shapely legs. She called the cat Loverboy. Once she was gone, I resumed my conversation with Lolek, and in this way a few hours passed. I could hear Edgia's voice coming from the kitchen as she talked to her cat, and I found myself imagining that she was preparing some poisonous dish for Lolek and me. With feigned cheerfulness I called out to her, "Edgia, what are you doing there? Why don't you come in and join us?"

Her head peeked out from behind the kitchen door and she favoured me with a crooked little smile. "I'll be right there. I just want to feed my Loverboy first."

I continued my chat with Lolek and waited for Edgia to join us. I expected — like one condemned yet brave — that at any moment she would appear before us with the poisoned dish, that she would fix me with a vengeful look and compel me to consume what she had prepared. That she craved vengeance — of that I had no doubt. I subscribe to the old adage which says that we resent most those whom we have the most reason to thank.

But Edgia did not emerge from the kitchen until just before I left. "Go in good health," she said. "Thanks for coming."

At this moment Lolek declared that my visit had so refreshed him that he felt ready to walk me home. We stepped out of the door onto the landing and remained standing in front of the winding staircase that led down to the street. Edgia and the tomcat came out to say another goodbye, and Loverboy began to rub against my legs. I was afraid that he would start a run in my nylons. I had an abhorrence for this black monstrosity of a cat, this disgusting pussyfooting spying devil with its knowing eyes which crept all over me like two green searchlights.

Edgia was well aware of how repulsive I found her cat. When she saw him winding in and out between my legs, she broke into giggles, then gave him such a powerful kick that he gave a shriek in a voice so high-pitched that it sounded nearly human. In the blink of an eye, the cat had vanished into the depths of the apartment. I was stunned by Edgia's brutality. In that moment I understood how much more I feared Edgia than I did her cat.

I carefully descended the stairs, fighting the feeling that at any moment a hand would push me from behind and I would roll down onto the sidewalk. I turned my head back and saw Edgia on the landing above leaning against the doorpost with the tomcat in her arms. She pressed him against her breast and I overheard her murmur to him, "Oh what have I done to you, Loverboy? Forgive me. I didn't mean to hurt you. Now hush, Loverboy, hush." When her eyes met mine, she waved her hand and called after us, "Go in good health and enjoy yourselves!"

I recall another time when I visited Lolek and Edgia alone and not with the rest of our group. On that occasion, Lolek had not yet returned from work. I had arranged with him to drive to a restaurant for dinner and then to the vernissage of an avant-garde artist who experimented with various kinds of chemical reactions to produce colour. Lolek's car had broken down and I was supposed to pick him up in mine at his apartment. Edgia received me as usual with exaggerated friendliness and invited me to make myself comfortable on the sofa. After a few minutes, she approached me, a smile both childish and cunning playing on her lips. She held a small faded photograph in her hand and showed it to me.

"See what a relative has sent me from Argentina?" she asked in a solemn whisper. "The little girl that you see here is me. I was ten years old then. I'm holding an award in my hand. I was the best student in my class."

My little sister Maniusha had been ten years old when she perished. The little girl in the photo brought back her memory with painful clarity.

"As you know, when we got to Auschwitz, they took everything away from us, the photographs too," I heard Edgia saying.

The name "Auschwitz" spoken aloud, and the remembrance of our arrival there, which Edgia's words so unexpectedly evoked, took my breath away. I wanted to block my ears, to stop her mouth with my hand, to run away. I grew stiff at the thought that at any moment Edgia might start to say more about Auschwitz, even though she had never done so before. Like me she never spoke about those days. Fortunately, she did not do so now either. As soon as we heard Lolek running up the outside stairs, she grabbed the photograph out of my hand and quickly hid it under the doily on the commode.

Lolek burst into the apartment like a tornado. Everything began to vibrate with excitement and expectation. He waved at me gaily and ran into the bedroom to change. I managed to avoid Edgia's glance, yet I did not want her to leave the room. Next to me on the sofa lay a book called *Epochs in Chaos* by somebody called Velikowsky.

"Are you reading this?" I asked Edgia with surprise.

Edgia bent her head to her shoulder and assumed the look of a moron. "I just look at the pictures," she giggled.

With a strange sense of revulsion I began to flip through the pages, just as Edgia stretched out her hand and took the book away from me. I noticed a small bandage sticking out from underneath her sleeve. Out of politeness, I asked, "What did you do to yourself?"

"Oh, it's nothing." She quickly pulled her sleeve over the bandage, adding in a whisper, "It's Lolek ... ."

I raised my eyebrows, ready to spring to Lolek's defence. "What do you mean?" I nearly shouted. "Does Lolek hit you?"

"Heaven forbid," she quieted me. "Lolek would never touch me. What are you thinking? He is the very embodiment of delicacy. You should know that by now. And the way he behaved as a partisan .... Why books could be written about that! He is too modest to talk about such things, but I know my Lolek. I'm the one who is the *shlimazl*. You know me. I cut my hand on the mirror, if you can imagine such a thing. It's my own stupid nature. Whenever Lolek makes the least remark, my head begins to spin. I've lived with him for so many years, and I still can't get used to his sense of humour. Whenever he calls me by his favourite nickname for me — he calls me 'holy Cunegunda' — I drop whatever I'm holding in my hands. You understand? I was combing my hair in front of the mirror. He was in a hurry to leave and wanted me to iron his pants. So he teased me. 'Why do you waste your time standing in front of the mirror? Do you think that the mirror will help your looks? Nothing can help a holy Cunegunda like you.' And he's right after all. So I threw away the comb, but so clumsily that my hand bashed into the mirror. The mirror was cracked, so it shattered."

I remember particularly the "historic" occasion of my birth-day, which for the first time Lolek forgot. His passion for me had by then started to cool, a fact of which I was ignorant at the time. That evening I could not bring myself to stay home alone, and decided to mark my so-called holiday with a visit to Lolek and Edgia. I put on a new white dress, and took along a box of chocolates, even though this was one day when I was the one who should have been receiving gifts.

Lolek was not at home. Edgia took the box of chocolates from my hand and put it on the table. "Lolek will thank you for this. He has a sweet-tooth, as you probably know." She left me sitting on the sofa, disappeared into the kitchen, and did not come out again. I found it a little tedious waiting for Lolek, but mostly, on that particular day, I felt drawn to

Edgia. In my mind, I went over all the birthdays of my child-hood, and I was particularly oppressed by the memory of my birthdays in the concentration camp. I got up from the sofa and went over to the kitchen door. I saw Edgia standing in front of a basin filled with water. Next to her on the table lay a gleaming knife and a large turnip, which reminded me both of my days in the ghetto when turnip was the staple of our diet, and of that monster Albert's grey shaven head.

"Today is my birthday," I said to Edgia.

"Oh, you don't say!" she exclaimed, wiping her palms against her dress and extending a damp hand. She kissed me. "I wish for you everything that you wish for yourself." She pressed me so tightly to her bosom that I had the impression that she would gladly have suffocated me.

I freed myself from her embrace and asked, "Why do you wash the clothes by hand and not in the machine?"

She began to titter. "These are not just any clothes. These are Lolek's shirts. Lolek likes me to wash his shirts with my own hands. This one, for instance ... ." She pulled a dripping shirt from the basin and showed it to me. "I'm washing this one for the third time. He wasn't satisfied with the way I tried to rub out the lipstick stains."

I had the feeling that at any moment Edgia would snatch the knife from the table and hold it against my throat. I left the kitchen and returned to the sofa in the living-room. Edgia fol-lowed me without the knife, drying her hands on a small towel.

"I am so grateful to you," she whispered, before coming to an abrupt pause, as if she lacked enough air to finish the sen-tence. "Grateful for what you do for Lolek. Be patient with him. People like him require a great deal of patience. He will soon be here and then he will also wish you a happy birthday. Personally I don't celebrate any birthdays. I have too many dates of birth to remember. You were the midwife at one of my births, or rather rebirths, remember Rella?" She stared at the black tomcat who was rubbing against her legs, as if she were addressing the question to him and not to me. Then she pointed her chin at the window, through which we could see the cross on top of the mountain. Illuminated by electric bulbs, it shone into the room through the navy blue darkness of evening. "Do you see that cross up there? Beautiful, isn't it? But I have the impression it's missing something. Guess what?"

"Jesus!" I exclaimed and burst into awkward laughter.

She nodded. "Yes, Jesus. Every cross should have its Jesus, and every Jesus should have his cross. Do you understand, Rella? The cross is the question and Jesus is the answer. Sometimes I believe that I am just such a cross and that I carry my Jesus on my back."

I looked at her inquiringly. Did she really mean what I thought she meant? But how could she, in her otherworldliness, ever have fathomed the depths of Lolek's tormented soul? I again gave an awkward laugh.

"Believe me, it's not a joke!" Edgia shook her head and put her hand to her breast. "I know Lolek's kindness, his generosity of heart. He would take the shirt off his back for you, for his friends, for all of humanity."

"But mainly for you," I ventured to give her a little prick.

"Certainly, mainly for me. For me he takes his shirt off so that I should wash it. He knows how I love to wash his shirts. It makes me so happy that he has chosen me to do this for him. You could search high and low and you would never find such another good man like Lolek. Why he's practically another Jesus!"

She sounded so sincere that the laughter died within me as a chill passed up and down my spine. I was gripped by apprehension that at any moment she might start to extol my kindness as well.

Later that evening, when I finally went out into the street with Lolek, he began to complain that Edgia was the major cause of his depressions, that something was terribly wrong with her physically and mentally, that she was absent-minded, lost in her own world, that she talked to her cat as if it were a person — friend and enemy at the same time. She kicked and caressed the cat, laughed at him and cried over him. Lolek said that he had no common language with Edgia, that her mind was mired in the nineteenth century, that she read and reread Tolstoy's novels, sighed and lamented over Dostoevsky's victimized and degraded characters. On those nights when Lolek did not eat dinner at home, Edgia's own meal consisted of nothing more than a turnip, as if she were still living in the ghetto. And sometimes she did not even eat that. If she did not go into work, then she did not see another human being all day long, nor take a breath of fresh air. It was no wonder, then, that she was always sick and that her head did not function properly.

"She can sit for hours by the window and stare at the cross," Lolek complained. "When I ask her what she's dreaming about, she answers that she is dreaming of a time when all the world's Jesuses will climb down from their crosses, become astronauts, and move to other planets. Because here on earth they don't fit in properly, and they do great harm without meaning to, and for this reason they are idolized. Those are the kinds of idiocies she tells me! As for the way she looks and the way she dresses, you can judge that for yourself. I know that all this is a hangover from the camps, and it's not that I am purposely impatient with her, but if a person behaves like a worm .... She looks like such a martyr with her saintly Cunegunda face and her frightened mousy eyes."

"Maybe if she had a child she would recover more quickly," I suggested hesitantly.

"What do you mean, Rella?" Lolek looked at me with reproach. "She herself is worse than a child, and certainly more helpless. Years ago she used to nag me about having a child. So I told her quite openly, 'First you yourself must grow up!' Do you understand, Rella? I could never have forgiven myself if such a thing happened. I don't want to have the responsibility of a child on my conscience. Fortunately, she no longer mentions it. But I still have the feeling that I don't treat her well enough."

"You treat her very well!" I jumped at the chance to defend Lolek against himself. "I see the sensitivity with which you treat her. I'm full of admiration for your patience and consideration. The very fact that you don't leave her... . You sacrifice yourself for her."

Gratefully, he kissed my hands with cold dry lips. Then he continued talking: "You have no idea what talent these broken people have for provoking feelings of guilt in those nearest to them. I would do anything to escape the guilt. I would run as far away as I possibly could." Lolek smiled sadly, like a little lost boy. "But how does a person escape from guilt? Can one escape from one's self?"

I felt an ache in my heart. I made an effort not to think of myself but to concentrate on Lolek instead, which was much less painful. "You don't have the least reason to feel guilty," I consoled him. "You yourself say, and rightly so, that this is all the fault of the camps. That's what broke Edgia, not you. On the contrary, you are what keeps her alive."

That evening Lolek was so serious, so immersed in his existential sorrow, that I gave up the idea that I had had earlier of going with him to a nightclub to celebrate my birthday. Instead we drove up to Mount Royal and took a walk around the lake and through the woods. The air was pleasant, mild and caressing. It was late in June, one of the first true summer evenings. But our mood was not at all summery. Lolek's despair was contagious. My heart overflowed with compassion for him — yes for him, not for Edgia. For her I felt only jealousy mixed with contempt. Her pathetic behaviour at once pleased and irritated me. I could not forgive the power that she had over Lolek — the brutal power of her weakness.

I turned Lolek's situation over in my mind until I came to this conclusion: "For you," I said, "it would certainly be better to leave her. No person has the right to poison the life of another. She is destroying you. I can see it clearly. She clips your wings. You will end by losing your joie de vivre, your interest in life. She might, heaven forbid, drive you to who-knows-what!"

Lolek waved his hand dismissively. "I'm a coward. I don't want to have her on my conscience. She would never be able to survive a single day without me. She is the cross that I must bear."

"You call this cowardice?" I exclaimed, full of admiration. "I am speechless ...."

I kissed Lolek by the light of the lamps on the mountain, kissed him with more tenderness than ever before, even though his lips remained dry and cold. We were standing under the illuminated cross on the mountain top. I looked at Lolek's pale suffering face in the glow of the electric lights which outlined the cross in liquid gold. I was ready to give myself to him right there in the dark shadows which the cross threw over the blue bushes. More than at any time previously, the torments of his soul made the blood boil in my veins and I was overcome by a passionate longing for him.

After a while I succeeded in convincing him that we should go to my apartment — it would be his present to me on this special occasion. I found it humiliating to have to resort to this particular argument, when not very long before he had been so eager to spend an evening at my place. But I also derived pleasure from my humiliation, which helped me to mobilize all my female charms. Thanks to them I even managed to talk him into staying with me the entire night! It was one of the most beautiful nights of my life, because if I still envied married women it was only for the reason that they spent entire nights next to the warm body of a man. Despite the fact that I had lived alone for so many years, I was still beset by a terrifying loneliness every night when I lay alone in my empty bed. It seems that, just like hypochondria, the craving to be with another person is an affliction for which there is no cure.

At the beginning of this night with Lolek, images frequently flashed through my mind of Edgia lying alone in her bed the way I usually did. But after a while I imagined that she was not alone, but lying together with Lolek and me, entangled in desperate proximity.

In the morning, after I had gaily chattered away an hour at breakfast, while Lolek sat across from me, sleepy and somewhat bewildered, the moment finally came when he had to leave me and face the harsh realities of life. He went home to change for work. Not long after he left, Edgia called. Her voice grated hoarsely.

"Is Lolek all right?" she asked.

"Why do you ask if he's all right?" I asked her back, in order to gain time while I decided what to tell her. The receiver in my hand seemed to weigh a ton.

"I understood that he is with you," Edgia went on. "This is the first time that he hasn't come home to sleep. I stayed up all night looking out the window for him. He didn't even phone, so I began to worry whether — God forbid — something might not have happened to him." Suddenly she cried out in an exaggerated tone of childish delight. "Oh, he's just come in! Guess who I'm talking to on the phone, Lolek sweetheart?" I heard her exclaim. Then she shouted into the receiver, "I must hang up! He won't let me talk to you. He says that you are a creative and productive person, and you are in a hurry to get to work." She hung up.

I was surprised when, late that same day, Edgia called me again. "Lolek wants me to invite you to our place for breakfast tomorrow," she mumbled. "Tomorrow is Saturday, and he wants me to tell you that you must on no account refuse."

"What do you mean?" I stammered. "What for? And why doesn't he come to the phone himself?"

"He says that he's in a bad mood. A deep depression ... . And he wants me to invite you myself in order to show that I am not angry at him and not at you. So I'm inviting you."

I understood what was at issue. Lolek needed this gesture on my part. So I suppressed the unease that I felt in my heart, and the next morning went off to take my breakfast with them.

As we sat down at the table in Edgia and Lolek's kitchen, Lolek — with extreme politesse — bade Edgia prepare a glass of hot chocolate for me. I usually drank hot chocolate with my breakfast every Saturday morning. Edgia had also prepared my favourite Saturday breakfast, pancakes with maple syrup. Lolek complimented me on my figure, telling Edgia that I never needed to count calories, because I was a creative and productive person. I burned them off with all my energy and accomplishments.

The pancakes tasted heavenly. You could say what you liked about Edgia, but not that she was a bad cook. As usual, somewhere in the back of my mind there nagged the suspicion that Edgia had put poison in the pancakes. And she looked so awful in that faded housecoat of hers — her pale face had a bluish cast, and her small mousy eyes were rimmed with red — that I almost lost my appetite.

That summer went by like a dream. It was a glorious joyful time, followed by a long golden autumn. I felt wonderful. The air around Lolek and me vibrated with something close to incipient love — at least I thought it did. I was looking forward to an interesting winter season. Lolek made sure to buy our theatre tickets well in advance, so that the members of our group would have good seats next to one another.

That winter began with a series of snowstorms followed by a spell of brutally cold temperatures. The outside staircases of buildings like the one in which Lolek and Edgia lived had to be regularly scraped clean of the accumulated ice and snow. But even then, they were dangerous because they were very slippery, making it imperative to hold on to the railing. But whenever Lolek was with me, and even when he was in the company of other women, he would run down — virtually fly down — the stairs so skillfully that the neighbourhood children would gape with admiration.

That was how the tragedy occurred.

Lolek slipped while running down the stairs, not of his own building, but of a building of questionable reputation in Old Montreal by the port. His head knocked against the iron banister with such force that he got a hemorrhage. His wallet appeared to have been stolen even before he fell, because there were no identifying documents on his person when he was found. It took thirty hours before his identity could be established.

After Lolek failed to come home to sleep that night, Edgia called me the next morning to ask how Lolek was feeling. Stunned and deeply hurt, I told her the truth — that I did not know, because I had not seen him. When she began to whimper and moan that her heart was full of foreboding, I first tried to calm her, then lost patience and banged down the receiver.

I was in turmoil myself. At first I thought that something had in fact happened to Lolek — that was the effect which Edgia's apprehensions had on me. But then I calmed down. There was only one thing that could have happened to Lolek, I told myself: He had spent the night with another woman. But this was not a happy thought either. After all, the past summer and fall had had a particular emotional significance for me; it had been the time when my love for Lolek had started to germinate. His disappearance this night was proof that he did not take me seriously and had not been sincere with me. I recalled what Pavel had told me about Lolek and his attempt to fool the world into believing that he had been a partisan. It suddenly dawned on me that a man who was false about one aspect of his life could be just as false about any other aspect.

That whole day I kept to myself. I did not call Lolek and Edgia. The next day, Sylvia, Pavel's wife, phoned to give me the news of Lolek's death with all the gruesome details.

Our group of friends was in shock. The guiding light of our small familial circle had been extinguished. Lolek, who had been so full of life, of curiosity and playfulness, of ideas and idealism, who had been so greedy for joy and pleasure, was no more. It was difficult to make peace with the fact. We felt orphaned. But whatever grief the others felt, I felt doubly. With Lolek's passing from the world, fate had played me a spiteful trick. Lolek, dishonest and false though he was, had been a light in my life. I had never gotten to the point of actually loving him — another proof that the camps had forever deprived me of the ability to love — but I had badly wanted to love him. I had taken delight in the pretense of being in love with him. Now the abyss of my loneliness yawned before me and I was engulfed by darkness.

During those days of mourning, we all worried about Edgia. We were afraid that she would have a complete breakdown. How would she ever be able to go on living without Lolek? She had worshipped him. And how, in practical terms, would she manage? She had never made the slightest move without Lolek. She had always lived in the clouds. Nor was she physically very strong.

But after a while, as often happens, our friends stopped calling or visiting Edgia. Nor did she keep in touch. Other dramatic events in the lives of this friend or that took priority and our contact with Edgia was completely broken. The group hardly noticed this. Just as we had once hardly noticed her actual presence, we now did not notice her absence. She would, in any case, not have fitted into our group without Lolek.

As for me, I did remember her. I remembered her very well, and in a strange way I began to miss her, even more than I missed Lolek. Deep in my heart I felt some satisfaction that Edgia, the living proof of my humanity, existed in this world, and I felt relief that the tragedy had occurred to Lolek and not to her. More than once I had the impulse to visit her, but forbore because I could not predict her reaction to such a visit, nor how I myself would handle it.

In this way more than a year passed. I heard from acquaintances that Edgia was beginning to return to normal, that she went to the factory every day, and that somehow she was learning to master the handbag business. People started to say that she had a strong character. Then I heard that her factory was growing and that despite the recession, she had been able to hire two more artisans. Word also went around that she was exploiting her workers.

Time went on. I found myself thinking often of Lolek, but more often still of Edgia. I still intended to call her. More than once I already held the receiver in my hand when a warning voice ordered me to put it down. What should I call her for? What would I say to her? Should I ask her to forgive me? Did I really regret my conduct with Lolek, even if strictly speaking it had not been morally *kosher*? Did I not hold dear all my memories of the hours that we had spent together? And why willingly throw myself to the wolves? I expected that now Edgia would point her accusing finger at me — and so take her revenge.

So things went until one evening I suddenly found myself face-to-face with Edgia during an intermission at the theatre. She was standing in the middle of a group of men and women, total strangers to me, holding a glass of liqueur in her hand. Of course I did not have the slightest doubt that I was looking at Edgia, although the sight of her stunned me. Before me stood someone entirely different from the person I remembered — a blooming attractive woman, an apparent reflection of myself.

She was wearing an elegant suit, and my professional eye immediately discerned that it was made of the most expensive imported fabric, and that it was cut in the style which I myself had introduced into fashion. In her high-heeled shoes, which were very similar to mine, with her thin shapely legs, her perfect posture, with the head carried proudly above the shoulders, she seemed taller than the shrunken Edgia I had known. In fact she seemed almost as tall as I was. Her small face, with its delicate features, its short nose and tiny mouth, was framed by a halo of wavy hair, dyed black — my hair colour— and it was combed in my style. She reminded me of an unfurled flower. Only a few deep wrinkles on her forehead, which I noticed beneath the strands of hair, bore witness to the fact that it had not been easy for the flower to straighten itself.

The odd thing was that despite our strange resemblance it took Edgia a long time to recognize me — or perhaps she only pretended not to know who I was. But when she noticed that I remained rooted in one spot gaping at her, she gave a gasp of surprise and hurried towards me with a radiant face. She threw her free arm around me and pressed me so tightly to her bosom that, just as in the past, I was afraid that she would crush me. She then ordered a liqueur for me and introduced me to her companions. She praised me so effusively to her friends, with such eloquence and humour, that the blood rushed to my face, and I felt embarrassed and uncomfortable.

"Rella is a creative and productive person," she concluded. Then she asked me what I thought of the performance. "Pinter really gets to me," she said. "He's as powerful in his way as Tennessee Williams is in his, don't you think?" She discoursed enthusiastically on Pinter, displaying such erudition that I was overcome with envy. Her eyes glistened with delight.

"Why don't you ever come to our get-togethers any more?" I felt prompted to ask.

She answered defensively that she had no time. "The days are too short now that I have to manage the factory, and I have no end of things to catch up on. But let me know the next time you go somewhere. I will gladly join you. I haven't seen you all for so long!"

Our group of friends began to meet with Edgia again. After all, there was so much which tied us — and especially me — to her. And every time that we met with her she rose another notch in our esteem. Of her former giggling, stammering self not a trace remained. On the contrary, she was forceful and convincing in what she said. She was clever, profoundly knowledgeable, and had a wonderful sense of humour. She contributed the salt and pepper to our table talk. Even the reticent Pavel took her seriously, and because of her, began to participate in our discussions. We started to sense that without Edgia our get-togethers lacked lustre, even more than had been the case with Lolek. Somehow Edgia's presence added weight and meaning to the friendship of our group.

I would say that the only obstacle to our getting along harmoniously with Edgia was the fact that she was a woman. What an irony! We women noticed that she bewitched the men — and especially Pavel — with her cleverness and charm. This meant that a gradually lengthening shadow of jealousy fell across our admiration for Edgia. We were ashamed of this feeling. After all, this was the same Edgia as of old.

As for me, I felt even worse than the other women. Edgia humiliated me by usurping my position in the group. I certainly did not lag behind her in intellectual matters, especially not when it came to contemporary issues. But just like Pavel, Edgia mocked modern culture and the group's tendency to be swept up by the latest trends in books, paintings, plays and music. She thought all this flimsy and irrelevant, just passing fancies, the result of the post-war confusion of values in all spheres of human endeavor. She held fast to her Shakespeare, her Tolstoy, Dostoevsky, Thomas Mann, and the like. And the upshot of it all was that I, who had once taken such an active part in our discussions, was now afraid to open my mouth. I was afraid that at the least provocation Edgia would contradict me with some devastating argument, that she would discredit me in front of everyone, or that in the heat of discussion she would point an accusing finger in my direction and exclaim, "How dare you speak! You were a *kapo*!"

But the mysterious power of attraction that existed between Edgia and me ensured that, despite all complicating sentiments, it was precisely at this time that she and I should become truly intimate friends. In addition to the past, which bound us so closely, we now had a business connection through my fashion boutique and her handbag factory. We understood each other's business problems, and we inspired one another in matters of style and advertising. I was flattered as well — although I sometimes suspected that she was mocking me — that she religiously followed my advice on how to dress and on fashion in general.

Edgia was in the best of health both summer and winter. I never heard her utter so much as a sigh. When I once mentioned her former illnesses, she replied as if she herself were surprised, "Yes, they have all disappeared. Maybe I was too spoiled." She winked at me. "Taking up sport must have done me some good."

Edgia had become a disciplined sportswoman, displaying an unexpected skill in whatever she attempted. She tried tennis, and talked me into playing with her. She and I also met first thing every Saturday and Sunday morning, rain or shine, at the top of Mount Royal, just below the cross. Dressed in our sweatsuits, we would jog the few kilometers down to the lake and then up again to the cross. This done, content and perspiring profusely, we would set out for my apartment, take a shower and busy ourselves in the kitchen. Edgia prepared her famous pancakes and I prepared my specialty, a delicious cup of hot chocolate. Then we stretched out on the bed, put on a record of classical music to please Edgia, and another of modern music to please me, and chatted and joked, some-times also discussing more serious matters of the heart — but we never touched on anything remotely related to the camps.

If the topic of Lolek came up, we did not try to avoid it. On the contrary, we both became very involved in the con-versation. There was not the least hint of reproach in Edgia's attitude towards my relationship with Lolek. At times I had the impression that his memory was dearer to me than it was to her. When we spoke of him my voice sounded less steady than hers. At such moments, I felt more than ever that I was in her power, but somehow this no longer bothered me. And so our conversation would flow on in a tone of heartfelt regret. We would analyze Lolek's complicated tragic person-ality, and then let him swim away on the current of our words while we concentrated on people and events more closely connected to our present-day lives.

I began to need Edgia more and more, and she seemed to need me. I felt acutely not only Edgia's intellectual superiori-ty, but her superiority as a person of clean conscience. I was always alert to what she might say or do. I became her echo. I copied her wisecracks and witticisms. I craved her praise, and gave in to her in everything. For her part, she seemed to copy my mannerisms and my style. She copied my appearance, my bearing, and my attempts to keep up with the times in mat-ters of fashion. From time to time we felt the urge to needle one another with sarcastic questions or remarks, but I was always careful not to arouse her anger.

One day when I was at her apartment, I suddenly realized that the black tomcat was nowhere in sight. So I asked her, "Edgia, I don't see your Loverboy anywhere. What happened to him?"

She stared at me as if she did not understand what I was talking about. Then my meaning dawned upon her, and she burst out laughing. "Oh my tomcat, you mean? He's been gone for three years. I accidentally scalded him with a kettle of boiling water."

I shuddered, as if she had at that very moment poured a kettle of ice-cold water over me.

Every year, the pages of the calendar seemed to flip by with greater speed. My complicated friendship with Edgia flourished, but her friendship with the other women in our group faded because of her aggressive behaviour and the attraction which she held for the men.

This was how things stood when we discovered that Pavel had fallen head-over-heels in love with Edgia. Pavel was in every respect Lolek's opposite. Despite his many good qualities, he had never occupied the same position as Lolek in our esteem. He did not possess Lolek's charm and boyish attraction. He was too sober, surpassing Lolek in one particular only — his honesty. He was, in fact, too forthright for my taste. More than once, one of his remarks threw cold water on the group's spontaneous enthusiasms.

It was not long before Pavel separated from Sylvia, a separation quickly followed by a divorce. Pavel went to live with Edgia, and as day followed night, they soon got married.

This dramatic romance in the midst of our circle of friends brought to the surface undercurrents of antagonism against both Edgia and Pavel. We stopped meeting with them.

As for my own reaction, I felt a double dose of that peculiar pleasure that one feels at the misfortunes of others. It always gave me a secret satisfaction to hear that a couple had separated. This was a proof to me that I had sacrificed very little by not marrying. But I was also pleased that Edgia had married again. I hoped that this would diminish her uncanny hold over me. I believed that I knew human nature well, and could predict people's behaviour. Edgia, according to my ideas, belonged to that type of woman who automatically assumes the same role with regard to every man with whom she has a relationship, even when the men are such contrasts as Pavel and Lolek. In my imagination, I saw Edgia stop imitating my looks and manners — which made me uneasy — and gradually revert to the servile, pathetically smiling, little mouse whom I remembered from the days of her marriage to Lolek. It gave me pleasure to fantasize how she would look in her shapeless clothes. In my head I dressed her that way, adding a new black tomcat at her feet to complete the picture.

For a long time I heard nothing from Edgia and Pavel, nor did I run into them. Not that Edgia had ceased to occupy my mind, or that I did not have the impulse to call. On the contrary, I could not stop thinking about her. But, for my own good, I forced myself to keep a distance in order to breath freely in an atmosphere where no-one knew of my past as a *kapo*, and no-one could point an accusing finger at me. I remained loyal to my group of friends. Anyway I disliked Pavel. I even began to believe that I had finally freed myself of Edgia, despite my obsessive thoughts about her.

But the day came when I could no longer restrain myself. I managed to convince myself that the demands of business made it imperative that I get in touch with Edgia. I called her, but a strange voice answered in Greek, and I understood that Edgia had moved away from Esplanade Avenue. I searched the phone book and discovered that Edgia now lived in the elegant residential district on the other side of the mountain. I called her. She was very friendly — too friendly. She invited me to her house, or more accurately, I saw to it that she should invite me. After all, she had done me no harm, nor I her. At my age and in my loneliness, I could not afford to lose good old friends. It was so difficult to find new ones.

So we stepped back into our friendship as if it were a pair of comfortable old slippers. I could once again keep an eye on Edgia. I was even more concerned than I had been with Lolek that Edgia should not reveal my secret to Pavel. I still felt a cold regard for him, and I was still frightened of his frank penetrating gaze. I also saw to it that our group of friends should again begin to socialize with him and Edgia. Edgia, by virtue of her relationship with Pavel, had been neutralized, and the women's jealousy of her had evaporated. Besides, Sylvia, Pavel's former wife, had moved to Florida where she had remarried.

As soon as we began to meet again at Edgia and Pavel's house, we noticed that between these two there bloomed a late and ardent love — although mainly this appeared to be Pavel's love for Edgia. It radiated from him with an intense glow, a flame permeating the entire atmosphere of their house.

Every time that we visited — they invited us quite frequently — Edgia sat at the head of the table and led the conversation, while Pavel served us, smiling with pleasure. Later, whenever we decided to meet at their place, we stopped saying that we were going to Edgia and Pavel's, but said only that we were going to Edgia's. And that was how it was. Edgia dominated our get-togethers. If the always-cheerful Pavel did venture to say something, Edgia jokingly finished the sentence for him, which amused all of us, including Pavel. And if Edgia held forth at the table, Pavel nodded his head encouragingly at her. If he made a remark to give her support, she tenderly put her hand to his mouth, and said lovingly, "Don't help me out, dearest."

I became a frequent guest at Edgia's. She felt at ease in my presence, had no secrets from me, and only wanted to know how I would do certain things if I had been in her place. We used to relax in the alcove off her bedroom, sprawled in comfortable black leather armchairs which stood next to the window. On the window ledge was arrayed a row of flowerpots. Edgia hated cut flowers. The mountain, topped by its large cross, loomed just outside the window.

"That cross follows me everywhere," Edgia complained. "It pierces my eyes. Maybe if I could hang a Jesus on it, it would leave me alone."

She said this in a whisper, as if she were afraid that Pavel, who was busy in the kitchen preparing tea, should hear her. I never knew what she meant by this, but I was afraid to ask.

Edgia often discussed Pavel with me. She poked fun at his appearance and his negligent manner of dressing. Once when the subject of masculinity came up, Edgia asked me, "What would you do if you had to deal with a loverboy who was constantly melting with tenderness and affection at the same time as he was shockingly shy and inhibited?"

She never raised her voice when she spoke about Pavel, but she developed the habit of speaking in a hiss whenever she was irritated with him, which she often was. She called him "loverboy" in the same grating tone she had once used for her cat.

Since I was under Edgia's spell, I viewed everything through her eyes. Her attitude towards Pavel appeared to me quite normal, and I was pleased with it. After all, I had never liked him myself. It now seemed to me that he acquired the look of a moron whenever he was in Edgia's presence, that he had become a mere rag of a man without a shred of self-respect, a nothing, a zero.

So I nodded in agreement whenever Edgia hissed out her complaints against Pavel, which occurred whenever something in their house was not in order, or when Pavel did not bring something she requested quickly enough, or when the photos he had taken of her did not turn out well. I consoled her as best I could. I sympathized with her. I understood her despair and the extent of her existential malaise.

"He hasn't got the faintest idea what I am all about," she would complain. "Not who I am, nor what I am. He never stops living in his own masochistic fantasies, beating his breast for having abandoned his wife and child forty years ago. He poisons my days. He clips my wings."

"You must break free of him," I advised her.

She stared at me with astonishment. "Break free of him? How can I? I would never forgive myself if I took such a step. Can't you see for yourself how attached he is to me and how much he loves me?"

I usually managed to avoid meeting Pavel, but one time I dropped in when Edgia had not yet returned home from the handbag factory. In order to have something to say, I asked him how Edgia was doing. His face twisted into a painful grimace. "Not too well," he answered and led me into the living-room. He turned to face me, and the deep blue of his eyes poured over me with bottomless sorrow. "That is" — he seemed to be forcing himself to speak — "that is, superficially, everything is fine, but deep inside her nothing has changed. Once she was servile, now she is aggressive, and it all springs from the same source, from her feeling of worthlessness. I had hoped that my love would cure her, but it seems that not even love can repair the wounds which she suffered in the camps. Maybe if she could just bring it all out from inside her ... . But she refuses to talk to me about it. Did she ever tell you anything about her experiences in the camps, Rella? You are such close friends."

"Never!" I said sharply, feeling my throat tighten.

"Not one word, eh?" he shook his head, and as if he had grown tired of the tension, he sank into an armchair and motioned me to sit down as well. So we sat in silence for a long time and looked at each other. I felt very uncomfortable. I longed to hear Edgia's steps on the landing. I was about to jump to my feet and run out of the room, when I heard him say, "She did once tell me about a strange dream that she had. In that dream she saw herself in the role of a *kapo*. She even described how she looked and — forgive me for telling you this — but the figure in which she saw herself resembled yours. I tell you this, Rella, not in order to pain you, but in order that you should understand her better. She picks the closest people, those most devoted to her, to avenge herself on for the wrong that was done to her. Basically we are all like that." Now the blue of his eyes embraced me with sudden touching warmth. "We must stand by her, Rella. She is dear to both of us. And who can know as well as we what goes on in the dark corners of her soul?"

I don't know why, but I started to cry. The first and only time in my post-war life that I ever cried was in front of Pavel, of all people.

A short time later I learned from Edgia that Pavel had high blood pressure and a weak heart. Edgia insisted that he give up his work, and she became the only breadwinner. Pavel took care of the house. He bought food, cooked and prepared the meals. Needless to say his cooking could not be

compared to Edgia's. I know this for a fact, because I frequently took my dinner with them. Edgia often forgot that
Pavel was forbidden to eat heavily salted foods.

"You put on too little salt, Loverboy," she playfully
caressed the top of his balding head. "What's the matter,
don't you love me any more?" Usually Edgia turned such
incidents into a joke and more than once when I was eating
dinner with them my sides nearly split with laughter as Edgia
comically mimicked her cook Pavel.

When we — I mean our group — drove out to the
Laurentians for the weekend, Edgia proved the most energetic mountain climber among us. She would insist that for
Pavel's good health he should climb with her on this or that
moderately steep slope, which she had picked out beforehand
to suit his capacity. She believed that he exercised too little
and that mountain-climbing would fortify him. When they
returned from climbing and Edgia sat down to rest, she
would send Pavel on errands — she required another pair of
shoes, a cold drink, a handkerchief with eau de cologne to
wipe away the sweat. When, panting, he finally sat down next
to us, Edgia would describe how clumsy Pavel was at climbing. She did this with so much bubbling humour that the
tears came to our eyes from laughing — and they came to
Pavel's too.

When we vacationed in the Laurentians, Edgia did not
neglect our usual routine of jogging in the morning. Seven
o'clock sharp, she would knock at the door of my motel room
and at eight o'clock we would meet on the road that passed
through a pine forest. Pavel waited for me along with Edgia.
He ran beside us for part of the way and when he got tired,
he sat down on the stump of a fallen tree to rest and wait for
us.

As we ran, Edgia took pleasure in every blooming bush

and every majestic tree. The sight of wild flowers awakened her enthusiasm. I nodded my head as she spoke, but I did not share her pleasure. When it came to the beauty of the Canadian landscape I might as well have been blind. I looked but I did not see. It was better for me that way. The landscape reminded me too strongly of the district that lies at the foot of the Carpathian Mountains, where I had used to spend summer vacations in my childhood. One time as we were running, Edgia pointed out a cluster of particularly colourful wild flowers and said, "In Auschwitz no flowers grew, remember Rella? But when I was there, in order to keep up my courage, I would conjure up just such clusters of flowers in my imagination, and I would decorate the entire globe with them."

The last time we drove out to the Laurentians was on the eve of a hot summer weekend. When I opened my eyes the following morning, I was drenched in sweat, and I could feel how heavily the air weighed on me. It was going to be an unusually humid day; the sky was preparing to storm.

That same morning, even before we began our jog, Pavel collapsed on the road, and Edgia and I could not rouse him. I ran back to the motel to call a doctor. When I returned to the road, I could hear Edgia's wailing from the distance. I saw her sitting in the middle of the road, Pavel's head and part of his body cradled in her lap, as if she were the Pietà and this was to be her last comment on the theme of the empty cross.

"What have I done? Oh my God, what have I done?" she cried.

Pavel was driven to the hospital. Edgia never left his side. Whenever I entered the hospital room to visit Pavel, I saw Edgia sitting in the same position, bent over her husband's body, swaying over him, mouthing half-phrases and broken words. As soon as she saw me, she would stop talking and stare at me though red swollen eyes. All the sorrow of the world screamed at me through those eyes. I realized that I had yet another Edgia before me, a completely new person with a new emotional make-up, a new knowledge, which had no connection to the sort of knowledge that I and our friends had so eagerly pursued. Who was this new Edgia? I was very much afraid of her.

The last time that I came into the hospital room, Edgia stared at me for a long time with those same eyes. A strange worshipful expression smoothed and relaxed her face. She straightened herself, came out from behind Pavel's bed, and approached me. So we stood, eyeball to eyeball. That was when I heard her dry heavy voice speaking those fateful words: "I thank you, Rella, for having saved my life. I thank you for everything. I have decided that we two, you and I, should never in our lives meet again. I no longer want your friendship, and I no longer want to give you mine. It was a sick, a poisonous, an impossible friendship."

Her words shattered my heart like an explosion. A pall of darkness fell over me. Edgia's sentence seemed to pulverize me, to reduce me to dust. The end flashed before my blinded eyes, and ever since that day I have peered into the depths of that end.

I never saw Edgia again. From acquaintances I learned that Pavel was out of danger. Edgia brought him home, took care of him day and night, watched and trembled over him. Friends told me of the atmosphere that permeated their house, and in my imagination I visited them, sensed the heavy silence, the expectation, as if someone were constantly praying. Then I heard that Pavel was much recovered, that he was walking around the house. Carefully, not wishing to betray the fact that Edgia had thrown me out of her life, I continued to seek out news of them. This was the thread that I tried vainly to hold on to. In this way I learned that Pavel could go out of the house and that he was well on his way to a full recovery; that in their home, there was now an atmosphere of peace and calm, that from both Edgia and Pavel there radiated joy and serenity. I was told that Pavel had become more talkative than he had been before, and that Edgia's humour was no longer so aggressive and biting, but had grown milder and gentler.

Not long after these events I began to lose the desire to join the others at our get-togethers. I hardly noticed how distant I had grown from them, nor how I was losing my passion for things that had once interested me. I no longer possessed the drive or the eagerness to chase after the always-changing times. Time became for me a stagnant water which had crystallized in one spot. I peered into it and saw that all that remained to me was the nakedness of my guilt, which I no longer had the means to dress. My loneliness no longer troubled me. I avoided people and at the same time took a dislike to my beautiful apartment and my "*boutique européen.*" I ate my meals in restaurants and sat there for long hours staring straight ahead and seeing nothing.

After a time I heard that Edgia and Pavel had also lost contact with the group. Like stars drawn towards different orbits, we had finally managed to tear ourselves away from the constellation of our friendship, which had held us together for so many years. The last news I had of Edgia and Pavel was that they had liquidated all their assets and set off on a long voyage around the world.

And now I too am about to embark on a long voyage, a voyage which Edgia precipitated by removing herself from my life. With this she cancelled my only moment of humanity, which I had thought would cleanse me of all sins. She had never pointed an accusing finger at me, and so she left me with the feeling that I must point the finger at myself, that I must let all the world know that I was a *kapo*.

This was Edgia's revenge. So be it. I am, in any case, sick and tired of the fear of being found out, sick and tired of myself. So I sit here and stare at my medicine, my vial full of sleeping pills, brightly coloured like beads.

Every criminal craves the moment of judgement, no matter how afraid of it he might be. I sentence myself willingly. I return to the camp, to the scene of my crime. The slice of life which I managed to sandwich in between the two camps — the camp that was forced upon me in the past, and the one which I am about to force on myself — was not tasty, nor worth the price I paid for it. I remove the lying inscription above the entrance to Auschwitz, *Arbeit macht frei*, work makes you free, and replace it with another, "death makes you free." I take the hand of my little sister Maniusha and promise her that I will never betray her again.

TRANSLATED BY GOLDIE MORGENTALER

A House with
Seven Windows

Kadia Molodowsky

❦

The story of Kadia Molodowsky's proud, strong heroine is played out against the background of the Khibat Tsion *period. A mid-19th century movement, it embraced and expressed the age-old dream of Messianic redemption and the desire to "normalize" Jewish life through a return to, and settlement of, the ancestral land of Israel.*

The drive towards self-realization was accelerated by the Russian pogroms of the early 1880's and widespread European anti-Semitism, resulting in the First Aliyah. Rosh Pina, settled by First Aliyah pioneers in 1882, was the first "modern" Jewish colony in the Galilee. Its symbolic name, "chief of all cornerstones," is derived from Psalms 118:22, which is recited regularly in synagogue.

BASHKE WAS THE ONLY GIRL in Grodno county who could sit a horse as well as any lord. Her father was a wealthy tenant farmer who rented fields and meadows from the lord of the manor and kept a hundred head of cattle.

When she rode out to nearby Brisk, it was in a chaise, no less, drawn by two fine horses. Yankl, her coachman, sat on the upholstered seat, holding the red-tasseled whip, as straight and as proud as if he were coachman to the daughters of the czar. He would polish his boots for half an hour before driving out with Bashke.

Bashke's blue eyes and small, upturned chin possessed a stubborn beauty that seemed to be teasing the whole wide world: "Well, who will outdo me?" On meeting her in the woods, the squire always found topics for conversation. He would stop his carriage to ask, "Where are you off to, Bashke? How is it you're so pretty, Bashke?" And once, "It would well become you, Bashke, to be a noble-woman." Bashke's eyes flashed, and the stubborn little chin seemed to challenge as she answered, "It becomes me just as well, my lord, to be the daughter of Mendl Shapiro."

The two coachmen, Vasil and Yankl, sat stiffly, neither uttering a word to the other. Yankl's broad back was clearly taunting Vasil: "You may be driving the squire, but I'm driving Bashke."

In the district, talk and speculation. "Whom will such a Bashke marry?" She married a young lumber merchant, a scholar, and she loved him. In Brisk, where she had moved with her husband, Bashke ran her house with great generosity: she had taken Yankl and the chaise with her and never went to town on foot except on *Shabes*. On *Shabes*, Bashke could be seen walking to *shul* or visiting her husband's family. When she stepped out with her husband, Reb Iser Paperno, it was all substance and status: she was Bashke Shapiro and he, a golden scion of Brisk already shaping his own rich future.

There were always guests at Bashke's table: merchants conducting business with her husband, emissaries soliciting for a *yeshive*, visiting rabbis, preachers, paupers and random travellers. Bashke greeted every stranger with respect. In the city her house was renowned; Jews called it "Jerusalem."

Once a Warsaw merchant came to Iser Paperno on business. Friday evening, after they had concluded the *Shabes* songs, he told about a newly-formed association of Jews in

Warsaw that was buying property in the land of Israel and emigrating to build a city there. Bashke's eyes brightened with an inner flame. "What type of Jews are they?" "Jews like all other Jews, " answered the merchant. "My brother-in-law is one of them. He's going with his wife and children." "How old is he?" asked Bashke. "He's twenty-eight and has four children."

Bashke served tea with cherry syrup and cookies. As the merchant prepared to leave, she said to him, "You've brought us glad tidings; may they come to fruition." Her husband, Reb Iser, gave her a puzzled glance but out of respect added, "And may there always be good tidings among Jews."

The business transaction with the Warsaw merchant was highly successful. In one year Iser Paperno doubled his worth but he took no joy in it. Bashke had been transformed. She frequently alluded to the group that was purchasing land in Israel.

One Saturday night, immediately after sundown, Bashke lit the lamps as if it were a holiday and sat down to write a letter to the group. The next morning she went off in the chaise to have it promptly mailed by Yankev Ravinovitsh, the postmaster.

Yankev Ravinovitsh knew all the town's secrets. When he was curious about the contents of any letter, he'd open it, read it, reseal it and then mail it; his curiosity, God forbid, harmed no-one. He read Bashke's letter as well. It pleased him greatly that Jews were buying land in Israel. "Just imagine! They'll overtake the Messiah — no joke!"

Within two weeks there was talk in Brisk that the Papernos were buying land in Israel. "The rich! What do they have to lose?" Then a rumour spread that the Papernos were leaving for the land of Israel. No-one had the nerve to ask either Iser or Bashke about it, but they fell upon Yankl the coachman like flies. "Are they really buying? Are they really going?" Yankl either knew nothing or was feigning ignorance. "No business of mine! If the master goes, I'll drive the horses."

A year passed. The town simmered like a stew. "Reb Iser doesn't want to go, but Bashke — steel and iron!" Everyone was curious as to who would prevail: Iser or Bashke?

Many of the town's families earned their livelihood from Reb Iser's lumber business: the agents, the bookkeepers, the brokers, the dray men and the watchmen. These, the stronger faction, were united in their belief that for Bashke this was a delusion that would pass, with God's help, as do the caprices of all rich women. The second faction, neighbours and relatives, said that if Bashke was caught up in the idea of building a city in the land of Israel, she would build a city. "Bashke is Bashke."

One sunny day before *Peysekh* Bashke went to Warsaw, not by coach like the merchants, but by train like her husband, Reb Iser Paperno. When she arrived at the train station in her chaise, driven by Yankl, the town's coachmen had already congregated to see whether she really would set foot on the train. Even those who had no passengers had cracked their whips and headed for the train station.

When Bashke came back from Warsaw, the secret was out. She had purchased land in Israel. Reb Iser Paperno would remain in Brisk and Bashke was "making *alie*." They started speaking of her emigration to the Land of Israel as "she is ascending."

After *Peysekh*, Reb Iser Paperno and Bashke went to the rabbi. They stayed there from after evening prayers until late. A decision regarding the children had to be made. Reb Iser was prepared to deed the purchased land for a *yeshive* and to pledge that he would send his oldest son to study there after his *bar mitzve*. Bashke argued that Jews were going there to build a city and she wanted to be among them with her children.

Reb Iser's mother burst into the rabbi's study. The prosperous Eydl Paperno, wrapped in a shawl, wailed, "Rabbi, they're taking my children from me!"

"I'm not, God forbid, leading them into idolatry," Bashke answered her. She rose from her chair and offered, "Sit, *Shviger*." Bashke remained standing. Her blue eyes were suffused with light and quietly she said, "Who will accuse me, God forbid, of leading my children into evil ways?" No-one replied.

The Papernos' house and large courtyard were cluttered as before a wedding. Crates stood braced with iron strapping. There was a pile of hay in the middle of the yard, and Yankl carried sacks stuffed full into the house. Dishes were being packed for meat, dairy and *pareve*, for *Peysekh* and for the whole year round; pots, pans, linens and bedding.

Reb Iser Paperno kept working at his business as if nothing were happening at home. His staff came in, he checked accounts with them, gave them letters and sent messages.

Neighbours commented more with glances than with words. "God help her; and him, the poor unfortunate, may God truly help, staying here alone! A saint! He's letting her take the children."

The crates were already loaded on one wagon, the bedding and food stuff — dried bread and cookies, cheeses and smoked meats and schnapps — on another. The children sat there, the older a boy ten years of age, the younger a little girl of four.

Reb Iser stood beside the wagon with the children. His eyes were wide open but he looked like a blind man who doesn't see the light. Beside him, almost shoulder to shoulder,

stood Yankl the coachman, confused and flushed like someone who'd just come out of a fight.

"We're going now," said Bashke quietly, as if pleading.
Yankl didn't move. "Yankl!" Bashke called, "Yankl!" And
when Yankl, his senses numb and disobedient, did not
respond, Bashke looked around, pressed her lips together and
said quietly, "The horses too will obey me." She got into the
wagon, sat down on the driver's box and pulled the reins.
Leaning down from the box, she said, "Iser, may we be
blessed with joy in our children, Iser!" and she drove out of
the courtyard.

Through their windows neighbours could see Bashke herself driving the wagon with her children. They pinched their
cheeks and covered their faces with their hands. "God protect her, such courage!" Some ran out and shouted after her,
"May you succeed! May you arrive safely!"

As the wagon went down the street, Yankl came to. For
the first time in his life he had not obeyed Bashke. Tearing
himself from his place, he ran after the wagon as if possessed,
calling, "Mistress! Bashke!"

In Rosh Pina, Bashke Paperno's house stands with its seven
windows. The courtyard is enclosed in tall eucalyptus trees
and it is known as "Bashke's Courtyard."

Her grandchildren and great-grandchildren with blue eyes
and up-tilted chins refuse to sell or rebuild the house. If a
wall sags, they repair it, so that it may continue to look as it
did when Bashke built it.

TRANSLATED BY ETHEL RAICUS

HER STORY

Chava Slucka-Kestin

❧

*"Her Story" introduces a fascinating spectrum of themes
and dilemmas in addressing the rarely discussed theme of
intermarriage between Arabs and Jews. Set at the incep-
tion of the State of Israel (1948), the story-within-a-story
structure simultaneously tells of its heroine's traumatic
survival of the Holocaust and of her experiences in Israel.
Throughout her difficult life, Paula must don one mask of
identity after another. As she peels them off, exposing herself in the recounting of her life story, the reader is confronted with both Paula's choices and her experiences.*

PAULA ALWAYS WALKED with head held high. Her pensive face
was suffused with a spirituality that not all in the community
could understand. She radiated kindness and love — a kind of
transcendence. Her love for humanity, rooted deeply in
childhood, had been planted by her beloved schoolteacher.
She felt enmity to no-one, except one person — Yekhezkl.

Years ago Paula had come with Mustafa to live with his
mother in this neighbourhood in Jaffa by the seashore. No-
one knew her real story. In the Arab community she was welcomed with love and trust; in the Jewish community they
could only gossip and invent stories about her. She had no
use for them. She would go about in her candid manner,
looking everyone frankly in the eye, head high. Let the
women satisfy their curiosity. Let them talk.

She would bow her head only when she noticed butterflies or bees hovering around her flame-red hair as if it were a red-flowering field. This was a habit from the times when she had had to hide her maturing body from all those around her, especially her breasts that filled out like two ripening apples. She had had to conceal her developing body, her joy in becoming a young woman. Her very life had been at stake.

Paula's only pleasure then had been in the beauty of the countryside around her. She would remember her teacher's words: "Put your ear to the ground and you will hear an entire universe." So she had lain on the grass, ear to the ground, and heard a world of sound. She had been happy to be still alive. Despite the loneliness, the surrounding beauty had heartened her, enabled her to go on, to persevere. At night, though the rumble of the death trains had filled her with dread, she hadn't given up, waiting for the day when she could once again become herself.

Although now she held her head high, a perplexed expression hovered about her lips. She carried too much within. "A hundred lives," she used to tell her husband, "they can tear you apart." From the Holocaust to this very day, conflicting experiences and struggles had been part of her life.

It was quiet now in the house. Her mother-in-law, old Fatima, was sleeping. Mustafa was at a meeting about the repeal of restrictions on Arabs. The children were sleeping and Paula didn't feel like reading. To this day she still read Polish books. Today she wouldn't read. She would mend some underwear for the little ones.

How strange fate was! How many characters can one person contain within, reshaping herself each time? How had it actually begun? She began to unravel the ball of suffering she had lived with until she met Mustafa.

The first time she had met him at his job in the laundry she had felt the intensity in his glance, and, uncharacteristically, she had surrendered to it. She had sensed in him an intimate friend.

Paula had come from time to time to bring her husband's clothes to be cleaned or washed. Had it not been for her simple and modest manner, one might have believed that she had deliberately stained the clothing in order to meet Mustafa. The truth was the stains had been the marks of too-frequent partying and drinking. Never from family celebrations. To Mustafa, these stains confirmed her weariness, the pensive loneliness on Paula's face.

Paula remembered her mother's saying: "A person's soul is reflected in their eyes. And the proof is that in Yiddish we call the iris of the eye a *mentshele*, a person in miniature." As a child she had thought that a person contained not one soul but two. She had also thought then that one needn't display one's soul to all and sundry. When she disliked or feared someone, she lowered her eyes. She had developed a habit of lowering her eyes with their thick golden lashes when she met a piercing glance. But Mustafa's gaze she withstood; never before had she seen such tender warmth in a pair of deep black eyes. The only language they shared was the language of eyes.

Every time Mustafa waited for Paula to arrive, he had felt the bond between himself and the married Jewish woman become more deeply fateful. Until finally he had summoned his courage and she had agreed to meet him.

How different this first meeting with Mustafa had been from that first tryst with Yekhezkl, the leader of the group in Cypress. From their first encounter, she and Yekhezkl had been afire. This passion had ended Paula's earlier interest in

Amos, the young Israeli who had come to Europe in search of family, and had fallen in love with her. Almost immediately Yekhezkl had the marriage sanctified with a borrowed ring and witnesses.

In the beginning she had been happy with Yekhezkl. For the first time after long wandering and loneliness she was close to another human being. She had found a brother. She had interpreted Amos' look of regret and warnings against Yekhezkl as mere jealousy. Amos had tried to talk to her, but Yekhezkl had created such warmth around her, gratifying all her wishes, that she didn't want to hear Amos' words, lest her happiness be shattered.

The first evening she had been together with Mustafa, they had sat on a rock under a eucalyptus tree. Both had been silent. Mustafa had put his hand boldly on her shoulder and asked, "Who are you? I feel the burden you carry robs all joy from your lips, and stifles the youth in you."

"It's a long story, Mustafa. I'm prepared to tell you if you have the patience. I don't know whether you can understand all of it. All those things were far from you: the Hitler war, all that the Jews lived through at that time."

"I've read of these things more than once in *Al Itahad*," he answered in his quiet way. "We feel for the brotherhood of all peoples; it's painful to us that Hitler's barbarism destroyed six million Jews as well as other peoples."

"I didn't mean to insult you, Mustafa. There are also Jews who haven't lived through all that and don't grasp the horror, the hell we lived through."

Both had again fallen silent. The full-branched eucalyptus tree blocked the moon, and they both felt it best that way. A bright moon might have kept them from the disclosures the evening was to bring to draw them together.

Paula looked up and glanced around the house. She had been so lost in her memories that she hadn't noticed her fingers moving automatically, mending the children's clothes. Again she went back to the thread of her first meeting with Mustafa. She remembered it all, word for word. She even heard his choked voice begging her, "Tell, Paula, tell it all."

"Yes, they discovered the granary. Mother, father, the children, all were sent away. I heard nothing more about them. Of the entire household, only Uncle Yoske and I remained. I was all of thirteen years old, and he was still a young man himself. We survived only by sheer luck. There wasn't enough room for everyone to sleep in the granary behind the barn, so every night we two hid in the haystack. On that terrible night I heard my family's screams and cries. I wanted to come out of my hiding place, but Mother's warning followed me: 'Paula, child, remember, even if you hear the worst, don't move, don't leave the hiding place, be strong.' Now I wonder, was it cowardice or perhaps a strong will to live? But I was trembling with fear. I thought the soldiers would hear my teeth rattle."

When Paula went back to the moment of how she had survived that night, her memories felt as alive, as real, as if it were today. She relived the past in all its intensity, in all its horror.

In the early morning stillness, as Paula followed the thread of her memory, she recalled coming out of her hiding place to find Yoske waiting for her. "No-one was in the house. We began searching for survivors. We went out to the fields. Maybe someone had hidden there. In the potato fields lay the Marusiaks, face down. By then I had already seen people shot, but the image of those two sturdy peasants with arms outstretched still pursues me.

"Their son Stashek had vanished. Once two years later when I was with the Sovitskis in Yanovke, partisans came looking for food. I thought I recognized Stashek amongst them. But that is another story, another transmigration in my path of suffering. At that time I was dressed in a peasant dress with a kerchief covering my head and much of my face."

She sighed deeply and couldn't continue her story.

"Something is disturbing you, Paula; perhaps another time?"

"No, my love," she had uttered for the first time, and nestled close to his chest which gave her the security and impetus to get past that anguished chapter in her life.

Paula had glanced at her watch and quickly taken leave of Mustafa. "I'll come back to this spot in three days."

At the agreed-upon time, Mustafa had already been waiting for Paula. As soon as she had arrived, she started.

"In Yanovke, near the Keltz forest, there were also partisans. At that time, the partisan section of the *Armya Krayova* still accepted Jews. My Uncle Yoske came upon this idea: he took a heavy peasant fur coat and hat from the Marusiaks, tied it around me with a leather thong, and we went along the edge of the forest to the third hamlet. As evening approached, we entered the first house along the outskirts of the village.

"At first the peasant thought that we were lost and wanted to stay the night. It never occurred to him who we really were. When the old lady Sovitski went into the kitchen to prepare something to eat, Yoske told Sovitski that Hrobri, the commander of the partisan unit, had sent us here, and that he, Sovitski, should hide the girl. Yoske would return in two weeks' time, and anyone who harmed her would put his own life in jeopardy.

"The suspicion that had crept into the old man's soul

intensified when I took the kerchief off my head; it was stuffy in the house. His eyes began to move restlessly from my head of wild red hair to Yoske. Fear of the partisans, who always carried out their threats, left him speechless. Yoske figured out the old man's dilemma and said to him, 'You, grand-dad, don't be so scared. We'll shave her head, dress her like a boy, and she'll be your shepherd.'

"Old man Sovitski remained silent. He was weighing his options. His son had gone to Keltz and hadn't returned. No-one knew what had become of him; not surprising in a war like this, thought Sovitski. Anyway, she could be helpful around the house."

Paula remembered that right after her first talk with Mustafa, he advised her to write it all down, at least her experience in the village as a shepherd. And she did. She had hidden the notebook in her room so Yekhezkl wouldn't find it. And now she kept it in her dresser at home, under the children's clothing. She put aside the mending and sewing. Everyone in the house was asleep. By the time Mustafa returned she would have managed to reread the memoir. The reading gave her a particular pleasure.

"And now I entered yet another incarnation. I was no longer a peasant girl, no longer Marta with the Marusiaks. I was now Yanek, though everyone called me 'Baldy.' In the village I had no other name. The Sovitskis kept me out of fear of the partisan's revenge and for one other calculated reason: if I were to leave and be caught by the Germans and under torture were to tell them where I had been hidden, the Sovitskis would have been incriminated. Then their fate would have been sealed. So I stayed.

"True, Yoske's threat to return also influenced them. Sovitski still waited for him, but I decided if he didn't come, I would look for him in the forest.

"My hard work won the Sovitskis' respect. The old man found books from an abandoned estate and while grazing the cow and his few sheep, I managed to read in hidden corners, taking care not to arouse suspicion. I had decided to find Yoske. And one evening when I was about to bring in the animals, Yoske appeared for a moment and told me to come to the woods.

"The story is so simple: I became a boy. This didn't mean merely wearing pants to enjoy freedom, as women do today. I had to learn to live not only in different clothes, but in a different skin — that of a slow-witted peasant.

"To make sense of the events in the forest, I must first explain that the character I had to play and become was the dull orphaned shepherd. Everyone felt free to make fun of me, to push me around. I learned to avoid people. In the village people didn't talk much to me; because when they did, the Sovitskis put finger to forehead, intimating that I was not right in the head.

"Finally I went into the forest to look for the partisans. From talk and stories I had an idea into which part of the forest they regularly disappeared. So I went poking about, deep in the forest, and it came to me that I didn't recall the Polish name Yoske had assumed. Despairing, I turned to retrace my steps out of the forest. As though to spite me, two armed partisans appeared. They shouted 'Halt.' My heart sank. What saved me was my looks. Everything I wore was too long, too big; the straw hat perched on my bald head was the final touch for a tattered scarecrow. As I came nearer, they burst out laughing. 'What kind of creature is this — neither man nor beast.' I stammered and told them that I was gathering mushrooms. They didn't answer, not a word, and left. I began gathering mushrooms ... .

"But I never saw Yoske again. I was left alone. What a lost opportunity — had I known Yoske's new name I would have revealed my whole secret story. But as it was — go tell them! They would never have believed me."

Here Paula had ended the story. Mustafa's devotion had unravelled the knot around her heart. Her spirits had lifted, she had returned to her home, where she waited long hours for Yekhezkl. It was late at night when he had finally come home after a "meeting." He smelled of whiskey.

Where had Yekhezkl gotten the energy to get up so early and go to work the next morning? He had apparently inherited a strong constitution. For her part, Paula had been glad that he left her alone. She had simply wondered what sort of party this *Yemay Kherut* was that it allowed its members to lead such a life? Before Yigal, their son, had been born, Yekhezkl had even introduced her into the party. She had sensed a great deal of materialism, but had also found decent people probably misled. Although she had suffered, her concern had been for the child. Little by little, Yekhezkl had totally neglected her.

All of this she had once told Mustafa. When he looked at her in amazement, she had explained that there are men who find their own wives intolerable once they have borne children. "It sounds strange, but it doesn't interfere with their love for their children. It is a particular form of degeneracy. My husband Yekhezkl is this type of man." She had continued the story. Publicly they had managed their family life so that no-one could fault Yekhezkl. "At the office, a diligent clerk; as to his habitual late-nights — he justified these to the neighbours as part of his community involvement. I wore myself out hiding everything from everybody. All this made me nervous and upset. This is why, Mustafa, our encounters are such a joy to me."

The meetings with Mustafa had become more frequent. Tsipe, the neighbour, took care of Yigal, and when Tsipe went out, Paula took care of her two children. As happens between neighbours, they quarreled. Actually, this was the issue: immigrants versus *vatikim*, early pioneers. Paula never let anyone belittle her, and she had been afraid of Yekhezkl, but not for herself, for the child.

This time Tsipe had maintained that the *vatikim*, the "chosen," had accomplished so much with such great suffering. Now the immigrants had come to profit from all their hard work. "And us?" Paula seethed in anger, "we who survived the seven fires of hell, we who came directly here and who love this land as much as you? We don't have to prove it. See how many of the *vatikim* deserted, not only to America, but even to West Germany."

In revenge Tsipe had told Yekhezkl about Paula's evening outings. Where to, she didn't know. But Yekhezkl had asked, searched and found her out. He had immediately raised an alarm in the entire neighbourhood that his wife was betraying him with a dirty Arab. He had reviled her using the most foul language.

Paula compared Yekhezkl and Mustafa, their morals, their behaviour towards her. How could she have joined Yekhezkl's party, even for a short while, when it sowed such hatred towards Arabs? Now Yekhezkl hit her, pulled her by the hair, and shouted, "You fake 'Mrs. Modesty,' a mother of a child and not even ashamed!"

That same evening she had fled to Mustafa's and had remained there. Once she was with Mustafa, Yekhezkl had become really wild, spying on them, spending entire evenings hanging around the laundry where Mustafa worked.

Mustafa had settled Paula at Matilda's, the Bulgarian woman who had once tried to sell her the Polish Communist newspaper *Volka*. Paula at that time still belonged to the *Yemay Kherut* party with Yekhezkl. She hadn't wanted to know or remember her past. Because of this, Paula didn't feel comfortable with Matilda at first. But within a day they had developed a mutual understanding and became closer. She wasn't Tsipe the snobbish *sabra*.

The persecution had intensified and Paula and Mustafa left the town for Jaffa, his mother's home.

But they had torn the child from her. Living flesh cut from her breast. Because she lived with an Arab. Although Yigal was still a minor he had been awarded to his father. This was the law. She obtained a *get*, and finished with Yekhezkl. He put Yigal into an institution. When and where she had never been able to find out.

When Mustafa came home, Paula was still sitting with the memoir in her hand. It had been almost eight years since she had been united with Mustafa. She had borne him three children, two girls and a boy; lively, happy, healthy children. Children raised with both parents. And the other, Yigal, was almost eleven years old. She looked into the distance; in the shallows of the stormy sea, ships sailed and approached the shore. But the sea forever beat the shore. And the thought never left Paula that Yigal still longed for her. So many years since she had seen him last.

The twins, the two girls Suad and Hadidja, were in school, little Akhmed was ill in bed, old Fatima had gone to see her son in Lod and the sea made Paula more restless than usual.

It was Yigal's absence that made her happiness incomplete. She had once again taken on a new way of life. Again she had

had to make herself over, to acquire new habits and undertake a way of life so different from the one she had lived till now. She spoke the language fluently, with the vividness embodied there by the ancient Arab people. It was unbelievable how this fair-skinned, red-haired woman lived with the joys and hardships of her husband's family. But as always she had no peace. Always longings, contradictions, complexities.

"Why are you so lost in thought, Paula?" She felt Mustafa's hand. She tore her gaze from the sea, looked at him confused for a moment, not knowing where she was. "Paula," he continued, "how is Akhmed?"

"Much better. Probably by evening he'll be fine. He's sleeping now; don't wake him."

"I took time off at noon; I was worried abut him." She felt a sharp pain in her heart. Maybe somewhere Yigal was sick, but who sat by his bed? Mustafa embraced in the restrained Moslem manner. Although Mustafa was not religious, he expressed his concern about his son by asking Allah's protection for Akhmed.

Paula contemplated. "What joy my two little girls are, and Akhmed, who's beginning to understand what's being said to him! But fate is not as kind to everyone." She would eventually have had to leave Yekhezkl, but how was Yigal to blame? "I'm a felled tree," Paula thought to herself. "The roots have remained but my oldest branch has been severed from me."

TRANSLATED BY RONNEE JAEGER

FIVE STORIES FROM "IN THE ALLEYS OF JERUSALEM"

Rikudah Potash

❧

As a Yiddish writer, Rikudah Potash is an anomaly. Born in Poland, she wrote in Yiddish about the mizrakhi *Jews from Turkey, Yemen, Salonika and Bukhara amongst whom she lived in her chosen city of Jerusalem. Her unique prose anthology* In geslekh fun Yerushalayim *[In the Alleys of Jerusalem], published posthumously in 1968, intertwines Yiddish with Sephardic Hebrew to portray Jerusalem life in the early days of the State of Israel.*

In "Jazal the Purim Player," Jazal dons a mask, a traditional component in the celebration of Purim, which allows her the creative and assertive expression denied to women of her time and culture. She becomes the heroic Queen Esther whose intervention on behalf of the Jews is recounted in Megilat Ester, *the text read on Purim.*

The protagonist from the story "Prikhah's Complaint to God" is an unschooled woman who wants to function more effectively in the world. Because she is a woman alone, she is thwarted and ridiculed.

"G'ula and Shulamit" is a sketch of two girls from different cultures who share their dreams and aspirations. In the presence of their families, however, they choose to silence their imaginations.

Rikudah Potash

In *"Pirkhah Ozeri,"* two sorrows unite to forge a new future through the act of naming. Destruction and oppression are thereby transformed into hope.

"Shraby's Daughter Comes Home" depicts generational differences between the traditional and observant world of Sephardic Jews and the new realities of the State of Israel. Underlying the story is the conflict between beliefs in messianic redemption and redemption by human intervention.

Jazal the Purim Player

A SOFT AND ROSE-LIKE SCENT drifted over the Bukharan quarter in springtime. Almond trees gave off this rosy scent and it was as if the heavens themselves were in bud. Birds chirped without end and the little sparrows lovingly took food from each others' beaks. They sang of a new spring day, though oftentimes there were still muddy and dirty pools of water left in the gutters from the severe winter. Even these were drying out, and you could see a coloured pebble which the children had tossed in together with their paper boats when pretending to sail far, far away, all the way to Sodom.

Mimosas veiled in soft yellow tulle bent and whispered springtime secrets to the breeze. The mimosas were so delicate, so playful in the wind, but you mustn't touch them or they'll droop. Into the midst of this duet of wind and mimosa shuffled the form of Jazal. Jazal was an old Yemenite woman who lived in the Bukharan quarter. Even though she frequently criticized the Bukharans, she wouldn't leave this place. Here she had settled, put down roots in this enchanted courtyard where only slender, delicate almond trees grow. Her kingdom was small and cramped.

Down below behind the great house, in the low road almost level with her window, Jazal had lived many a long year. Jazal didn't like to talk about herself. She lived her life according to her own view of the world. But somewhere lost within her was a classic among Eastern types, capable of performing theatre but not quite aware of it. Jazal remembered that when she was a young girl in Sanaa, in old Yemen, she had loved to mimic different types of people, to copy their expressions and sing their songs. Songs which sometimes told of drunkards, sometimes for no reason at all, of lunatics and also of buffoons. But that was long past, shadows really, like paper cut-outs wandering in her memory just as they do in everyone when they grow old. For Jazal, there was no great distance between her girlhood and the present. When she added it all up, by thirteen years of age she had already become a mother; it seemed to her that everything that had happened to her had been but a dream. Her husband the *shoykhet* believed that all the fowl he'd slaughtered would return during the *slikhes* period, shrieking and carrying on, demanding to know why he'd killed them. He himself was now in the "true world." Sometimes the *megile* of a wasted life would unroll before Jazal. It was, she thought, a life in which her years now returned to her, as the fowl had returned to her husband, crying, "Why did you slaughter us?"

Not a single line of bitterness, God forbid, had been etched on Jazal's face. The very opposite was true. Her face was smooth, dark-skinned and full of charm, with huge green eyes. Perhaps they were not green at all but their depth changed in the daylight. Perhaps she had chameleon coloured eyes which changed with her wisdom, becoming two deep reflecting wells containing the great mystery of the source of life which ebbs and flows, ebbs and flows, welling from unknown distances and depths. Alone, like a straw fallen into the sea that cannot escape the waves and is tossed about in the swirling waters. Year after year, Jazal swam within the enclosed borders of the Bukharan quarter. Her colourful clothing lay hidden in the carved Bukharan trunk, dreaming dreams about Jazal once young and beautiful, who had sacrificed her youth to the old *shoykhet*; he, who had taken her poor and barefoot and made her his wife. He, who suffered from lethargy, had nonetheless picked out as wife the most capable, the most beautiful. He knew that at first Jazal had laughed at him and mimicked the way he held the knife in his teeth between his withered lips. But he also knew that she would not be able to refuse him because he was wealthier than her own father and smarter than all of them. He had first noticed her when she came dressed in her red Yemenite trousers, carrying a little white hen to be slaughtered. There, at the huge green fence, his hands trembling, he had taken the little white hen from her, caressed her hands as no-one at home had ever done. Nor did he give the bird back immediately after slaughtering it, but wrapped it up in a big piece of paper so that she wouldn't soil her hands. After that, she never again wanted to go to the *shoykhet*.

When Purim came, Jazal wore her grandmother's special clothes. She would masquerade as an old Yemenite dancer whom she could imitate unbelievably well. She danced steps she had never seen anywhere. Jazal also went off with the other children to dance for the *shoykhet*. Perhaps because she was motherless, Jazal didn't realize that there was any other kind of life besides the one her grandmother and her father had taught her.

Sometimes years are a mirror of human reflection and soul-searching. On this first beautiful day of spring, among the delicate almond blossoms and veils of mimosa, Jazal began once again to unroll the *megile* of her youth. Three sons she had with the *shoykhet* but every one of them had died of trachoma: First they became blind, then they died of a variety of childhood diseases. Too young to fully comprehend how much anguish a mother can bear when she loses her children, she was not able to overcome the sorrow. She couldn't follow this sorrow to its end. She believed that God had punished her for marrying so young and especially to so old a man. But this sorrow was concealed within her and she was not even aware when it had actually begun. She only knew that when the *shoykhet* closed his eyes forever, the very next day she found his ritual knives lying at the head of the bed. She understood at once that they had come, sharp and thin, to slaughter her as well. She took them and hid them under her *Shabes* finery in the trunk which stood like a fortress, locked with all her secrets, all her sorrows, inside.

Once, when Sleyman the drunkard approached her with a marriage proposal from a Yemenite, Jazal replied, "My husband's sharpest knives will chase and slaughter you. Don't you dare enter my house!"

Since then, everyone knew that Jazal chased away all the matchmakers and lived a strange, reclusive life. She would often stroll about, hands on hips, especially in early springtime, but in fact she was strolling through her own wellsprings which bubbled with silent wisdom within her. But when the trees began to blossom and the mimosas donned their yellow earrings, Jazal was filled with a fantastic yearning. She wanted to play the role of Queen Ester going before the king to plead for the Jews. Jazal took out the antique, wondrously embroidered Yemenite clothes and put them on. She stood a big broom in the centre of the room, dressed it in an Arab sheikh's turban, combed her own greying hair and set upon it the headdress which framed her head and face and made her look years younger. She approached this effigy of King Akhashveyresh, bowed three times and said,

"Lord of all kings, my people, the Jews, are in great danger. Only you can save them." She embraced this costumed broom and called out,

"You will not disgrace Queen Ester!"

As she was expounding, Sleyman, who had staggered in, began laughing loudly; his hoarse, drunken voice shamed Jazal to the core and she exclaimed, "What are you doing here now? Where do you get such nerve? Don't you know that we Jews are in a time of trouble again? Pick up your feet and get out or I'll pour a kettle of boiling water over you!"

Sleyman stammered, "*Purim* is still a week away and look at you!" He roared with laughter and thumped his chest. "Upon my life! You're even more beautiful than you were as a thirteen-year-old. Dear widow, where did you get so much charm? From where?"

Silence descended. Jazal suddenly disappeared from the room, throwing off her *Purim* costume. She tiptoed back in with the beater used to pound the rugs in her hand, but Sleyman was no longer in the house. Then she vented her rage upon the broom which still stood atilt in its Arab clothing. She beat her anger into it so fiercely that its entire top scattered and only a few twigs remained. It fell over like a living thing beaten to a pulp lying face down on the ground. Jazal cried out, "So will all the enemies of Israel lie at my feet!"

TRANSLATED BY SHIRLEY KUMOVE

Prikhah's Complaint to God

WHEN PLUM SEASON CAME to the countryside, Prikhah sat herself down to figure out whether it would be worth her while to start again and become a businesswoman. She, Prikhah, didn't know how to write, so she went out into the courtyard which was full of neighbours. It was a summer night and Meyer Shushn happened to be sitting there puffing on his water-pipe after a hot day's work. He, Shushn, liked to look up at the stars, at the blue-green Jerusalem sky which was so beautifully engraved with all kinds of small and large white clouds. Prikhah, who was wearing a satin Persian housecoat, sat herself down near him on one of the well-scrubbed white stones which, in the moonlight, looked as if the Almighty Himself had washed them. She had brought pen and ink with her, and she said to him,

"Esteemed One, make me some calculations. Tomorrow, I want to start over again and deal in plums."

Meyer Shushn replied, "*Khabibati*, sit yourself a little further from me because you scorch me and I'm not so young anymore, so it's better that you sit across from me. My wife, Saadeh, will be here in a few minutes. She went to borrow a glass shade for the oil lamp because there were none left."

"I don't need Saadeh," answered an angry Prikhah. "I need only your calculations." She would, she said, go to Tankhum the Lame, and buy from him both the very large plums, the real Santa Rosas, and also the smaller ones which are juicy but don't have the sheen of the Santa Rosas. She would also take the big white plums which are a little bitter. It didn't matter, however, she must know how much to earn so that she wouldn't be stuck with only the leftovers, the half-rotten ones.

Shushn puffed pleasantly on his water-pipe and stretched out his hand to show Prikhah the miracles of the Creator. "*Khabibati*, just take a look at what's going on in the sky. The angels are getting ready to recite *khtsos*. They're soaring, . that's why the sky is so clear! And if the Almighty should hear that at Shushn's they're making calculations about plums, He'll become angry and make such a storm! The wind will come, God forbid, and shake up everything and nothing will remain for you of the plum trees."

Prikhah saw clearly that this was a bit of trickery; that Shushn was in fact refusing to make the calculations for her. So she picked herself up and strode off without so much as a "be well." On the way, she met Yikhiyeh the shoemaker. Yikhiyeh was all too willing to stop and listen to her request. Yikhiyeh the shoemaker was the blackest Yemenite in all of Jerusalem.

Prikhah said to him, "Oh, Wise One, perhaps you have time to do some calculations for me? Tomorrow, I want to begin again as a plum dealer. It's now plum season and this year the harvest is a big one. I'll make conserves because I have a good location to work where nobody has the right to sit near me because it's my very own place. I bought it when the English left the country."

Yikhiyeh stood there somewhat bewildered. First of all, Prikhah pleased him because she was so beautiful. Secondly, it pleased him that a woman had a man's head on her shoulders and wanted to be a merchant.

"Do you already have the merchandise at home? How much did you pay and how much do you want to earn?" he asked.

Prikhah laughed lightly and replied, "They're still on the trees! If I were certain of the price, then very early tomorrow morning I would pick them off the trees. Shaar Ephraim is not far and by seven in the morning I could already be sitting doing business."

"Are you then the only person at the market who deals in plums? What will you do if others sell the plums even cheaper? *Khabibati*, Makhne Yehuda is a huge abyss. There the competition is as keen as at a sporting event ... ! You'd better think it over very carefully."

Yikhiyeh was speaking but at the same time he was thinking to himself that if Prikhah wanted to be his wife, he would be the buyer. Even though his own wife was still quite young, she did not have the healthy beauty of Prikhah. Why, Prikhah could mesmerize even an angel! All this was going through his mind but he was afraid to speak a word of it because the look on Prikhah's face never gave a hint as to what she might be thinking. His mind was thinking but his tongue wagged.

"I've already got your calculations but if I write it down on paper you'll see it doesn't pay. Plums can't lie around for long. If they don't sell quickly you'll have a real loss. Plums are such a seasonal item; once the season is passed, it's over."

Prikhah stared at him. She wasn't, heaven forbid, frightened, but she did note how black he was, and said, "*Khabibati*, it seems to me that you've never been a businessman. If a merchant has no courage, he's a shoemaker not a businessman! If I could make my own calculations I wouldn't need to ask you and the plums would already be in the crates."

"*Khabibati*," Yikhiyeh replied helplessly, "Let's go over to Meyer Shushn. He's got a clever brain and he'll know what to advise."

"I'm almost ready to give up on the thought of plums."

Yikhiyeh smiled. "When plums are finished, then come apples. Apples are no good? And lemons and oranges are no good? Everything the Lord created is beautiful. And a woman ...?"

Prikhah instinctively moved away and said nothing. Yikhiyeh was not the man who could please her.

Silently, they approached Meyer Shushn, who sat squinting. He laid aside the water-pipe saying, "If there weren't such a sky, Prikhah wouldn't have plum trees in her head! It's all thanks to the Holy One and His deeds! Prikhah makes the calculations in her head, she can't even write; but the Holy One, blessed be He, will soon tell her what to do. So don't you mix in, Yikhiyeh. She is, thank God, a clever woman; she's managed to take care of herself quite well until now and she'll continue to look after herself."

Prikhah now became very angry, saying, "If God is so all-knowing, why didn't He arrange for Prikhah to be able to make her own calculations?"

Meyer Shushn looked at her, smiled and said, "Does my Saadeh know how to add? No! But the Holy One, blessed be He, gave her a husband, a good man, and he does the figuring. So, Prikhah sweetheart, go find yourself a man. Get that matchmaker from Salonika. He'll know how to fix you up."

Shushn ordered black coffee to be brought out. A container of sunflower seeds was at his side.

Prikhah sat, asking nothing and answering nothing. Seeing that she was so self-absorbed, the two men struck up a conversation between themselves and sipped their coffees. Prikhah also sipped coffee, becoming melancholy. Every now and again, she raised her eyes to the night sky and complained to the Almighty: Why couldn't she make these foolish calculations by herself? Why did she have to depend on others?

TRANSLATED BY SHIRLEY KUMOVE

G'ULA AND SHULAMIT

"THE WIND HAS GONE TO SLEEP," said the two little girls sitting together on a doorstep. In that same conversation they told the following:

"Once upon a time two little alley-ways, Gedem and Tsipore, quarreled. When they quarrel, it is different than with people. They speak through a messenger, the wind. Little pieces of paper, potato peel and, especially, bird feathers blow back and forth ... and if they make up, the wind has nothing to do. Then the sun comes out and sits down in Gedem Street. She sits there for a few hours, then leaves to sit in Tsipore Street. The sun stays overnight in Tsipore Street because the Tiferet Synagogue is there and she goes into the synagogue. After all the people have finished their prayers, she hides in the Holy Ark. They even say that she fills in missing letters in the *Toyre* scrolls and letters that are worn from being read so often."

Shulamit, who was a little cross-eyed and had thin braids tied at the ends with bits of torn ribbon, said, "When I'm as big as my mother, I'll dress like Malke from the grocery store. I won't wear clothes that make me look old, only clothes that'll make me look like a princess."

G'ula, a blond little girl, was earnest and silent, but when Shulamit uttered the word "princess," she woke from her trance, "Princesses have nothing to do; they're lazy, they loll about all day in easy chairs! It's nicer to be a teacher or even a pharmacist. A teacher educates children so they get knowledge, and a pharmacist has the great responsibility of making medicine for the sick! When I grow up, I'll study the science of nature, I'll write books about grasses and after that, I'll be a professor at the university!"

"And I will be a duchess!" said Shulamit, undoing her braids and tossing her hair over her shoulders. She bowed then and picked up a stick, "This is how I'll walk and order people around!"

They both laughed and then suddenly grew silent. From a green verandah, mother called "G'ula!" That green verandah was like an ingenious toy. No-one on Tsipore had a verandah and no-one had a blond little daughter named G'ula. There all the children were dark skinned.

The green verandah was now lit up. G'ula and her mother were eating their supper. Her mother wore a green dress with a white collar; mother-of-pearl earrings hung from her ears. When the electric light hit the earrings, a white glow reflected on her cheek. G'ula looked at her mother and said,

"One of your cheeks is covered by a cloud. Brush it off!"

Her mother didn't understand and asked, "What new ideas have you picked up from your girlfriends this time?"

Offended, G'ula dropped the bread she was holding, stopped eating and sat silent.

In Gedem Street electricity hadn't yet been installed. A kerosene lamp was used in Shulamit's parents' home. It stood on a high cupboard and threw a giant umbrella shade over everything. Shulamit sat under the umbrella doing her lessons. On the floor five children ate from a common dish. Shulamit's mother, pale, sallow, thin, had opened her blouse to pacify a little one. Her husband had just come in; he was in uniform — a policeman.

"Daddy!" they cried out in unison, "Daddy!" But Daddy had no time. He had hurried in with time only to pat Shulamit and each of the smaller children, smile at his wife, Hadase, and rush out the door again.

Shulamit stopped her writing and turned to her mother, "Why don't you ever have time to talk with me? I want that so much. Your face is tired; maybe I should help you? I know you're always too busy. When I grow up, I won't let you have any more children. They're the reason you never have time. A mother should be beautiful and not tired!"

A fear that could be seen in her eyes took hold of Hadase; she understood full well what Shulamit had just said. She washed her hands and dried them on a piece of a child's woollen undershirt. Now she would take the time. She drew on her prettiest blouse; she buttoned it crooked, so tired were her hands. But her eyes now cleared of all shadows. She sat down beside Shulamit, unbraided and combed her hair, rebraided it and tied it with a fresh ribbon. Shulamit watched, watched and permitted it all.

"Take your father's mirror and look at yourself!" said her mother. Shulamit stayed seated. She understood her mother was offering compensation for something owed her, something she should have given her and hadn't. Shulamit remained sitting there, silent.

TRANSLATED BY NORMA FAIN PRATT

Pirkhah Ozeri

A LARGE, VERY LARGE MOON rose over the courtyard where Pirkhah was sitting, bare feet on the stone stoop.

She stared, lost, at the moon. The courtyard was white and clear; Pirkhah had swept and washed it clean. She was preparing for a guest.

The hot summer evening had drawn Pirkhah into longing and desire. She was restless and her thoughts were wrapped in a peculiar veil. No-one knew that she had tied a knot of friendship with a soldier from Shkhunat Akhuva. She feared her own would throw stones at her because everyone knew that only *shikanazim* lived in Akhuva.

How did it happen that it was from Shkhunat Akhuva of all places that she found her destined one? She rubbed her bare feet on a freshly washed stone, rubbed them in fearful apprehension. She examined her toe nails: they had white, round half eyes like young chestnuts. The darkish, mossy hair on her shins disgusted her. But thoughts of her feet soon vanished. She took out her little square mirror and examined her face in the moonlight. She had a fresh, dark face with wide, large almond eyes. Her neck was long, even a bit too thin; it stretched her slim, elegant body. She smiled into the little mirror because it was Shimon the soldier she really saw there. True, he came from another community but he belonged to her, to her alone.

Shimon the soldier arrived with a package under his arm. Pirkhah leapt up like a wild doe and quickly stepped into her green slippers.

As soon as Shimon appeared, the white courtyard came alive with faces. Eynee, the shoemaker, opened the window a crack. He measured the soldier with a sullen glance and disappeared. Simkha the sorceress opened a squeaky door. She held a flowerpot in her hand and with a mouthful of water sprayed the little sprig; squinting with her clever little eyes, she meanwhile caught a quick look at Shimon the soldier. She had more than once earned a lira note for working her magic. Heaven forbid that Pirkhah loose her beauty in Shimon's eyes. He would have forbidden Pirkhah to visit the fortune teller had he been aware of it. But Pirkhah, though still very young, wanted to do everything in her power to keep him.

She knew all the ways and wiles to hold him so he'd have no regrets. For what prospects did a Kurdish girl have, an orphan, with two uncles in Nakhlat Sheva, both porters? When they sometimes met her on the street — they berated her for wearing high-heeled shoes and combing her hair like a movie actress.

Uncle Yusuf had one eye and used to whine as he moralized for her benefit. Uncle Tsadok didn't even look like a Jew. He was always girded with a rope as if prepared to carry a heavy trunk. He always asked whether she remembered her father's death; he was snatched away one winter while lighting a *yortsayt* candle for his mother. No-one could find out what had caused his death.

Pirkhah loathed her uncles. They always ran into her as she was buying ointments, cosmetics. These purchases of ointments to beautify herself cost her much heartache. Her uncles were crude people compared to Shimon the soldier who always spoke with examples from the *Tanakh*. He was from a *khasidic* home, religious and observant.

Shimon the soldier sat down opposite Pirkhah. From paper with the printed letters KAPULSKY he unwrapped round cheese buns and from another paper, a bunch of green grapes. Pirkhah bounded into her room and brought out a large plate decorated with little figures on which she laid out the buns and grapes. Quickly realizing that the grapes had to be washed, she said, "Shimon, it's cool inside; we can sit in the room."

So Shimon got up, went in with the plate and sat down on a low stool. His feet were stretched out in front of him. He studied Pirkhah, how she dressed up for him and he called her to him,

"Pirkhah, from today on I will call you Frume. My father called my mother Frumetl. You probably don't know what 'Frume' means. In Yiddish 'Frume' simply means 'pious,' 'Datiyah' in Hebrew. It's good that you'll be called by my mother's name because she was a woman of valour, a dear mother. She died young, tortured to death by Hitler. My father promised her to remain true and never to re-marry. He's kept his word: sits studying in a *yeshive* to commemorate her pure soul. I'm less pious. I cause my father great distress because he doesn't want me to serve in the army. But I'm discovering that to serve the State is an obligation. And when you turn eighteen you too will go into the army, if you don't get married first."

Pirkhah remained silent, drinking in his every word. Then, "What will your father say?" she asked shyly. "Will he be forever angry that you love a Kurdish girl? Won't he tear you away from me?"

"And what will your uncles say? Will they consent to your going through life with a *shikanazi*?"

"My uncles will merely pay out the money my father left for me until I'm grown. In the bank where I work everyone likes me. They're always asking whether I have a boyfriend yet! And I say, 'An *Ashkenazi*, a sweetheart!' Then the manager closes his ledger, looks at me with calf's eyes and I smile, but it's to you."

"Frume, you'll be embarrassed to tell them at the bank that your name is 'Frume'? Then demand that I change my name and be called by your father's, exactly! Do you remember him?"

"My father's name was Gamliel. If you agree I'll call you Gamliel and Shimon! No-one will know about it, only the two of us. My entire family were porters. My father's life was cut short; but we won't have to be porters."

Shimon took Pirkhah's face, kissed her eyes and said again,

"We'll be the children of the dead. They'll come to see whether we live fine and faithful lives. We will be children bearing their names. And when we have children they'll know that Frumetl's name has not been lost; Gamliel's name hasn't disappeared. We'll immortalize them and they will come to our bedsides every night. They will bless us. Frume will rock a child and Gamliel will rock a child."

The white courtyard was silent and forbidding by the time Shimon left Pirkhah's room. They waved to one another until he disappeared from view.

Pirkhah went off to see the fortune teller, a white-haired woman with a red birthmark on her left cheek. She had a pail full of water in which lay a playing card, a red king. The king was soaking in the tin pail.

"Do you see the card?" the fortune teller asked. "Do you see the red king?"

"Yes, I see the red king," Pirkhah repeated.

"Look into the water. Dip your little finger in and say to the king of the card, 'Counterfeit king, reflected in the pail. Water is shallow, sorrow is deep. The ear is deaf. Do not intrude in my fate.' "

Pirkhah repeated everything that Simkha the fortune teller had told her. Simkha then put both hands into the water, drew them out and sprinkled Pirkhah's head. From her bosom she pulled a worn yellow amulet and said, "Tie this onto one of your long hairs and give it to your destined one. He must wear it always against his bare chest. Your hair won't break, God forbid. Hair and amulet will always remind him that you are his."

Pirkhah trembled, her eyes filled with tears. Her fine hair would bind him to her forever.

TRANSLATED BY NORMA FAIN PRATT

Shraby's Daughter Comes Home

Nakhlat Akhim is a treasure of alleyways. The alley called Tiberias Street, may no evil eye fall upon it, is filled with neighbourhood people, with children, and with grown daughters who come home from the army for *Shabes*. By Friday noon, Shraby's courtyard is washed sparkling clean. Even the broom becomes something different on *Shabes*. Malke, Shraby's wife, stands there, bent over, pours water and swishes the broom back and forth. The broom knows it's all for the sake of a guest. So when a few twigs fall out of its whiskers, it doesn't mind. Malke surveys her courtyard and notices that the yellow fence is splattered with mud. She turns and splashes a pailful of water over it. Malke is pockmarked, has short, crooked feet and a nose like a *shoyfer*, but when she pours a dipper of water over her face, wetting her crown of black hair, she takes on a different appearance.

Shraby's house is known all over Tiberias Street. Although poverty dwells within, the walls radiate comfort. Malke cooks so much cabbage with rice and cinnamon that the odor of cabbage remains lodged at the door. Malke peels a large onion, puts it on the kerosene burner and this smell of onion spreads with such force that you could imagine that the cabbage is a step-child allowing itself to be overpowered by the scorched onion. However, all is not quite as it seems. Here comes Shraby himself. He looks like a biblical Abraham in a painting by Rembrandt. His beard is impressive, spreading broadly over his entire face and flowing over his neck. He wears a large woolen scarf around his neck. His beard looks like soft dough rising; the small growths on his face like tiny potatoes.

Moments earlier, in the Yemenite synagogue, he was arguing with his drunken friend, Yerukham. Yerukham drinks not from pleasure; Yerukham drinks to intoxicate the worm that gnaws, that bores into him. Shraby is absorbed in prayer for his only child, his daughter, who is serving in the Israeli army. His fatherly heart is worried and sad. What kind of a world has it become (says Shraby to Yerukham the drunkard) when girls go into the army?

Yerukham the drunkard, lying on the floor of the Yemenite synagogue, sighs and spits. Hearing Shraby talk, he lifts his bloodshot eyes, and says, "Ya, *khabibi*, the Messiah doesn't want to come; he's afraid that girl soldiers will come out to meet him — Jewish girls in military dress. He would have come long ago but what kind of Messiah will risk his life to come to a country where girl soldiers march around with guns?"

That was earlier. Now, when Shraby goes into the house, his daughter comes toward him, tawny-skinned, brown-haired, with the same eyes as Shraby himself. Shraby stops, looks at his one-and-only daughter and says,

"So, when will the Messiah finally come?"

Khasudah humbly kisses his hairy hand, not knowing how to respond to such a question.

"What do you do there in that army of yours? What kind of work does my one-and-only daughter do?" he asks again.

"*Aba, Abale*, it's very difficult, it's very hard to be a soldier but one must, one must! Every Jewish girl must do her duty because we must be prepared for war."

"We?" Shraby asks again and begins to laugh. "We? You think maybe I should also serve in the army? How exactly will all of you defend the country? You with your painted faces will welcome the Messiah? Upon my life! The Messiah will fall off his horse this very evening! Oh Khasudah, my daughter, don't be foolish! Shraby still has his wits about him. He won't let himself be led around by the nose. My daughter, you're dear to me, but you're not strong enough to wage war on behalf of the State of Israel! You can sooner wage war with your predestined one that you'll probably bring home from the army. Just don't forget that we, the Shraby family, do not mix with *shikanazim*!"

Khasudah stands pale and downcast, tears welling in her eyes. Malke covers the table with a Turkish shawl, places two brass candlesticks on top and says, "When the child comes home you should be glad and not shout or talk like you do to Yerukham the drunkard. Whoever the Holy One, Blessed Be He, destines, that's who she'll marry. The matchmaking for Khasudah is not in our hands."

"Be quiet, Malke. Yerukham is a drunkard but he knows what he's talking about. He also says that the Messiah won't come because girls serve in the army. He says they will delay the Redemption!"

Suddenly, all is quiet in the house. Shraby begins to prepare himself for the synagogue. He pulls on the white stockings, dons the black and white striped robe over his clothes and slips his feet into soft slippers. Before leaving, he says, "It's time to go and welcome the Sabbath Queen. She's already on her way but if, God forbid, She has become a soldier, then I'll stop going to prayers!"

Outside, the winter evening has already spread. A silver grey sky hangs by a mere hair. The moon looks down, counting Shraby's footsteps as he plods along to the brightly lit synagogue.

TRANSLATED BY SHIRLEY KUMOVE

Authors' Biographies

LILI BERGER (1916 –)

A prolific literary critic and essayist, as well as a novelist and playwright, Lili Berger has written in a variety of genres: journal articles, works of literary criticism, short stories, novels, plays and translations. Her novels and short stories often include very real, human characterizations of people in unbelievable circumstances. Her work has been hailed as original, Kafkaesque minus the bizarre element. An important critic on contemporary and classical European literature, her insights into the work of Sholom Aleichem have been lauded.

Born December 30, 1916 in the Malkin, Bialystok region, Berger received a religious education and completed the Polish-Jewish *gymnasium* in Warsaw in 1933. She studied pedagogy in Brussels and then settled in Paris at the end of 1936. There she taught in Yiddish supplementary schools and became a contributor to the *Naye prese*. Later she wrote for the monthly *Oyfsney* and the weekly *Di vokh*, both important Yiddish publications in Paris.

During the nazi occupation of France she was active in the Resistance movement. After the war she returned to Warsaw where she lived until 1968, then again in Paris, where she presently resides. Her works have been published in journals in Israel, South Africa, France, Mexico and the United States. Although most of her writing has been in Yiddish, she has also had two books published in Polish.

ROKHL BROKHES (1880 – 1945)

Born September 23, 1880 in Minsk, Russia, to a poor family, Rokhl Brokhes was educated by her father, an adherent of the *Haskole*, who taught her Hebrew and the Bible. He died when she was nine, and shortly thereafter Brokhes went to work as a seamstress. Later she taught needlework at the Minsk Jewish Vocational School for Girls.

At nine years of age she began writing in a diary. Her short story "Yankele" was published to acclaim in *Der yud* when she was nineteen. Her work continued to appear in Russian and American periodicals including *Fraynd* and *Tsukunft*.

Brokhes married a dentist and they moved to a small town isolated from the Yiddish literary environment. There she wrote much but published little. In 1920 the family returned to Minsk where she resumed her writing: novellas (some of which were translated into Russian, German and English), theatre pieces and children's stories.

A realist with an inclination to lyricism and fine psychological insight, Brokhes depicted Jewish family life, particularly the Jewish woman as mother and worker. The first volume of her collected works, including over two hundred short stories, was to be published by the State Publishing House of White Russia — indeed they were already typeset — when the nazi invasion put an end to the project.

Rokhl Brokhes was tortured and murdered by the nazis in the Minsk ghetto in 1945.

CELIA DROPKIN (1888 – 1956)

Born Celia Lenin on December 18, 1888 in Babroysk, White Russia, Dropkin was raised by her mother. Her father, a lumber merchant, had died at a young age, leaving behind his wife and two daughters. Up to the age of eight, Dropkin studied with the rabbi's wife and then attended a Russian school. She wrote her first Russian poem at the age of ten.

At seventeen years of age, Dropkin moved to Kiev, Ukraine where she finished *gymnasium* and continued to write with the encouragement of her mentor, the Hebrew writer A.N. Gnessin, who translated some of her early Russian poetry into Hebrew. Her poetry, however, did not receive a positive response and, discouraged, she stopped writing for a while. She then moved to Warsaw where she became a teacher.

Her husband fled to the United States as a political refugee and Dropkin followed in 1912. Here she took up writing again and was influenced by the Yiddish writer Avrom Leyesin to write in Yiddish. She began by translating some of her Russian poems into Yiddish. In 1917 her Yiddish poetry appeared for the first time in *Naye velt*. She was associated with *Di yunge* and the *Insikhists*, two important Yiddish literary groups in America at the time.

A poet as well as a visual artist, Dropkin pioneered eroticism in Yiddish poetry. She is considered one of the most talented Yiddish writers and is acknowledged for her poetic rhythms and intensity of feeling. Dropkin contributed her stories and poetry to many prestigious Yiddish publications, yet only one volume of her poetry appeared during her lifetime. A volume of her collected poems and short stories was published posthumously in 1959. Both volumes bore the same title: *In heysn vint* [In Hot Wind]. She died in New York on August 17, 1956, eighty of her poems still incomplete.

SHIRA GORSHMAN (1906 –)

Gorshman, who also wrote under the names of Shirke Goman, Szyrke Gorszman and Shire Gorman, was born on April 10, 1906 in Krock, a small town near Kovno, Lithuania to a poor family. During the First World War, she and her family were evacuated to Odessa, where she finished elementary school. By age fourteen, she left home and at sixteen gave birth to a daughter. In 1924, she immigrated to Israel and worked there in the home of the poet Khayim Nakhmen Bialik. In 1930, she returned to the Soviet Union to help build the Jewish agricultural collectives in the Crimea. Later she lived in Odessa and Moscow, where she began writing short stories about Jewish life in the *shtetl*, as well as in the new Russia, Crimea and Israel.

Gorshman inherited her mother's gift for language: a traditional, unaffected Yiddish, ironic yet gentle, melancholy but playful. Her writing is concise, visually rich, and poetic. She has an eye for both nature and humanity; her written dialogue is sharp and intimate. Rarely able to write full-time, her work has a fresh, almost improvisational quality.

Gorshman's *33 noveln* [33 Short Stories], did not appear until 1961, when she was fifty-five. Some of her short stories were included in the anthologies *Tsum zig* and *Heymland*; her work also appeared in the journals *Shtern, Emes* and *Eynikeyt*. She is presently living in Israel.

SARAH HAMER-JACKLYN (1905 – 1975)

Born in Novoradomsk, Poland in 1905, Sarah Hamer-Jacklyn immigrated with her parents to Canada in 1914 at the age of nine. She was educated in the public schools of Toronto and received private Jewish lessons. Captivated at an early age by the Yiddish theatre in Toronto, she began her career as an actress and singer at sixteen, travelling with a troupe across North America.

Hamer-Jacklyn made her writing debut in 1934 with the story, "A Shopgirl," which was serialized in *Der tog*. Her work continued to be published in the *Tsukunft, Yidisher kemfer, Kanader odler, Der forverts* and other periodicals in North America. Her first book, *Lebns un geshtaltn* [Lives and Portraits], and the two that followed portray life in the *shtetls* of Eastern Europe and in America.

Hamer-Jacklyn's writing was praised by the critics for its richly coloured terrain, full-blooded characters and fluent dialogue; she was attuned to the life around her, whether in the rootedness and intimacy of the *shtetl* or in the raw and bewildering world of immigrants.

Author and critic Yankev Glatshteyn marvelled at Hamer-Jacklyn's capacity to capture, decades after her emigration, the spiritual climate, daily life and family portraits of the *shtetl*. Her use of local dialect and idiom and of folklore contributes not only to the authenticity and freshness of her stories but also to the preservation of the linguistic aspect of pre-Holocaust Eastern European Jewish life.

The dramatic impact of Hamer-Jacklyn's old world stories reflects her background in theatre; they are, at the same time, true childhood memoirs.

Hamer-Jacklyn later lived in New York. Her marriage ended in divorce, and she raised her son alone. She died on February 9, 1975.

RACHEL KORN (1898 – 1982)

Born in 1898 near Pokliski in East Galicia, Rachel Korn grew up among farmers and peasants. At a time when nearly all European Jews lived in cities or *shtetls*, her family had owned farmland for several generations. The great love and understanding of nature so prominent in Korn's poetry can be attributed to her childhood experiences.

Korn learned to read and write in Yiddish as an adult, taught by her husband. Though her first publications were in Polish, she chose to become a Yiddish writer because of the pogroms that followed the First World War. Soon thereafter the Yiddish literary world recognized her talents. The powerful vibrancy and boldness of her nature imagery were a new phenomenon in Yiddish literature.

When the nazis invaded Poland, Korn fled to Uzbekistan in the Soviet Union with her young daughter. Her husband was killed by the Germans as were most other members of her family. After the war, Korn returned to Poland, resuming her literary career in Lodz where she was elected to the executive of the Yiddish Writers' Union. In this capacity she attended a PEN conference in Stockholm. Korn never returned to Poland, spending some time in Sweden before immigrating to Montreal in 1949. Here she remained productive as a Yiddish writer of poetry and short stories. As a Holocaust survivor, she often wrote about her grief and isolation. Though she had lost her family, her social context and most of her Yiddish readership, she continued to write poetry and short stories of great eloquence and poignancy in the language of her youth.

In the course of her writing career, Korn wrote nine volumes of poetry and two of short stories. Her works have been translated into a variety of languages including English, Hebrew, Polish, Russian, German and French. Two collections of her poems have been published in English: *Generations* and *Paper Roses*. Korn's short stories appear in translation in *Canadian Jewish Short Stories* and *Canadian Yiddish Writing*. She was awarded numerous literary prizes, including the prestigious Manger Prize for Yiddish Literature presented to her by the State of Israel in 1974.

ESTHER SINGER KREITMAN (1891 – 1954)

Esther Kreitman was born Hinde Esther Singer on March 31, 1891 in Bilgorey, Poland into an intellectually gifted literary family. Her brothers, brilliant Yiddish novelist and journalist Israel Joshua

Singer and Nobel laureate Isaac Bashevis Singer, became eminent Yiddish literary figures. Kreitman herself never received recognition for her literary talents. Intellectually capable, her literary aspirations were frustrated by the limitations imposed on women in a Hasidic home. Kreitman's parents refused to encourage or even to educate their obviously talented daughter. Kreitman, called a "Hasid in skirts" by her brother Isaac Bashevis, was the inspiration for the protagonist depicted in his short story "Yentl the Yeshiva Boy." While Kreitman sought independence and self-expression, she was thwarted throughout her life by the social constraints on women.

A born storyteller, at age twenty Kreitman had already written an impressive collection of short stories, the first among her siblings to begin a literary career. On a train trip to her arranged marriage, however, she threw out the notebooks containing all her literary work. This was done at the suggestion of her mother, who thought the Yiddish writing might be wrongly identified as "socialist revolutionary writings" by the czarist train officials.

Kreitman began her married life in Antwerp, Belgium, where her son was born. At the beginning of the First World War, the family fled to London to escape the German invasion. Her husband, a diamond cutter, was conscripted by the czar's army and deported from England.

For most of her life thereafter, Kreitman lived in London. She was unhappy with her marriage and would periodically leave her husband to go to Warsaw, intending to become independent and support herself as a writer. She always returned.

While in Warsaw, Kreitman supported herself by translating Dickens and Shaw into Yiddish. In England, she wrote short stories that were published in Yiddish dailies and literary journals around the world. In 1936, her semi-autobiographic novel *Der sheydim tants* [The Devil's Dance] was published in Poland to favourable reviews. However, no literary critic gave this work its proper recognition as the first Yiddish novel written by a woman in support of the *Haskole*. *The Devil's Dance* was translated into English by Kreitman's son and published in 1946. It was later republished as *Deborah* in 1983 by Virago Press, a feminist press. Both her novel *Brilyantn* and the collection of short stories *Yikhes* [Status] received good reviews in the Yiddish press.

Plagued by illness from the age of twelve, Kreitman died in 1954 at the age of sixty-three.

MALKA LEE (1904 – 1972)

Malka Lee was born Malka Leopold on July 4, 1904 in Monastrikh, Galicia to a Hasidic family. During the First World War she fled with her family via Hungary to Vienna, where she lived from 1914 to 1919 and graduated from *gymnasium*. She was fluent in Hebrew, Polish and German and began writing German poetry as a young child, despite her Hasidic father's strong disapproval.

After returning to small-town life in Poland with her family following the war, she immigrated to the United States on her own in 1921 at the age of sixteen. In New York, she continued her education at the Jewish Teachers' Seminary, Hunter College and City College. Though her initial poetry was written in German, she soon began to write in Yiddish, her mother tongue, in order to communicate to people of her own background in America.

Married to the writer Aaron Rappaport, she was part of the flourishing Yiddish literary circles of the time in New York City and her poetry was well regarded by important literary critics such as Shmuel Niger. Author of at least seven volumes of poetry published in New York, Buenos Aires and Tel-Aviv, she later turned to autobiographic writing in her book *Durkh kindershe oygn* [Through the Eyes of Childhood] and continued her prose writing with a book of short stories written for her son called *Mayselekh far Yoselen* [Little Stories for Joseph]. Her work also appeared in many important Yiddish periodicals throughout the world.

BLUME LEMPEL (1910 –)

Blume Lempel was born on May 13, 1910 in Khorostov, Galicia. Her education included a girls' *kheder* and Hebrew *folkshule*. She immigrated to Paris in 1929, but in 1939, on the eve of the Second World War, immigrated once again, this time to New York City. She debuted in 1942 in *Der tog* under the pseudonym Rokhl Halperin. In 1947, *Der morgn-frayheyt* serialized her novel *Tvishn tsvey veltn* [Between Two Worlds]. Her fiction and stories have appeared in major Yiddish journals and newspapers, including *Tsukunft, Der tog, Di goldene keyt* and *Der morgn-frayheyt*. She is the author of two collections, *A rege fun emes* [A Moment of Truth] and *Balade fun a kholem* [Ballad of a Dream]. She currently resides in Long Beach, New York.

IDA MAZE (1893 – 1962)

Born July 9, 1893 in the village of Ogli, White Russia, Maze studied in a *kheder* to the age of thirteen; from then on she was self-taught. In 1907, at the age of fourteen, Maze immigrated to the United States. She came to Canada in 1908. Maze lived first in Toronto and then, for the rest of her life, in Montreal.

Maze was active in all aspects of Jewish cultural life. Her generosity was extended to all, particularly Yiddish writers. Maze fed, advised, and helped promote and publish the works of her protégés. During and after the Holocaust, she was instrumental in obtaining visas for Yiddish writers and cultural workers in the refugee camps.

Maze began writing lyric poetry in her early youth. *Lider vegn mayn kind* [Poems about My Child] was published in 1925, its subject probably based on the loss of one of her three sons. These unique elegies were considered an innovation in Yiddish poetry. Maze's best writing was modest, natural and simple, reading much like folk song.

Maze contributed articles, essays, stories and poetry to periodicals in Montreal, Toronto, New York and Paris. In addition to the four further volumes of poetry she published, Maze coedited the literary journal *Heftn* with E. Korman and N. Gotlib in Montreal from 1935 to 1937. Her work was translated into Hebrew, Russian, French and English and is represented in Leftwich's *The Golden Peacock*.

In preparation at the time of her death were *Geklibene lider* [Collected Poems], *Mayses far kinder* [Stories for Children], and the autobiographical novel, *Denah. Denah* was published in 1970 through the efforts of the Montreal poet Moshe Shafir.

Ida Maze's writing was a natural outgrowth of her consuming interest in the writing of others. Her friend, writer Rachel Korn, said of Maze, "She, the gentle poet, was for a whole generation the refuge and mother in Israel-Montreal."

KADIA MOLODOWSKY (1894 – 1975)

Born in Bereza-Kartuska, Lithuania, Kadia Molodowsky studied Bible and *Gemore* alongside her father's students, and later graduated from Warsaw's Hebrew Teachers' Seminary. In the early Twenties, she was part of the Yiddish writers' group in Vilna where her first poems were published. She returned to Warsaw to teach in the secular Yiddish schools, then immigrated in 1935 to the United States. From 1950 to 1952, Molodowsky lived in Israel; the remainder of her life was spent in New York.

Molodowsky's work is informed by a passion for justice and a preoccupation with the history and survival of her people and its culture. She veers between thematic seriousness and, in her works for children, charm and playfulness.

Molodowsky was known as the "First Lady of Yiddish Poetry." Her works include the early *Froyen lider* [Women Songs], a series of feminist poems, and numerous volumes of poetry. *Kheshvndike nekht* [Nights of Kheshvan] was published in 1927; *Likht fun dornboym* [Light from the Thornbush] in 1965. In the genre of fiction, Molodowsky published the novel *Fun Lublin biz Nyu York* [From Lublin to New York] and the collection of short stories *A shtub mit zibn fenster* [A House with Seven Windows]. Molodowsky also turned her hand to the theatre, publishing two plays, and to children's literature. For years Molodowsky edited the New York literary periodical *Svive* as well as the Tel-Aviv journal *Heym*. She was a contributor to many other periodicals and anthologies.

Molodowsky was the recipient of many awards including Israel's Manger Prize for Yiddish Literature in 1971.

RIKUDAH POTASH (1903 – 1965)

Born in Tshenstokhov, Poland to a prosperous and enlightened family (her father was a journalist, her older brother was a director of the National Museum in Jerusalem), Rikudah Potash was raised in Skale-Bayvidov, a beautiful natural setting commonly referred to as the "Polish Switzerland." Though she received the traditional Jewish education given to girls at the time, she became enamoured of Polish culture and at age sixteen began to write nature poetry in Polish. In the aftermath of the Lemberg pogrom she drew closer to the new Yiddish literature and started writing and publishing in Yiddish.

In 1924, Potash moved to Lodz and became part of the Lodz Young Poets Group, making her writing debut with two poems in the literary journal the *Lodzher folksblat*. Her works were later published in literary journals all over the world. Potash wrote poetry on nature, *Shabes* motifs, children's stories, short stories and novellas about girls' lives. These works appeared in various Lodz publications. Her theatre works include dramatic mystery and comedy.

In 1934, Potash left Europe for Israel and became a librarian for the art division of the Jewish Art Museum in Jerusalem. Short-story writer, essayist, storyteller, poet, translator and dramatist, the multi-faceted Potash was a resident of Jerusalem for thirty years. Sholem Ash dubbed her "the Jerusalem poetess." In her last years, still writing in Yiddish, Potash dedicated herself to depicting the various nationalities of Israel in a prose that retained the dream-like qualities of her poetry.

MIRIAM RASKIN (1889 – 1973)

Miriam Raskin was born in Slonim, White Russia. As a young woman, she became a member of the *Bund* and was imprisoned for her political activities for one year in St. Petersburg.

In 1920 she immigrated to the United States where she wrote about Jewish life in czarist Russia as well as about the immigrant experience in America. She made her writing debut with short stories in *Tsukunft* and her novels were serialized in *Der forverts*. Her work was also published in the *Kinderjurnal*.

Three volumes of her work were published, each one steeped in *Bundist* politics and outlook. *Tsen yor lebn* [Ten Years of Life] is a series of diary entries, while *Zlatke*, a full-length novel, depicts life on the brink of change in czarist Russian and Jewish revolutionary politics. In her book of short stories, *Shtile lebns* [Quiet Lives], Raskin portrays with great compassion simple people of varied backgrounds — Blacks, Italians, as well as Jewish immigrants — all working people trying to make a living as factory workers, maids, housekeepers in America.

Miriam Raskin died on October 8, 1973.

CHAVA ROSENFARB (1923 –)

Prize-winning writer of fiction, poetry and drama, Chava Rosenfarb was born February 9, 1923 in Lodz, the industrial centre of Poland before the Second World War. She completed Jewish secular school and *gymnasium* in this community where several hundred thousand Jews lived — nearly half the population of the area.

The Holocaust put an end to one of the richest centres of Judaism in all of Europe. Like many Jews of the city, Rosenfarb was incarcerated in the infamous Lodz ghetto. She survived there from 1940 to 1944, when she and her sister Henia became inmates of the concentration camps of Auschwitz, then Sasel and Bergen-Belsen.

Even in the ghetto Rosenfarb wrote, and she hasn't stopped since. Her first collection of ghetto poems, *Di balade fun nekhtikn vald* [The Ballad of Yesterday's Forest] was published in London in 1947. After the liberation Rosenfarb moved to Belgium. She remained in Belgium until 1950, when she immigrated to Montreal. In Montreal, Rosenfarb obtained a diploma at the Jewish Teachers' Seminary in 1954.

Rosenfarb has produced a prolific body of writing, all of which speaks from her experience during the Holocaust. Her work has been translated into both Hebrew and English. Rosenfarb has been widely anthologized and has had her work appear in journals in Israel, England, the United States, Canada and Australia in Yiddish and in English and Hebrew translation. Among the many prizes awarded her work, she has received the I.J. Segal Prize (Montreal, 1993), the Sholom Aleichem Prize (Tel-Aviv, 1990) and the Niger Prize (Buenos Aires, 1972). She has travelled extensively, lecturing on Yiddish literature in Australia, Europe and South America as well as in Israel and the United States.

FRADEL SCHTOK (1890 – circa 1930)

Fradel Schtok was born in Skala, Eastern Galicia into a cultured family. She was a gifted student who played the violin and was familiar with German poetry. Both parents died while she was still in her youth.

Schtok immigrated to the United States in 1907 at the age of seventeen. Her first poems, published three years later, brought her immediate attention. Yankev Glatshteyn, the poet and critic, said of her work: "Her poetry is elegant, original ... masterful ... capable of inscribing a beautiful chapter into Yiddish poetry."

Thereafter, Schtok appeared regularly in various Yiddish-American periodicals such as *Dos naye land*, *Di naye heym*, *Inzl* and *Tsukunft*. In 1919, her volume of collected stories, *Gezamlte ertseylungen*, was published in New York. Despite a series of favourable reviews, a negative article by one critic led Schtok to abandon writing in Yiddish. *Musicians Only*, a novel published in English in 1927, received poor reviews. Schtok withdrew into a depression and died in a mental hospital in New York.

Schtok was supreme in her portrayal of Galician *shtetl* life, Hasidim, Germanophiles, young girls cramped by *shtetl* life and longing for Vienna, dancing, poetry, music. She wrote poetry and short fiction which was inventive, finely nuanced, revealing and ironic.

Schtok was among the first to introduce the sonnet form to Yiddish literature. Her poetry was widely anthologized, notably in *500 yor yidishe poezye*, *Di yidishe dikhtung in Amerike biz 1919*, and in Rojansky's *Di froy in der yidisher poezye*.

A number of Schtok's poems in English translation were included in *Great Yiddish Poetry*, *Modern Yiddish Poetry* and *The Golden Peacock*.

DORA SCHULNER (1889 – ?)

Dora Schulner was born in 1889 in Radomysl, Kiev province. Her father, an adherent of the *Haskole*, was a school teacher, a cantor and a scholar with a worldly, progressive bent. He imbued in Dora, his favourite child, a love of Yiddish literature.

Her mother, Schulner recalled in her autobiographical writings, was a wonderful storyteller, a woman of the people who endured a life of continuous hardship and toil. Without a reliable source of economic or emotional support, Schulner's mother became the family mainstay, baking and selling honeycake.

Schulner's father died when she was still a child. She was apprenticed to a tailor at the age of ten, while continuing to help her mother with the honeycake business. At fourteen, Schulner began working in a textile factory and at the same time joined the *Bund*, where in time she became an organizer.

At sixteen, Schulner's mother's will prevailed and she was married to a religious man with whom she had little in common. Her husband, a tailor, worked in Kiev and came home from time to time. In five years they had four children. Schulner remained active in the *Bund* throughout this period.

In 1914, days before the outbreak of the First World War, Schulner's husband left for America, where she and the children joined him after the war. Schulner was an activist in the Yiddish cultural life of Chicago and worked to establish Yiddish schools and to organize reading and study groups as well as other activities.

Her first stories were published in the *Frayheyt* in 1940. Later her work appeared in *Chicago Jewish Courier*, *Undzer veg*, *Kalifornye yidishe shtime* and other periodicals in Toronto, Winnipeg and Mexico.

Drawing on her background, which comprehended both the *Haskole* and observant religious life, she depicted in her writing a full range of Jewish expression: from the *shtetl* where modernity was encroaching, to the idealism and optimism of the early revolutionary period, to the new Jewish community being forged by her immigrant generation.

Her autobiographical work, *Azoy hot es pasirt: 1905 – 1922* [This is How it Happened], received an Institute for Jewish Research (YIVO) award. Two novels, *Miltchin* and *Esther*, followed. *Geshtaltn un dertseylungen* [Portraits and Stories], a collection of short stories, was published in 1956.

YENTE SERDATZKY (1877 – 1962)

Yente Serdatzky was born September 15, 1877 in Aleksat near Kovno, Lithuania, into a poor family distinguished for their love of literature and learning. In her youth, she read widely in German, Russian and Hebrew and received a secular as well as a basic Jewish education. Her father was a used-furniture dealer as well as a scholar and her parents' home was the gathering place for young Yiddish poets in Kovno. From these poets Serdatzky learned about the new Yiddish literature of the time. After marriage, she ran the family grocery store.

At the time of the first Russian revolution in 1905, Serdatzky was inspired to become a writer. In her late twenties and already the mother of two, she moved to Warsaw to further her writing career. Here she made her literary debut in the Yiddish daily *Der veg* and was encouraged by its literary editor, I.L. Peretz. Serdatzky attracted much attention for her short stories and novellas.

In 1907, Serdatzky immigrated to America, first settling in Chicago, then in New York where she ran a soup kitchen to support herself. Meanwhile, she continued writing fiction — sketches, short stories, one-act plays — in journals and magazines. Serdatzky eventually became a regular contributor to *Der forverts*, a relationship which ended in 1922 in a conflict about an honorarium. Serdatzky then stopped writing for twenty-seven years and withdrew from Yiddish literary circles. During her silence as a writer, she supported herself by renting furnished rooms. Serdatzky resumed writing in 1949 at the age of seventy-two and subsequently had thirty stories published in the *Nyu York vokhnblat*.

Geklibene shriftn [Selected Writings] was published in 1913, when Serdatzky was thirty-six. Serdatzky's stories about the lives of women and other Jewish intellectuals in Europe and America provide a critique of the radical and progressive movements. Although Serdatzky wrote from a modern feminist perspective which was not always accepted by male literary critics, she was nevertheless considered by the poet and critic Yankev Glatshteyn and others as the most talented woman fiction writer of her generation. Though Serdatzky was a great writer, her works were never translated during her life time; she died lonely and unknown.

CHAVA SLUCKA-KESTIN (1900 – 1972)

Born December 24, 1900 to an impoverished working-class family in Warsaw, Poland, Chava Slucka-Kestin nonetheless managed to receive both a Jewish and a secular education. From 1936 to 1938 she studied history and pedagogy at the University of Warsaw.

While she pursued a master's degree earned in 1939, Slucka-Kestin undertook a myriad of involvements. She graduated from the Jewish Teachers' Seminary (where she later became an instructor) and interned at the Institute for Jewish Research (YIVO) in Vilna. Slucka-Kestin also taught at the secular schools organized by the *Bund* and Borokhov socialist parties, founded a school for retarded children, and was active in the cultural section of the *Poaley tsion*, the Zionist socialist party in Warsaw.

When the nazis took over Poland in 1939, Slucka-Kestin escaped to the Soviet Union, where she continued to work as a teacher. In 1946, after the war, Slucka-Kestin returned to Poland where she taught at the Jewish Teachers' Seminary and was an active member of the Central Committee of Polish Jewry.

Throughout her life Slucka-Kestin was a prolific writer of pedagogical and political material, children's stories, literary criticism and fiction.

From 1950 to her death on March 1, 1972, Slucka-Kestin lived in Tel-Aviv as an active member of the Communist Party of Israel (MAKI). A surviving daughter lives in Israel.

CONTRIBUTORS' BIOGRAPHIES

ROMA ERLICH

Roma Erlich was born in Wroclaw, Poland. In 1948, speaking only Yiddish, she immigrated to Montreal with her family. She has worked as a clerk for Revenue Canada Taxation for almost twenty years. Erlich developed spinal meningitis as an infant and consequently suffers from petit-mal epilepsy. She has devoted her time extensively to volunteer activities at the Hemophilia Society, the Canadian Cancer Society, the Board of Mental Health and other associations and has received many awards for her volunteer contributions.

FRIEDA FORMAN

Frieda Forman was born in Vienna into a Yiddish-speaking family. During the war years, spent in francophone European countries, she was the family translator. After attending Hebrew Teachers' College in Boston, she taught Hebrew and Jewish Studies from 1958 to 1964. She established, with one other faculty member, the Women's Studies program at the Ontario College of Art where she also taught literature and philosophy. She founded Kids Can Press, a Canadian children's book publisher, which continues to this day.

For the past twenty years she has been associated with the Ontario Institute for Studies in Education, where she developed curriculum resources in women's studies and founded the Women's Educational Resource Centre, which she currently heads. She has been, and continues to be, an activist in progressive movements: feminism, peace and New Jewish Agenda.

Her publications to date include: *Taking Our Time: Feminist Perspectives on Temporality* (Pergamon Press, 1989); *Feminism and Education: A Canadian Perspective*, edited with Mary O'Brien (Centre for Women's Studies in Education, Ontario Institute for Studies in Education, 1990); *A Play About Bread and Roses* with Margot Smith (Kids Can Press, 1973); *Teddy and the Moon*, a children's book adapted from the German (Harvey House, New York, 1972).

Forman attended Yiddish language programs at Oxford and at the Hebrew University in Jerusalem. Her research during the past five years has focussed on Yiddish women's literature of the 20th century .

SHARI COOPER FRIEDMAN

Shari Cooper Friedman first studied Yiddish at the Institute for Jewish Research (YIVO) Yiddish Summer Program at Columbia University in 1982. She has a BA in Journalism and a Diploma in Education. She received her MA in East European Jewish Studies from McGill University. Friedman wrote the chapter on Montreal poet J.I. Segal in *An Everyday Miracle: Jewish Culture in Montreal* (Véhicule Press, 1990). She taught Yiddish and Jewish studies in Montreal Jewish day schools before coming to Toronto and teaching Yiddish at the University of Toronto. She currently teaches primary school for the Toronto Board of Education.

BARBARA HARSHAV

Barbara Harshav's recent translations, with Benjamin Harshav, include: *American Yiddish Poetry: A Bilingual Anthology* (1986), Yehuda Amicha's *Even a Fist was Once an Open Palm with Fingers* (New York: Harper Collins, 1991), and *A. Suzkever: Selected Poetry and Prose* (Berkeley, CA: University of California Press, 1991).

RONNEE JAEGER

Born and raised in the Jewish left-wing world of immigrant Winnipeg, Ronnee Jaeger attended Hebrew religious day school and was an active member of *Hashomer Hatzair*, a marxist Zionist youth movement. She is currently a social worker at the Jewish Family and Child Service, and has been active in progressive Zionist groups as well as Jewish feminist groups. Her history of political activism is a long and varied one. Her interest in Yiddish did not begin until the Seventies, sparked by a love of Yiddish literature and song.

IRENA KLEPFISZ

Irena Klepfisz was born in Poland in 1941 and in 1949 immigrated (via Sweden) to the United States. She attended New York City public schools and Workmen's Circle *shules* and *midl-shul*, graduated from City College and received her PhD from the University of Chicago. She was a post-doctoral fellow at the Institute for Jewish Research (YIVO) and also served as its translator-in-residence. She has taught English literature, creative writing, Women's/Judaic Studies and Yiddish women writers and has received a National Endowment for the Arts fellowship in poetry.

For the past twenty years Klepfisz has been an activist in the lesbian, feminist and Jewish communities and has written and lectured on Jewish secular feminism, Yiddish women writers, class, anti-Semitism, women and peace in the Middle East, Jewish lesbians and homophobia. She was a founding member of the lesbian journal *Conditions* and of the Jewish Women's Committee to End the Occupation of the West Bank and Gaza (New York City) and served as Executive Director of the New Jewish Agenda for two years.

She is the coeditor of *The Tribe of Dina: A Jewish Women's Anthology* (Beacon) and *Jewish Women's Call for Peace* (Firebrand). Her two collections, *Dreams of an Insomniac: Jewish Feminist Essays, Speeches, and Diatribes* and *A Few Words in the Mother Tongue: Poems Selected and New 1971–1990* were published by Eighth Mountain Press in 1990. Her article on the lives, political work and writing of four Eastern European women activists, *"Di mame, dos loshn/*The mothers, the language: Feminism, *Yidishkayt*, and the Politics of Memory" appeared in *Bridges* (Winter 1994).

SHIRLEY KUMOVE

Shirley Kumove is the author and translator of *Words Like Arrows: A Collection of Yiddish Folk Sayings* which was published in Canada by the University of Toronto Press, (1985), in the United States by Shocken Books/Warner Books, and in Germany in German translation by Ferlag Volk un Welt (1992). A second volume, *More Words, More Arrows* is ready for publication.

Kumove is presently completing a translation from the Yiddish of the collected poetry of Anna Margolin. She has received translation grants from the Multiculturalism Department, Secretary of State, Government of Canada and from the Ontario Arts Council.

Kumove lectures frequently on Yiddish language and literature and on the art of translation in Canada, the United States and abroad. She has appeared on national radio and television in Canada and is the author of articles and reviews which have appeared in numerous publications. Shirley Kumove was born and educated in Toronto; Yiddish is her mother tongue.

GOLDIE MORGENTALER

Goldie Morgentaler lives in Montreal. She had translated Michel Tremblay's play *Les Belles-Sœurs* from French into Yiddish for presentation by the Yiddish Theatre of the Saidye Bronfman Centre in June 1992. She is also the translator from Yiddish into English of several stories by I.L. Peretz in the *I.L.Peretz Reader* (Shocken, 1990), and of the three-volume novel by Chava Rosenfarb called *The Tree of Life* (Scribe, 1985). She has taught Yiddish language and literature both in Montreal and at the National Jewish Book Centre in Amherst, Massachusetts, and has contributed articles and reviews of various subjects to the *McGill Journal of Education; Prooftexts: A Journal of Jewish Literary History*, and *The Victorian Studies Newsletters*. She is a contributor to the language column of *The Montreal Gazette*.

NORMA FAIN PRATT

Norma Fain Pratt graduated from Sholom Aleichem Folkshule in the Bronx, New York and also has a PhD in History from the University of California, Los Angeles. She has taught women's history at UCLA, Sarah Lawrence College and Mount San Antonio College since the mid-Seventies. She has published two books: *Morris Hilquit: A Political Biography of an American Jewish Socialist* (Greenwood Press) and *Jewish Women in Los Angeles* (Legacy: Southern California Jewish Historical Society).

Fain Pratt's article "Culture and Radical Politics: Yiddish Women Writers in America, 1890 – 1940," (1980) was one of the pioneering feminist literary-historical studies to rediscover and analyze the works and lives of Yiddish women writers. Subsequently, she has published articles about the poet Anna Margolin and about the earliest Yiddish women writers in the New York immigrant press. In 1991 she edited a special volume of essays dealing with Eastern European Jewish women for *Shofar: An Interdisciplinary Journal in Jewish Studies.*

Fain Pratt has published several short stories; her play about the Yiddish poet, *Margolin*, was filmed by the UCLA Educational Media Center. She is the recipient of post-doctoral grants for her work from the National Endowment for the Humanities, the Littauer Foundation Grant at the Institute for Jewish Research (YIVO) and Hebrew Union College and American Jewish Archives in Cincinnati Grant.

ETHEL RAICUS

Ethel Raicus has lived in Toronto for all but two years which were spent in Israel working on a kibbutz and teaching in the children's village Hadassim. Yiddish was her first language. She is a graduate of the Farband Folkshule (Labour Zionist school system), where the language of instruction for *Tanakh*, Yiddish and Hebrew literature as well as history was Yiddish. In 1989, she received the certificate in Yiddish from Oxford University's summer program.

She has enjoyed a two-fold career: in education and simultaneously in art. She was the first woman to graduate as an industrial designer from the Ontario College of Art. A member of the Canadian Society of Painters in Watercolour and of the Ontario Society of Artists, Raicus is represented in many collections and has received numerous awards, including a Canada Council Grant.

She has taught design and painting at Queen's University, Guelph and in the community.

She was on staff at Holy Blossom Temple Religious School for thirty-five years, at different times teaching Jewish Studies and Hebrew. Her last position was that of Director of the Hebrew Department.

HENIA REINHARTZ

Henia Reinhartz was born in Lodz, Poland where she received her primary education in a Yiddish day school. After the war, she studied Yiddish, Yiddish literature and related subjects at the Ecole Pedagogique in Paris from which she received her teacher's certificate.

In Toronto, Reinhartz obtained a BA degree in psychology from York University and an MEd degree from the Ontario Institute for Studies in Education in Toronto. She taught Yiddish for many years at the Workmen's Circle Peretz School and at the Senior Division of the Bialik Hebrew Day School.

BRINA MENACHOVSKY ROSE

Born in Poland of parents who were both Yiddish teachers and Yiddish activists, Brina Menachovsky Rose received twelve years of education in Yiddish schools in Poland and Canada. Menachovsky Rose taught General Studies for thirty years in Jewish day schools in Montreal and Toronto. She earned a BA (Honours) in Social Science in 1973. Menachovsky Rose has been active in translating Yiddish to English. Her translations of Israel Emiot's poetry have appeared in the *Seneca Review* (Vol. XXI, No., 1991) and in *Siberia* (State Street Press, 1991); she has also published various memoirs.

SARAH SILBERSTEIN SWARTZ

Author of *Bar Mitzvah* (New York: Doubleday, 1985) and editor of several books and cassettes on Jewish and feminist topics, Sarah Swartz's interest in Judaica stems from the traditional Yiddish home in which she was brought up and the progressive Jewish home in which she is bringing up her two daughters, Rebecca and Hannah. She is a founder of the Downtown Jewish Community School in Toronto, an alternative Jewish supplementary school. Swartz was presented with the Tom Fairley Award for Editorial Excellence by the Freelance Editors' Association of Canada for her professional work.

Daughter of Holocaust survivors Menakhem and Regina Silberstein, Swartz has spoken Yiddish since childhood and has recently refined her knowledge of the language by completing the Uriel Weinreich Program in Yiddish Language, Literature and Culture at Columbia University.

MIRIAM WADDINGTON

An acclaimed author of twelve books of poetry, most recently *The Last Landscape* (Oxford, 1992), Miriam Waddington has had her work translated and published in Russia, France, Germany, Hungary, Japan, Romania, Italy and South America. Her poems have been incorporated into the work of Canadian artists, and more than twenty of her poems have been set to music by various Canadian and American composers. In addition to her poetry, Waddington has published collections of stories and essays. She has translated both poetry and prose from Yiddish and German. Waddington was the editor of *Canadian Jewish Short Stories* (Oxford, 1990), to which she contributed two translations from Yiddish. She has published a critical study and edited *The Collected Poems of A.M. Klein*. She is currently Professor Emeritus and Senior Scholar at York University, and is the recipient of two honorary doctorates (DLitt).

MARGIE WOLFE

Margie Wolfe has been a feminist publisher since 1977, first at Women's Press and presently at Second Story Press. She has sat on numerous advisory committees and boards of directors for government and the book publishing industry and has written teacher's guides and articles on women's studies as well as coedited several book collections.

Born in Germany, but a resident of Toronto since the Fifties, Wolfe has discovered while working on this book that there is much she still needs to learn about Yiddish and Yiddish literature. She is the daughter of survivors Toby and Joseph Wolfe and the granddaughter of Bayla and Margula who did not.

BIBLIOGRAPHY OF AUTHORS' WORKS

LILI BERGER

Eseyen un skitsn (Warsaw, 1966)
Fun haynt un nekhtn (Warsaw, 1965)
Nokhn mabl (Warsaw, 1967)
Opgerisene tsvaygn (Paris, 1970)
Tsvishn shturems (Buenos Aires, 1974)
In gang fun tsayt (Paris, 1976)
Fun vayt un fun noent (Paris, 1978)
Nisht farendikte bletlekh (Tel-Aviv, 1982)

ROKHL BROKHES

A zamlung dertseylungen (Vilna, 1922)
Nelke: dertseylungen (Moscow, 1937)
Shpinen (Minsk, 1940)

CELIA DROPKIN

In heysn vint (New York, 1935)
In heysn vint (New York, 1959)

SHIRA GORSHMAN

Der koyekh fun lebn (Moscow, 1948)
33 noveln (Warsaw, 1961)
Lebn un likht (Moscow, 1974)
Yontev in mitn vokh (Moscow, 1984)

SARAH HAMER-JACKLYN

Lebns un geshtaltn (New York, 1946)
Shtamen un tsvaygn (New York, 1954)
Shtot un shtetl (Tel-Aviv, 1965)

Rachel Korn

Dorf (Vilna, 1928)
Erd (Warsaw, 1936)
Royter mon (Warsaw, 1937)
Heym un heymlozikeyt (Buenos Aires, 1948)
Bashertkeyt (Montreal, 1949)
Nayn dertseylungen (Montreal, 1957)
Fun yener zayt lid (Tel-Aviv, 1962)
Lider un erd (Tel-Aviv, 1966)
Di gnod fun vort (Tel-Aviv, 1968)
Oyf der sharf fun a rege (Tel-Aviv, 1972)
Farbitene vor (Tel-Aviv, 1977)

In English translation:
Generations: Selected Poems (Oakville, 1984)
Paper Roses (Toronto, 1985)

Esther Singer Kreitman

Der sheydim tants (Warsaw, 1936)
Brilyantn (London, 1944)
Yikhes (London, 1949)

In English translation:
Deborah (London, 1983)

Malka Lee

Lider (New York, 1932)
Gezangen (New York, 1940)
Kines fun undzer tsayt (New York, 1945)
Durkh loytere kvaln (New York, 1950)
Durkh kindershe oygn (Buenos Aires: 1955)
In likht fun doyres (Tel-Aviv, 1961)
Mayselekh far Yoselen (Tel-Aviv, 1969)
Untern nusnboym (Tel-Aviv, 1969)

BIBLIOGRAPHY OF AUTHORS' WORKS

BLUME LEMPEL

A rege fun emes (Tel-Aviv, 1981)
Balade fun kholem (Tel-Aviv, 1986)

IDA MAZE

Lider vegn mayn kind (Montreal, 1925)
A mame (Montreal, 1931)
Lider far kinder (Warsaw, 1936)
Naye lider (Montreal, 1941)
Vaksn mayne kinderlekh (Montreal, 1954)
Denah (Montreal, 1970)

KADIA MOLODOWSKY

Kheshvndike nekht (Vilna, 1927)
Mayselekh (Warsaw, 1931)
In land fun mayn gebeyn (Chicago, 1937)
Fun Lublin biz Nyu York (New York, 1942)
Der meylekh Dovid aleyn iz geblibn (New York, 1946)
A shtub mit zibn fenster (New York, 1957)
Nokhn got fun midber (New York, 1949)
A hoyz oyf Grend Strit (1953)
Likht fun dornboym (Buenos Aires, 1965)
Baym toyer (New York, 1967)
Martsepanes (New York, 1970)

RIKUDAH POTASH

Vind oyf klavishn (Lodz, 1934)
Fun kidrun tol (London, 1952)
Molad iber Timna (Jerusalem, 1959)
Lider (Tel-Aviv, 1962)
In geslekh fun Yerushalayim (Tel-Aviv, 1968)

MIRIAM RASKIN

Tsen yor lebn (New York, 1927)
Shtile lebns (New York, 1941)
Zlatke (New York, 1951)

CHAVA ROSENFARB

Di balade fun nekhtikn vald (London, 1947)
Di balade fun nekhtikn vald un andere lider (Montreal, 1948)
Dos lid fun dem yidishn kelner Abram (London, 1948)
Aroys fun gan-eydn (Tel-Aviv, 1965)
Der boym fun lebn (3 Vols.) (Tel-Aviv,1972)
Bociany (2 Vols.) (Tel-Aviv, 1983)
Brif tsu Abrashen (Tel-Aviv, 1992)

In English translation:
The Tree of Life (translation of *Der boym fun lebn*) (Melbourne, Australia, 1985)

In Hebrew translation:
Ets hakhaim (translation of *Der boym fun lebn*) (Tel-Aviv, Vol. 1, 1978; Vol. 2, 1979; Vol. 3, 1980)

FRADEL SCHTOK

Gezamlte ertseylungen (New York, 1919)

In English :
Musicians Only (New York, 1927)

DORA SCHULNER

Azoy hot es pasirt: 1905 – 1922 (Chicago, 1942)
Miltchin (Chicago, 1946)
Esther (Chicago, 1949)
Geshtaltn un dertseylungen (Chicago, 1956)
Perzenlekhkayten in yidishn lebn (Chicago, 1963)

Bibliography of Authors' Works

Yente Serdatzky

Geklibene shriftn (New York, 1913)

Chava Slucka-Kestin

In undzere teg: dertseylungen, miniaturn, skitsn fun yisroel lebn (Tel-Aviv, 1966)
Fun mayn notits-bukh

GLOSSARY

In this book, we have chosen to use "standard Yiddish" according to the Institute for Jewish Research (YIVO) transliteration system. Other words in parenthesis ( ) are alternative transliterations of Yiddish and Hebrew words as they appear in the English dictionary or as they are more commonly used in transliterations from the Hebrew.

Words from languages other than Yiddish are indicated as (H) Hebrew, (G) German, (R) Russian.

Diminutives for names and titles are indicated as (dim.).

Plural forms are indicated as (pl.).

Adjectival forms are indicated as (adj.).

Female and male forms are indicated as (f.) and (m.).

aba (H), abale (dim.) — father, papa

agune (agunah) — literally a "chained woman"; a woman unable to obtain a Jewish divorce because of desertion, unproved death or recalcitrance of her husband; according to traditional Jewish law a woman who can not remarry

Akh ti dolya moya dolya! (R) — "Oh you fate, my fate!"; lyric from a famous pre-revolutionary song about being sent to Siberia for political activity

alie (aliyah) — literally "to ascend"; immigration to Palestine or Israel; in a place of worship, the honour of being called up to say a blessing before and after the reading of the Torah

Armya Krayova — the Polish army under the auspices of the Polish government in exile

Ashkenazi, Ashkenazim (pl.) — Jews of Central and Eastern European descent, as distinguished from Sephardim, descendants of Jews from Spain and Portugal

babke — a sweet yeast cake

baleboste (f.) — boss, owner; accomplished housewife

bar mitzve (bar mitzvah) (m.) — literally "son of the commandment"; assuming at the age of thirteen the responsibilities of an adult in the Jewish religious community; ceremony marking this event

besmedresh (beit midrash) — house of prayer and study

bobe (R), *bobinke* (dim.) — grandmother, granny

bobe-mayse — literally "grandmother story"; nonsense, fabrication, "old wives' tale"

Bund — literally "association"; the Jewish socialist labour movement founded in 1897, influential in Eastern European countries until the Second World War

dos folk — the people

eynikl — grandchild

folkshule — public school

Fräulein (G) — formal form of addressing an unmarried woman or girl

gabe (gabbai) — trustee of a synagogue charged with supervision of religious services

gefilte fish — literally "stuffed fish"; delicacy made of finely ground fish eaten on the Sabbath and holidays

Gemore (Gemara) — the part of the Talmud that consists of a commentary on the Mishna (laws and rabbinical discussions), disputatious in style

get — Jewish writ of divorce

gmiles khesed — loan without interest provided by the community; the name sometimes given to the benevolent society which distributes these loans

goy, goyish (adj.) — literally "nation"; non-Jew, gentile; can be used pejoratively

guten Morgen (G) — Good morning

gymnasium (G) — an academic high school in Europe

hagode (Haggada, Haggadah) — literally "a telling"; relating a tale; a collection of historical and biblical texts, psalms and songs recited at the seder on the first two nights of Passover

Halokhe (Halachah) — Jewish Law

hamavdl ben koydesh lekhol (H) — "who separates the sacred from the profane"; a portion of the Havdalah prayer traditionally recited at the end of the Sabbath, separating the holy (Sabbath) from the secular (weekday)

hamoytsi (hamotzi) — literally "who brings forth"; the blessing recited over the bread; the portion of that bread given to everyone at the table

Haskole (Haskalah) — the Jewish Enlightenment; nineteenth century movement amongst European Jews to integrate into Western culture

Hatikvah (H) — literally "the hope"; song expressing Jewish yearning for the land of Israel and hope for freedom and independence; adopted as Zionist anthem at the end of the 19th century and in 1948 as the Israeli national anthem

havdole (havdalah) — literally "separation"; ceremony marking the end of the Sabbath and the beginning of a new week

HIAS — acronym for the Hebrew Immigrant Aid Services; international organization which has helped facilitate Jewish immigration throughout the world, especially during times of crisis

Ich liebe dich (G) — I love you

kadesh (kaddish) — derived from the word "holy"; portion of the daily prayer praising God; mourner's prayer for a deceased close relative traditionally recited daily for a year after the death and then on each anniversary; traditionally the son who recites the prayer

kale moyd — girl of marriageable age

kapo (G) — camp inmate put in charge of other inmates by the nazis in concentration camps *kayn eyn hore* — literally "no evil eye"; invocation like "knock on wood" used to ward off bad luck for those favoured by beauty, intelligence, success

khabibi, khabibati (H) — Israeli idiom for "my dear"

khale (challa) — braided egg-bread traditionally eaten on the Sabbath and other holidays

khasidic, khasidim — SEE khosed

kheder (heder, cheder) — literally "room"; traditional religious elementary school in which children were taught to read Hebrew, the Torah and other religious books

Khibat Tsion (Hibbat Zion) (H) — literally "love of Zion"; a mid-19th century movement which promoted a return to the ancestral land of Israel for the Jewish people

khosed (Hasid, Chassid), *khasidim* (pl.), *khasidic* (adj.), *khasidism* — a member of several mystical sects based on the religious movement founded in Eastern Europe in the late 18th century by the Baal Shem Tov; a populist movement stressing joyous worship over learned observance

khtsos — literally "midnight"; refers to custom of rising at midnight for study and prayer to commemorate the destruction of Jerusalem

Khumesh — the Torah, the Five Books of Moses (Pentateuch)

khupe — ceremonial wedding canopy

khutspe (chutzpah) — excessive self-confidence; nerve, gall

kidesh (kiddush) — literally "sanctification"; blessing recited over the wine

klezmer — Jewish musicians who performed on joyous occasions in Eastern Europe; the style of music played by these musicians

kosher — according to the requirements of Jewish law, for example dietary laws such as separating meat from milk and abstaining from certain kinds of meat and fish

krayz — circle; group; often a study group

kreplekh — three-cornered dumpling filled with meat or cheese, boiled or fried

kursistke (f.) — a woman who studies (takes courses) and prepares herself for revolution

kvas — a Russian fermented drink

Lag Boymer (Lag b'Omer) — minor Jewish holiday, marking a break in the mourning period between Passover and Shavuoth

lamdn — scholar

landsman — countryman; compatriot

latke — potato pancake traditionally eaten on the holiday of Chanukah

loshn-koydesh — holy language; refers to the Hebrew-Aramaic study language

mame-loshn — mother tongue; refers to the Yiddish language

maskil, maskilim (pl.), *maskilic* (adj.) — an adherent of the Haskole movement

matse (matzo, matzoh) — unleavened bread eaten on the holiday of Passover; used ceremonially at the Passover seder feast

mazl tov (mazel tov) — good luck; congratulations

medresh, medroshim (pl.) (midrash) — stories which explain, interpret or expand on the Torah

megile (megilah) — literally "scroll"; used in reference to the Book of Esther, text read on Purim recounting the story of Queen Esther and the Jews of Persia

mekhitse — the curtain or division which designates the women's section of the synagogue

melamed — teacher of children

mentsh (mensh), *mentshele* (dim.) — literally a "person"; used to mean a decent person, responsible, humane, etc. depending on the context

minyen (minyan) — quorum of ten required for communal worship; traditionally adult males

mizrakhi — literally "eastern"; refers to Jews from Asia

nign (nigun) — literally "melody"; a Hasidic melody or song repeated over and over again into a state of ecstasy

Oder (Adar) — sixth month in the contemporary lunisolar Jewish calendar; coincides with February, March, or April in different years

olevasholem (Alov hashalom) — literally "may he rest in peace"; a term of respect used after the name of a dead person is mentioned

pareve — neither dairy nor meat nor their derivatives; includes fruit, vegetables, fish, eggs and bread

Peysekh (Pesach) — festival of Passover, celebrated in the spring to commemorate the liberation from slavery in Egypt

Purim — festival celebrating the deliverance from threatened extinction of the Jews as recounted in the Book of Esther

Rassenschande (G) — literally "racial disgrace"; the nazi proscription against sexual relations between aryans and Jews

rebe (rebbe) — teacher or scholar; Hasidic rabbi

rebetsn — rabbi's wife

Reboyne-sheloylem — Master of the Universe, the Almighty

Reshkhoydesh (Rosh Chodesh, Rosh Hodesh) — beginning of the month; celebration of the new moon, traditionally associated with women

Rosheshone (Rosh Hashanah, Rosh Hashona) — the Jewish new year; with Yom Kippur part of the High Holy Days; the start of the ten Days of Awe ending with Yom Kippur

sabra (H) — literally a type of cactus which is tough outside and soft inside; Jew born in Israel; used to describe the Israeli character

Shabes (Shabbat, Shabat) — the Jewish Sabbath; day of rest, renewal; a holy day

Shabes Nakhmu — the Sabbath following the fast of the ninth of Ab on which the fortieth chapter of Isaiah (which begins with the word "nakhmu") is read

shames (shammes) — the sexton or beadle of a synagogue

sheytl — wig worn by religious Jewish women after marriage as a sign of modesty

shikanazi, shikanazim (pl.) — slang for "Ashkenazim" used by Sephardim; can be used pejoratively

shive (shiva) — the traditional seven-day period of deep mourning observed in Jewish homes after the death of a close relative

shlimazl — ne'er-do-well; an awkward person; a person plagued by bad luck

Shoah (H) — the Holocaust

Shomrim (H) (pl.) — literally "the guards"; self-defense movement begun by the Jews in Europe and continued in Israel

shoyfer (shofar) — ram's horn sounded during the month of Slikhes, the High Holy Days and other solemn occasions

shoykhet — one who slaughters animals and poultry according to Jewish ritual laws

shtetl — small Eastern European town or village with a Jewish population

shul — synagogue

shule — school

shund — trash; refers to low-brow popular literature

shviger — mother-in-law

Slikhes teg — days of penitence leading up to the High Holy Days

Stubendienst (G) — barracks supervisor in a concentration camp

Talmud Toyre (Talmud Torah) — traditionally a tuition-free elementary school maintained for the community's poorest children

Talmud, talmudic (adj.) — body of Jewish civil and religious law and legend, comprising the Mishna and Gemara; literature interpreting the Torah, second only to the Torah as the central text of Judaism

Tanakh — the Jewish Bible which includes the Torah, the Prophets and the Writings

tashlekh — a ritual performed on the Jewish new year in which Jews gather at a running body of water and empty their pockets, symbolic of washing away the sins of the preceding year

Taytsh-khumesh — book of translation of the Torah into Yiddish used mostly by women

teygl, teyglekh (pl.) — a sweet served on Jewish holidays made of honey-covered dough

tkhine — Yiddish prayer written especially for women; prayer often invoking the matriarchs and other biblical heroines to intercede on behalf of the petitioner

Toyre (Torah) — the Law, the Pentateuch; the Five Books of Moses (Genesis, Exodus, Leviticus, Numbers and Deuteronomy); the central text of Judaism

tsadek, tsadikim (pl.) — holy man; wise man

tsu lernen toyre — to study Torah

umgekumene — those who have perished, especially in the Holocaust

UNRRA — abbreviation for the United Nations Relief and Rehabilitation Administration; a UN agency created in 1943 to assist war-ravaged nations with relief supplies and personnel

vatikim (pl.) (H) — early pioneers in the resettling of the land of Israel after 1881

Yemay Kherut (H) — precursor to the Likud party; initially an underground organization that resorted to violence against the British in order to bring refugees into Palestine during the Second World War

yeshive (yeshiva) — Jewish academy devoted to religious study; a rabbinical seminary until recently only for males

yidishe veltlekhe kultur — secular or "worldly" Yiddish culture

yidishkeyt — literally "Jewishness"; Yiddish culture

yisker (yizkor) — memorial prayer

yisker bukh (bikhl), bikher (pl.) — memorial book

Yom kiper (Yom Kippur) — Day of Atonement; solemn day of prayer, fasting and repentance; holiest day of the Jewish year

Yomim noroim — Days of Awe; believed by observant Jews to be the days when prayers of repentance are accepted and the Book of Life is inscribed for the coming year and sealed at the close of Yom Kippur

yortsayt — the anniversary of the death of a loved one often commemorated by the lighting of a twenty-four hour candle

Yudenrat (Judenrat) (G) — literally "Council of Jews"; governing body made up of Jews set up by the nazis in the ghettos and camps during the Second World War

zeyde, zeydenyu (dim.) — grandfather, grandpa

zhargon — jargon; pejorative name for Yiddish used in the 19th century

zogerin (firzogerin) (f.) — literally "foresayer"; woman prayer leader who read prayers aloud in the women's section for other women to repeat, often interjecting individual pleas

PUBLICATION DATA

Berger, Lili. "On Saint Katerine's Day." In *Fun haynt un nekhtn* [From Today and Yesterday]. Warsaw: Wydawnictwo Idisz Buch, 1965.

Brokhes, Rokhl. "The *Zogerin.*" In *A zamlung dertseylungen* [A Collection of Stories]. Vilna: Vilner Farlag fun B.A. Kletskin, 1922.

Dropkin, Celia. "A Dancer." In *In heysn vint* [In the Hot Wind]. New York: Shulsinger Brothers Publishing Co., 1959.

Gorshman, Shira (Gorszman, Szyrke). "Unspoken Hearts." In *Lebn un likht* [Life and Light]. Moscow: Sovetski Pisatel, 1974.

Hamer-Jacklyn, Sarah. "My Mother's Dream." In *Shtamen un tsvaygn* [Stumps and Branches]. New York: Novoradomsker Society, 1954.

Korn, Rachel. "The Road of No Return." In *Nayn dertseylungen* [Nine Short Stories]. Montreal: 1957.

Kreitman, Esther Singer. "The New World." Published in English translation in *Lilith*, 16: 2 (Spring 1991), 10–12. In *Yikhes* [Status]. London: The Narod Press, 1949.

Lee, Malka. "Through the Eyes of Childhood." In *Durkh kindershe oygn* [Through the Eyes of Childhood]. Buenos Aires, Argentina: Editorial IDBUJ, de la Asociacion Pro-Escuelas Laicas Israelitas en la Argentina [Association of Jewish Secular Schools in Argentina], 1955.

Lempel, Blume. "Correspondents." *Yidishe kultur* [Jewish Culture], 5 (September/October, 1992), 21–23.

Maze, Ida. "Dina." In *Denah*. Edited by M.M. Shafir. Montreal: The Ida Maze Book Committee (with the help of the Canadian Jewish Congress), 1970.

Molodowsky, Kadia. "A House with Seven Windows." In *A shtub mit zibn fenster* [A House with Seven Windows]. New York: Farlag Matones, 1957.

Potash, Rikudah. "Jazal the Purim Player," "Prikhah's Complaint to God," "G'ula and Shulamit," "Pirkhah Ozeri," and "Shraby's Daughter Comes Home." In *In geslekh fun Yerushalayim* [In the Alleys of Jerusalem]. Tel-Aviv: Publishing House Israel-Book, 1968.

Raskin, Miriam. "Zlatke." From *Zlatke*. New York: Farlag Unser Tsait, 1951. "At a Picnic." In *Shtile lebns* [Quiet Lives]. New York: Group of Friends, 1941.

Rosenfarb, Chava. "Edgia's Revenge." *Di goldene keyt* [The Golden Chain], 126 (1989).

Schtok, Fradel. "The Veil." In *Gezamlte ertseylungen* [Collected Stories]. New York: Nay Tsayt, 1919.

Schulner, Dora. "Reyzele's Wedding." In *Miltchin*. Chicago: Group of Friends, 1946. "Ester." In *Esther*. Chicago: Dora Schulner Book Committee, 1949.

Serdatzky, Yente. "Unchanged." In *Geklibene shriftn* [Selected Writings]. New York: Hebrew Publishing Co., 1913.

Slucka-Kestin, Chava (Chawa). "Her Story." In *In undzere teg* [In Our Days]. Tel-Aviv: Farlag Meyer, 1966.

PERMISSIONS

Every effort has been made to contact copyright holders of the stories and photographs included in this collection, some of which are in the public domain. Since many of the works included were published privately or by companies no longer in existence, it has not been possible to obtain permission in every instance.

Edgia's Revenge translated with permission of Chava Rosenfarb.

Correspondents translated with permission of Blume Lempel, 415 East Olive Street, Long Beach, New York 11561.

Dina translated with permission of Dr. Irving Massey, son of Ida Maze.

The New World, reprinted here with permission, was originally published in *Lilith*, the independent Jewish women's quarterly. Subscriptions are $16.00 per year from *Lilith*, 250 West 57th Street, New York, New York 10107.

The Road of No Return translated with permission of Dr. Irena Kupferschmidt, daughter of Rachel Korn.

Photograph of Celia Dropkin used with permission of the photographer, John Dropkin, her son.

Photograph of Ida Maze, Kadia Molodowsky and Rachel Korn used with permission of Sylvia Lustgarten.

Cover photograph and photograph of Yente Serdatzky used with permission of YIVO Institute of Jewish Research.

Photograph of Esther Singer Kreitman used with permission of *Lilith*.

OTHER BOOKS FROM SECOND STORY PRESS